POSTCARD HISTORY SERIES

Danville

VIRGINIA

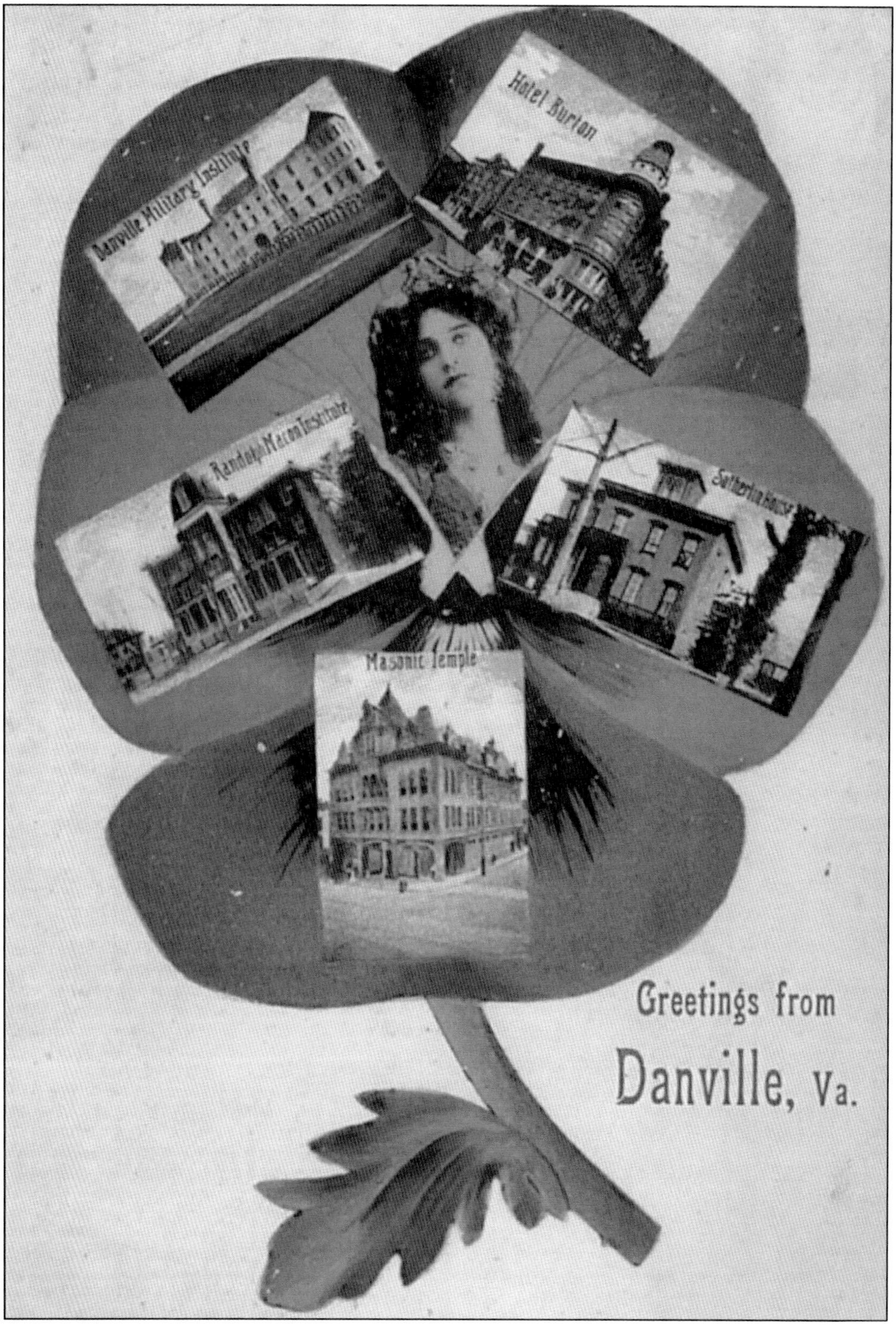

"Greetings from Danville, Virginia" is the sentiment expressed on early postcards long before the establishment of the Hallmark Company with its folded cards mailed inside colorful envelopes. Every imaginable category was issued in postcard format in the first half of the twentieth century.

POSTCARD HISTORY SERIES

Danville
VIRGINIA

Clara Garrett Fountain

ARCADIA
PUBLISHING

ISBN 978-0-7385-0652-4

Published by Arcadia Publishing
Charleston, South Carolina

Printed in the United States of America

Library of Congress Catalog Card Number: 00-107122

For all general information contact Arcadia Publishing at:
Telephone 843-853-2070
Fax 843-853-0044
E-mail sales@arcadiapublishing.com
For customer service and orders:
Toll-Free 1-888-313-2665

Visit us on the Internet at www.arcadiapublishing.com

To Marc

Contents

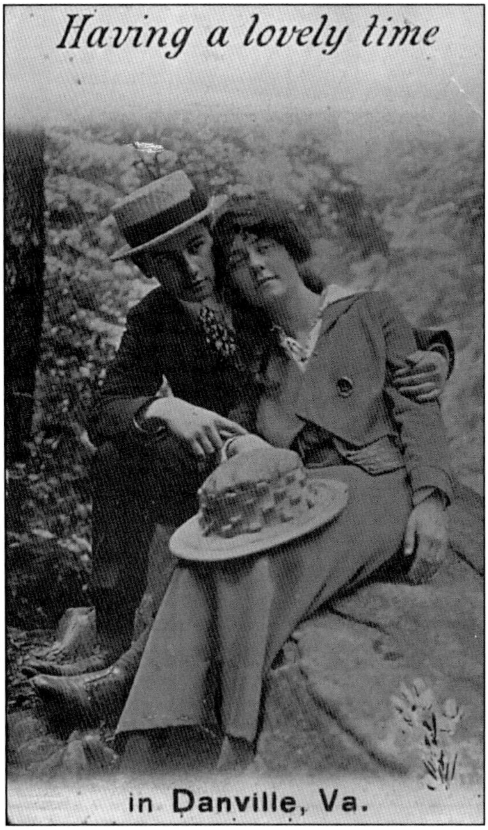

Early greeting cards favored by many young correspondents featured a romantic theme.

ACKNOWLEDGMENTS

Compiling the postcards and information for this book has been a delightful experience for me, thanks to the willingness of many people who have contributed their talents and knowledge. This is not a definitive history of Danville; too many people, events, and places were never recorded on postcards. It is simply a glimpse backwards into the past, to memories of a time well worth the remembering. Thanks to each of you who joined me in this pleasant journey: Florence Archer and the staff of the Danville Public Library; Carrie Ashe; Averett College Archives and staff of Mary B. Blount Library; Mark Berry, my editor at Arcadia; Carolyn and Bob Bouldin; Pat Brachman; Jean, Pete, and Tango Brown; Leona Buettner; Ronnie Burton; Stavros Calos; Tommy Cannon; Sharon Carney; Frank Carroll; Joey Cox; Darryl Dalton; Kim Demont; Louise Dix; Charles Dove; Marc Fountain; Martha Fowlkes; Helen Gantsoudes; Earle Garrett III; Evelyn S. Garrett; Mary and E.T. Glidewell; Gary Grant; Meredith Gravely; Kathy Allgood Graves; Bill Grier; Debra Gust; Marillyn Halstead; Reverend June H. Hughes; Isabelle and Henry Johnson; Anne Jones; Doris Jones; Bitsy Keeling; Zane Kinn; Lake County (IL) Museum / Curt Teich Postcard Archives; Lydia Landrum; Langhorne House Trust; Mark Lewis; Hortense P. Martin; Jean Martin; Lawrence McFall; Reverend David V. McGuire; Ricky McLaughlin; Betty Lou Giles Montgomery; Chris Palmer; Patsy Pickral; Linda Polhamus; Paul Shaip; Fran Skenderis; Edith Sorrell; Libby Spainhour; Susan Stilwell; Craig Stowe; Robert Stowe; Betty Updike; Dan Vaden; Margaret Wayland; Mildred Wilkerson; and Howard Woody.

Introduction

The intent of this book is to present the history of Danville, Virginia, through the medium of deltiology, or the collecting of postcards. The first chapter will hopefully provide the reader with sufficient knowledge of deltiology to enable new collectors to date and enjoy postcards that lurk in family scrapbooks and attics. Furthermore, the artistry of the photographers whose work is represented will record the history of a city in little vignettes that might have been forgotten but for the camera's eye. As the book is both a history of Danville and of an art form, a brief record of Danville's own history may benefit the reader.

Native Americans once crossed the Dan River at a shallow ford below a falls near the modern Main Street Bridge. Their trail led uphill along Main Street's steep climb. In 1738 this land was deeded to William Wynne by the Virginia Colony. Wynne purchased land on the south side of the Dan, calling this territory Wynne's Falls, Danville's original name.

The early inhabitants of Pittsylvania County raised tobacco as their principal means of support. Transporting it to Richmond was difficult, so in 1793 the State Legislature set up a tobacco inspection station at Wynne's Falls. On November 23, 1793, the town was founded and the name changed to Danville. In 1816 a canal was constructed around the waterfalls of the Dan, allowing farmers to transport tobacco down river on flat-bottomed boats.

By 1830 Danville had nearly 500 inhabitants. In 1833 James Lanier was elected Danville's first mayor by the newly formed town council of 12, who met at Bell's Tavern. As the population continued to grow, schools and churches were constructed. Several lower grade schools were followed by two colleges: Danville Female College (Stratford) opened its doors in 1854, then Union Female College (Averett) in 1859.

Formed in 1826, the First Presbyterian Church was Danville's first religious organization, and it was soon followed by the Baptists (1834), Methodists (1834), and Episcopalians (1840). By 1856 the first railroad rolled into town by charter of the Richmond and Danville Railroad. This accomplishment of Whitmell P. Tunstall gave impetus to further community growth. Tunstall became the first president of what evolved into the great Southern Railway System.

Until 1858 tobacco was sold by samples brought to local inspection stations in hogsheads. Thomas D. Neal perfected the idea of Dr. J.B. Stovall of Halifax County, Virginia, putting into practice a new tobacco sales system that spread rapidly. Loose-leaf piles of tobacco were set out on an open floor where buyers could examine and purchase them at auction. This "Danville System" became accepted throughout the South, and numerous warehouses and factories were opened in Danville, allowing the city to be called the "World's Best Tobacco Market."

Danville's prosperity waned during the Civil War, yet the city was not actively involved in the conflict. Danville only played a significant role during the last year of the war. Selected as a prisoner exchange center, Danville offered six tobacco warehouses as prisoner lodgings. Of the nearly 7,000 prisoners housed locally, over 3,500 died from cold, dysentery, and smallpox.

Confederate President Jefferson Davis fled Richmond during the last week of the war, bringing his Cabinet to Danville. Arriving on April 3, 1865, he established the last Confederate capital, residing at the home of Major William T. Sutherlin. Davis left the city on April 10, 1865, ending Danville's brief reign as the "Last Capital of the Confederacy."

After lean years following the war, Danville again began to prosper. The 1880s brought an awareness that water rights along the river could prove valuable. Six businessmen, including architect Thomas B. Fitzgerald, desired an industry to provide jobs for Danville's laborers, as tobacco was seasonal and provided small security. Thus, in 1882 a charter was granted to establish Riverside Cotton Mills, which opened in a single building on lower Main Street. The owners later took advantage of waterpower provided by a waterfall 2 miles upriver and built the Schoolfield Division of the mills. These two large companies merged in 1909 to become the Riverside & Dan River Cotton Mills, now Dan River Inc., and a village called Schoolfield emerged.

Danville's wealthiest period occurred between 1880 and 1920. Fast growth of the tobacco and textile markets at home and abroad allowed local businessmen to make fortunes. Large impressive homes constructed along Main Street are evidence of this prosperity. The mile-long stretch from Ridge Street to Broad was bordered with ornate Victorian houses and is often called "Millionaires Row." Sadly, parking lots and modern buildings now occupy the sites of many early mansions.

In 1892 Harry Wooding was elected mayor, a post he held for 46 years (and a record that is listed in Ripley's "Believe It or Not"). Danville had scored a number of "firsts" by 1938, the end of his term. In 1886 Danville was the nation's first city to own and operate its own utilities. In 1935 Danville was Virginia's first city to install a radio patrol system in its police department. A woman, Kerr M.Harris, became the first female magistrate appointed by the State of Virginia.

Following World War I, numerous public buildings and stores were constructed, and a large improved hospital was erected due to the generosity of John Edward Hughes. In 1929 an airstrip was opened. Danville's future seemed inevitable. The greatest change in size and lifestyle occurred following World War II when the population grew from 32,000 to 46,000 in 20 years. Danville began to provide small, low-cost housing to accommodate a growing population, and the local government annexed many areas including Schoolfield. In 1950 Ed Temple was named the first city manager and the council-manager form of government replaced the older council-mayor form. In 1950 Kroger opened Danville's first self-service supermarket. Motels and fast-food chains emerged in the 1950s. Expansion and leisure had returned to Danville, a city bound for post-war prosperity.

One

DELTIOLOGY

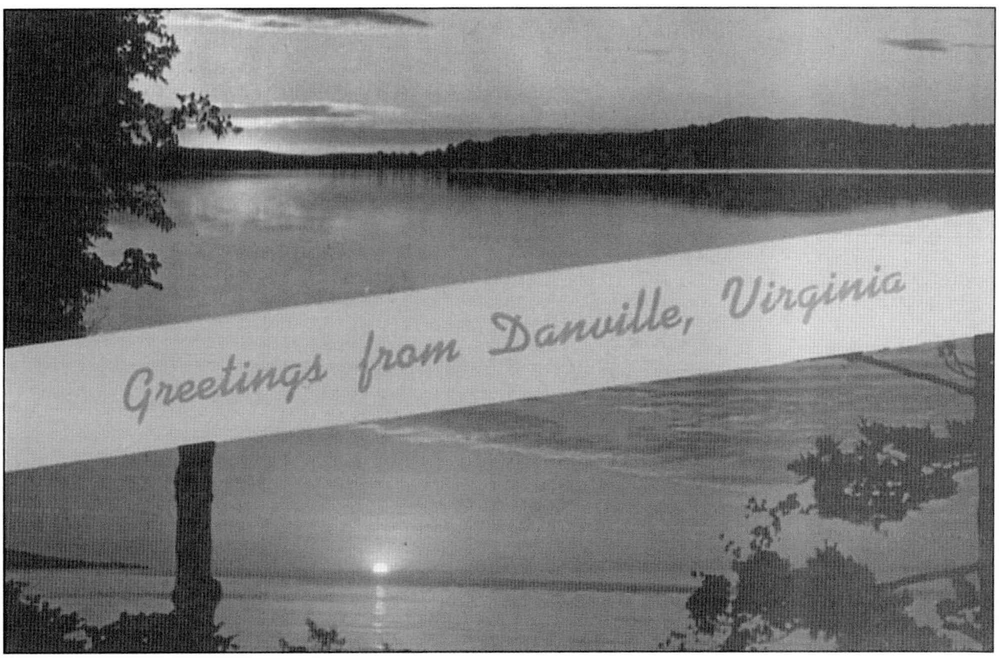

Deltiology is the American term used today to refer to the hobby of collecting postcards. The first picture postcards were "Gruss Aus . . ." or "Greetings From . . ." cards, souvenir cards that featured illustrations or photographs of specific places. Collecting picture postcards became a national craze in the last days of the Victorian era, a fad that mushroomed soon after 1900 and then almost died out by 1914. Yet, old view cards of hometowns are currently one of the most popular of collectibles. No one knows exactly how many postcards were published on any single place, but in the last century more than 1,500 cards were published on Danville, Virginia, alone.

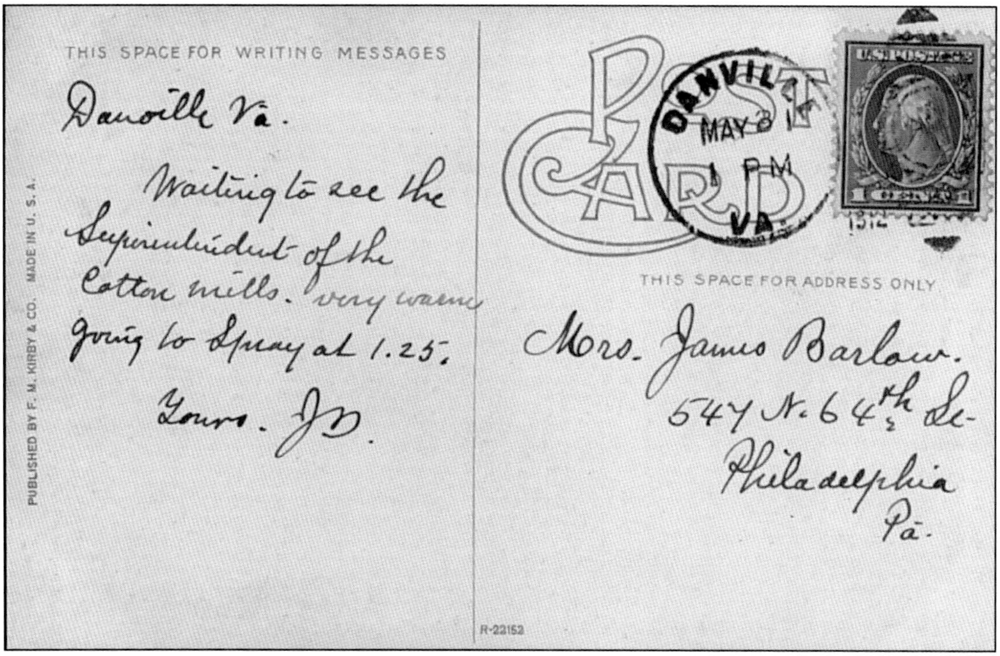

The postcard with its brief, hackneyed message used to be an integral part of the daily life of the American public. Postcards, public education, and literacy all evolved about the same time during the 1870s and 1880s. Before the advent of the telephone, television, or computer, the postcard was the chief means of communication for many people.

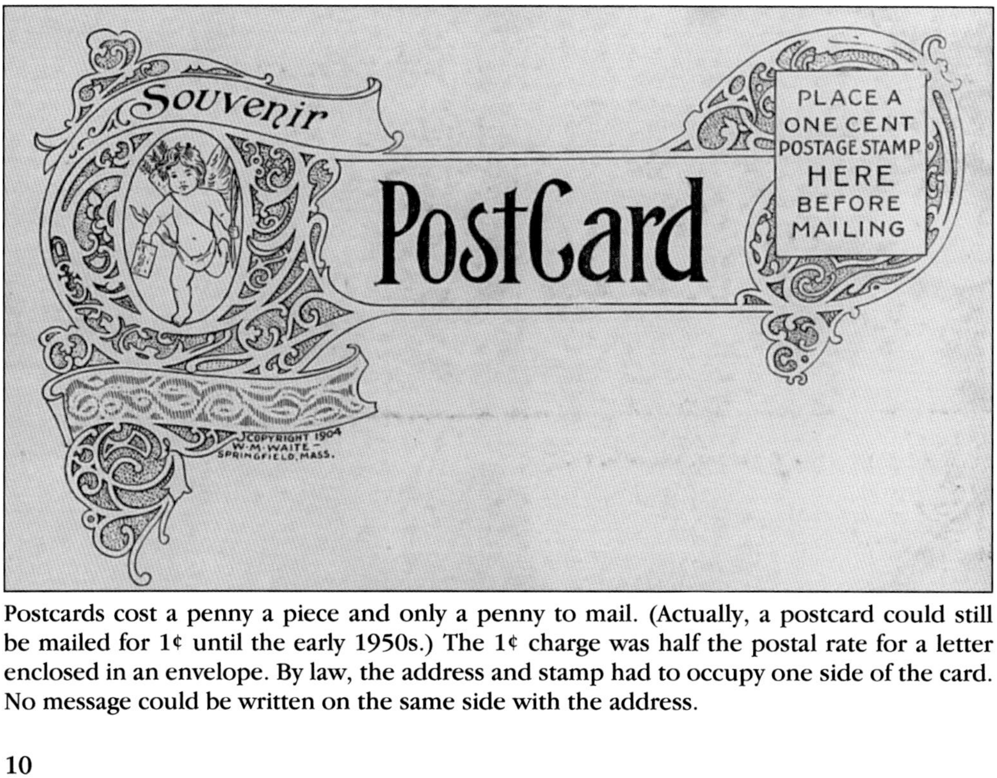

Postcards cost a penny a piece and only a penny to mail. (Actually, a postcard could still be mailed for 1¢ until the early 1950s.) The 1¢ charge was half the postal rate for a letter enclosed in an envelope. By law, the address and stamp had to occupy one side of the card. No message could be written on the same side with the address.

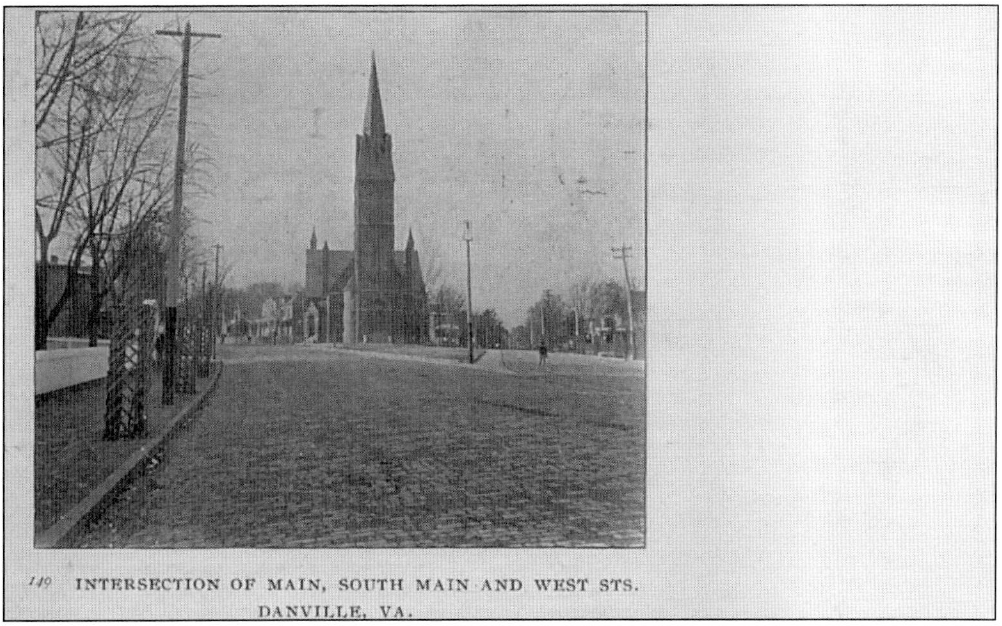

Thus, if photographs or illustrations were used, they had to be placed at the side or top of cards, leaving a blank space on which the message would be written. So far, the earliest postmark found on a Danville picture card in the author's collection of more than 900 postcards is this card, dated May 1904.

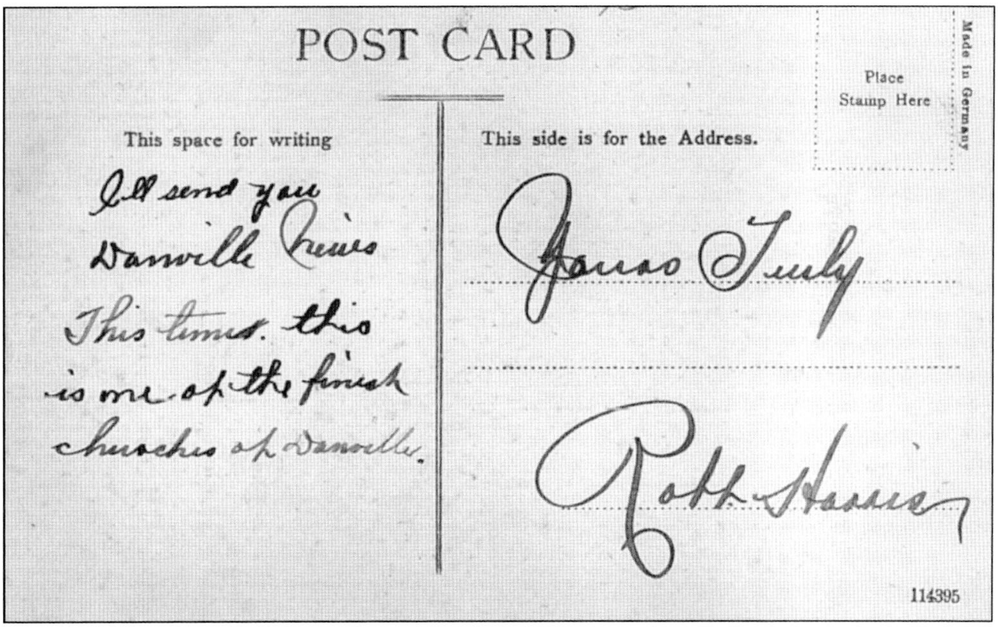

Great things happened for postcards in March 1907, when the United States government changed postal laws and allowed what was called the "divided" card where a line literally bisected the address side of a postcard. Space for a message was now allowed on that side of the card, freeing the entire front for pictures. Collecting and trading picture postcards quickly became one of the greatest fads to hit this nation.

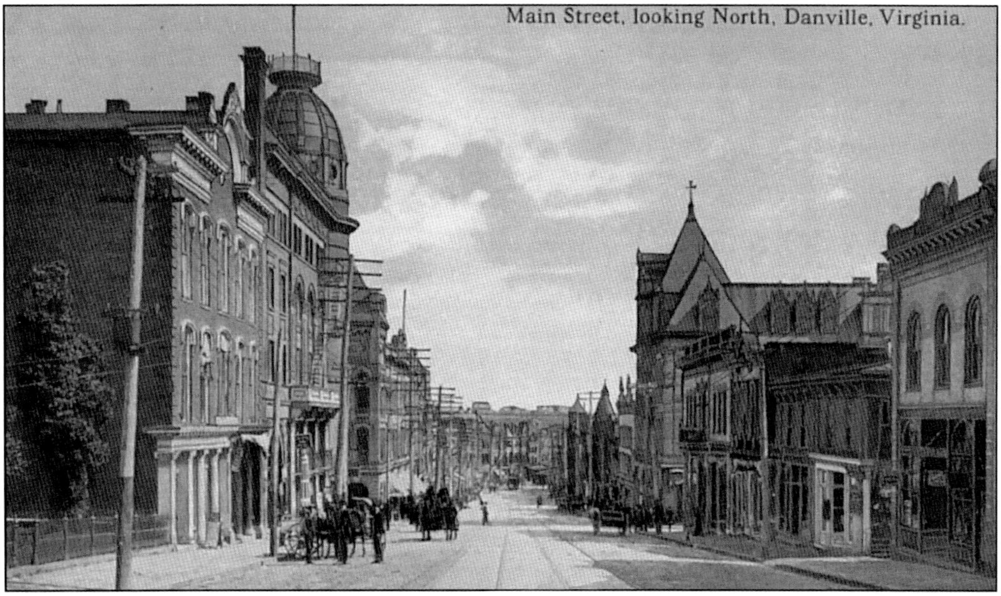

The blossoming of postcard companies paved the way for the emergence of freelance photography. An individual photographer could travel to remote places, take pictures of local buildings and events, and then send negatives to Germany to have lithographic plates made, and order as few as 100 cards. A local store could buy these cards and sell them for 1¢ each. All of the businessmen could make a profit.

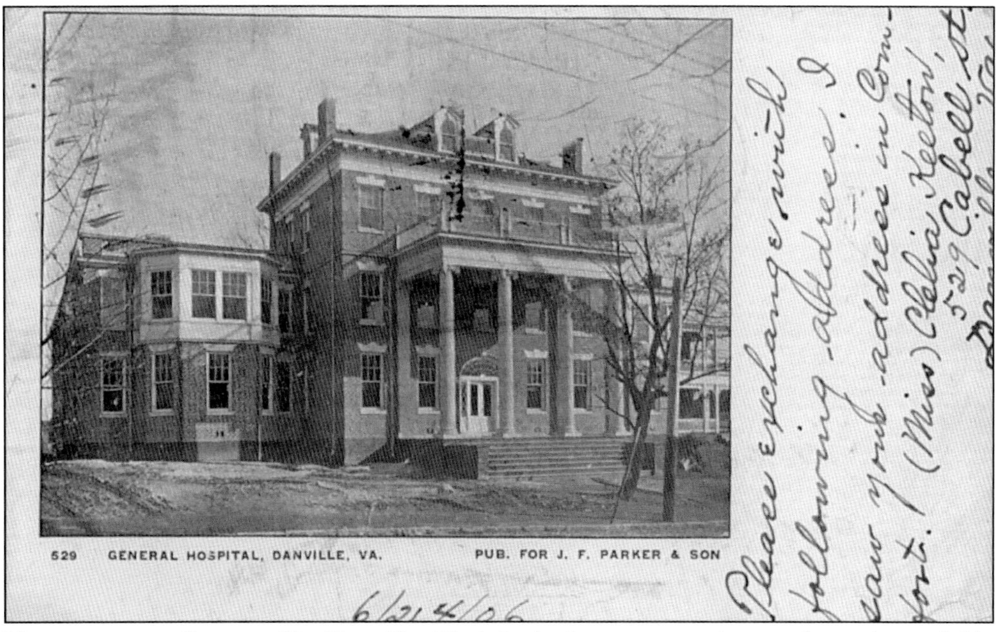

Thus, many small towns like Danville, Virginia, had numerous view cards made available to its citizens, who collected cards themselves or traded with friends and relatives all over the world. Various postcards were created by local photographers or businesses including Walter Smith, U.W. Clark, Raymond Hitchcock, Parker's Book Store, the Danville Book and Stationery Company, and J.T. Townes Printing Company.

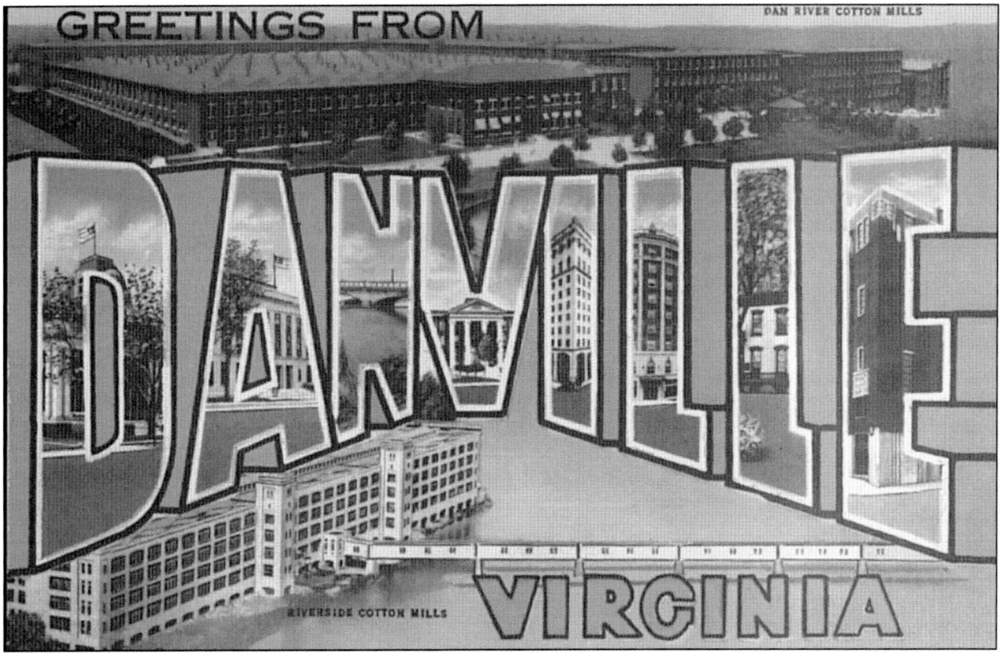

Multi-view cards were sometimes published that showed two or more scenes on one card. "Large-Letter" greeting cards contained a view within each letter of the name of the town or state. This practice may have grown out of the desire of the small shopkeeper of the 1930s to stock fewer cards but provide important views of the town.

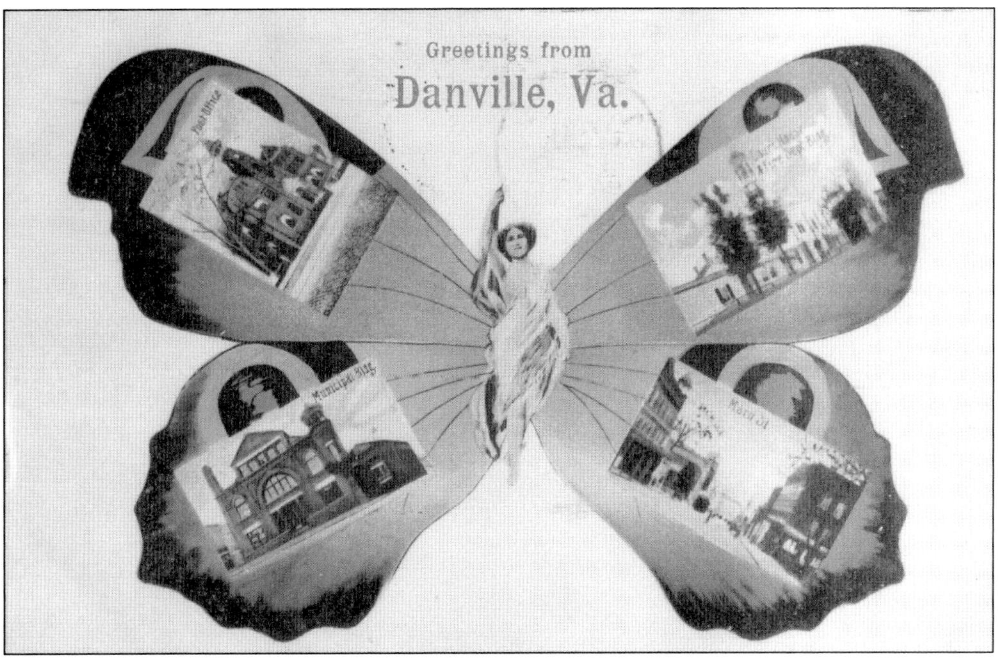

The multi-view cards eagerly sought by today's collectors are those that were published in the Golden Era years (from 1907 to 1914) and often show views of buildings placed within the butterfly wings of a Victorian lady, or a four-leaf clover, or a flower such as a pansy.

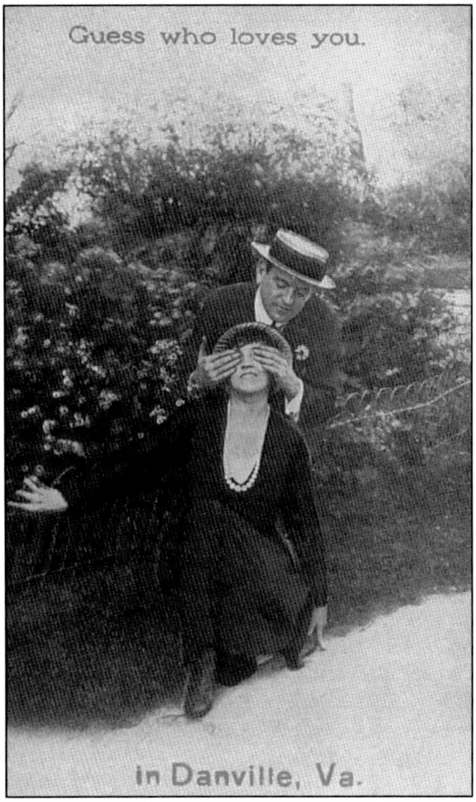

Postcards were produced in different shapes and sizes. Cards before the 1940s were 3 1/2" x 5 1/2" in size, and after World War II the dimensions were changed to 4" x 6" (the continental size). Two-fold or three-fold cards were printed, or small attachments were added like buttons, ribbons, or feathers. Greeting cards continued to be published in a variety of formats, especially humorous ones, until prices rose and Hallmark and other such companies took over the market.

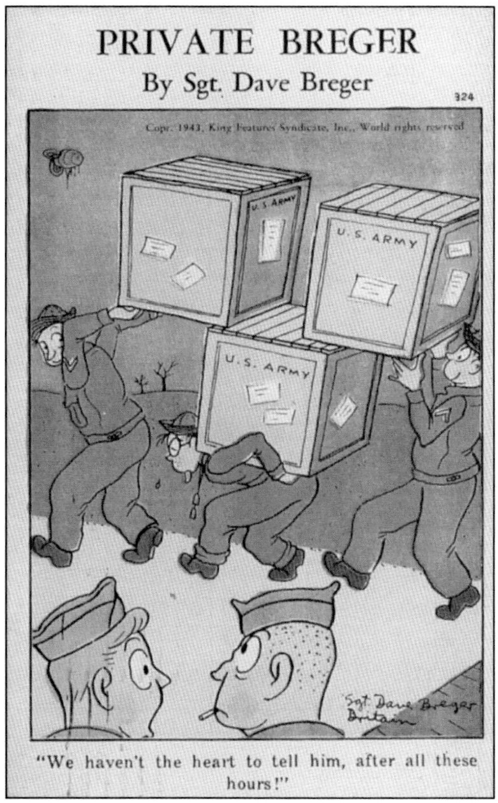

One set of humorous linen postcards published during World War II by Graycraft Card Company of Danville, Virginia, was a series of 24 hand-colored comic cards for King Features Syndicate, the "Private Breger" cards produced by Sergeant Dave Breger.

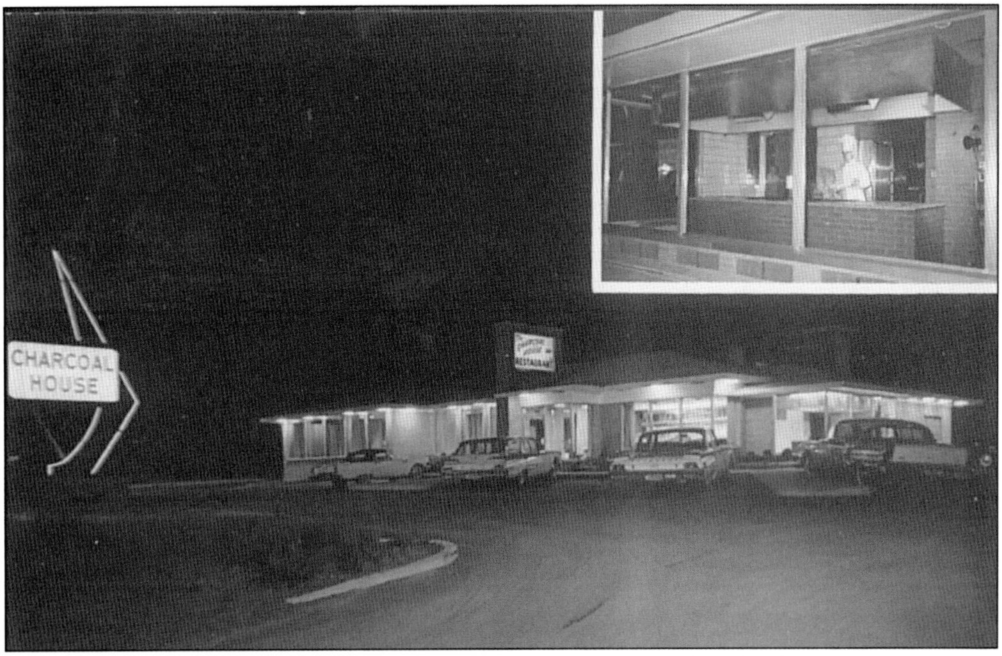

Today there is a renewed interest in collecting picture postcards (whether seen as antiques or historical artifacts), particularly view cards showing scenes of hometowns. People are discovering the excitement of finding inexpensive bits of their vanishing past, for instance when they find a card depicting a building that no longer stands or a business that is almost forgotten.

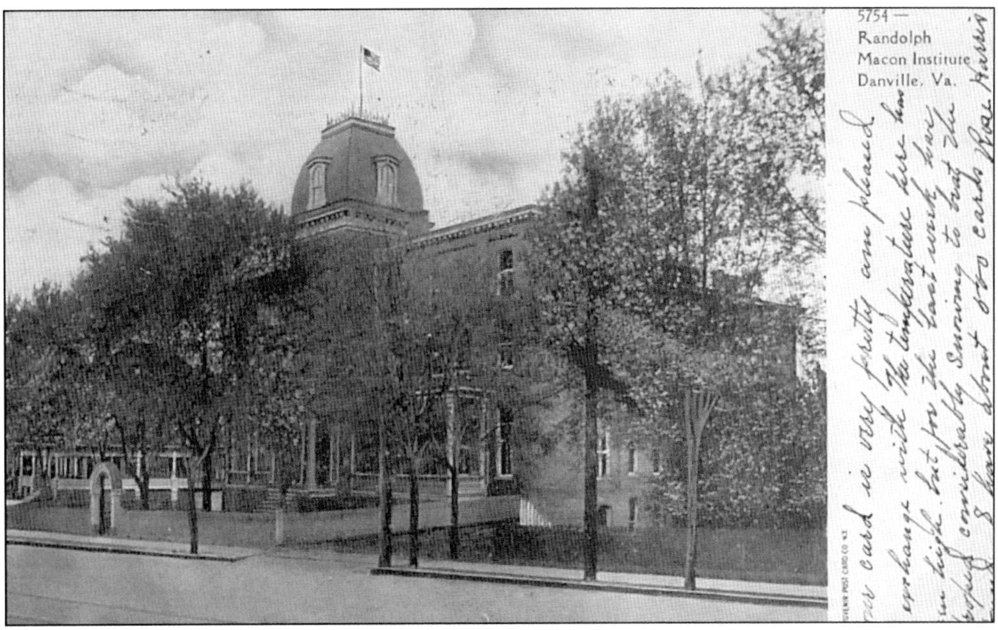

For the most part the dating of postcards is actually quite simple. Cards published up to March 1907 had some blank space on the same side with the picture (to be used for the message), and the address side was not divided.

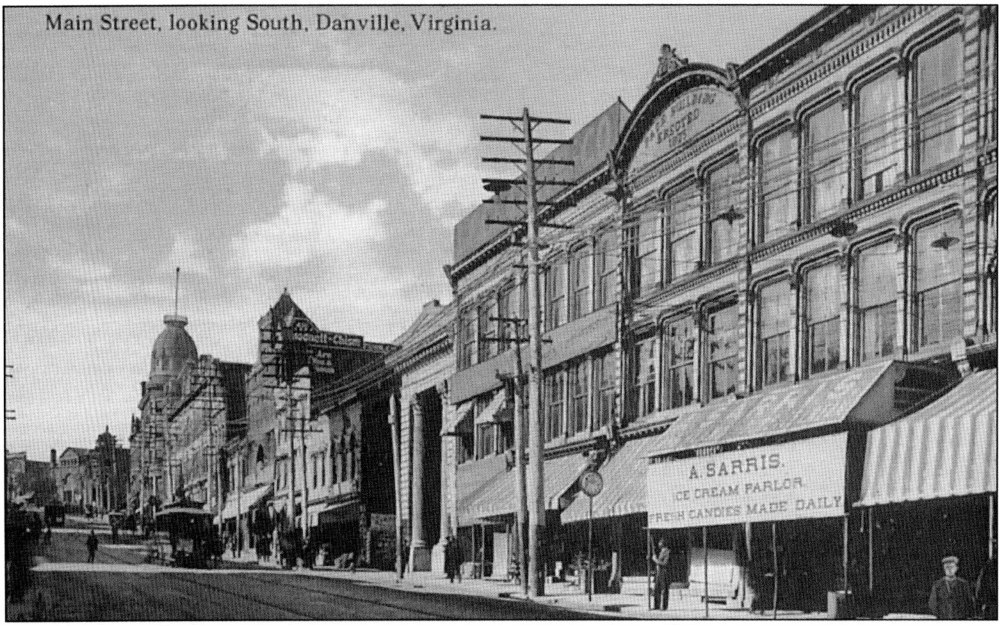

The Golden Era cards, from 1907 to 1914, show pictures that completely filled the front of the cards, their inks and illustrations representing the best printing techniques available. These are usually the most expensive cards to collect, but they are well worth the search, as they provide the best images of life as it was then in American towns.

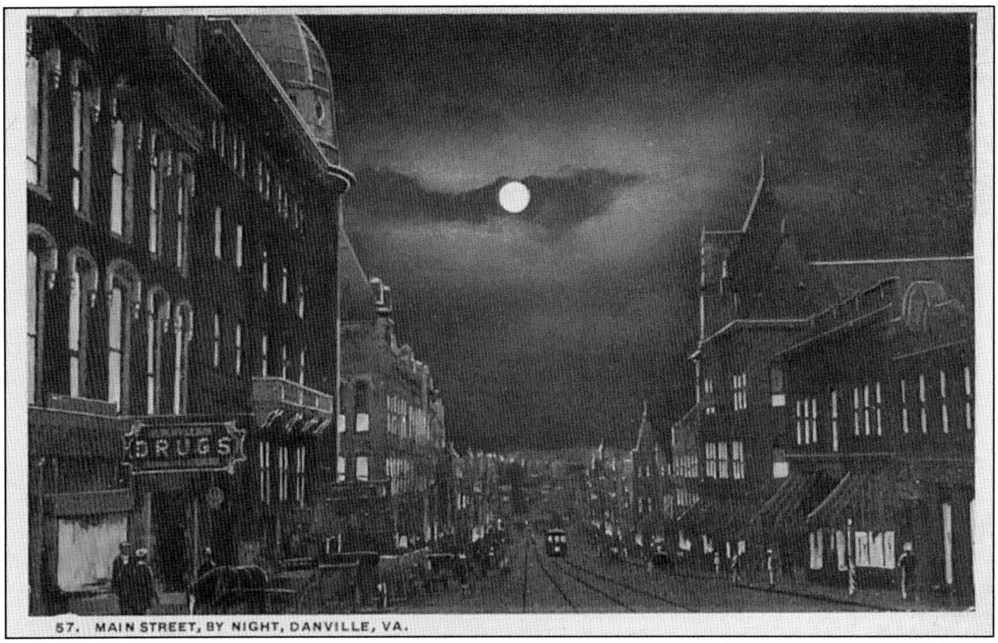

Most cards from around 1915 to 1930 had white borders around the pictures, an attempt to cut back on the cost of ink. This was true of both color and black-and-white postcards. After World War I, postcards were printed in the United States and their quality did not match the Europeans. Postal rates began to rise and postcard collecting as a hobby for the most part died out.

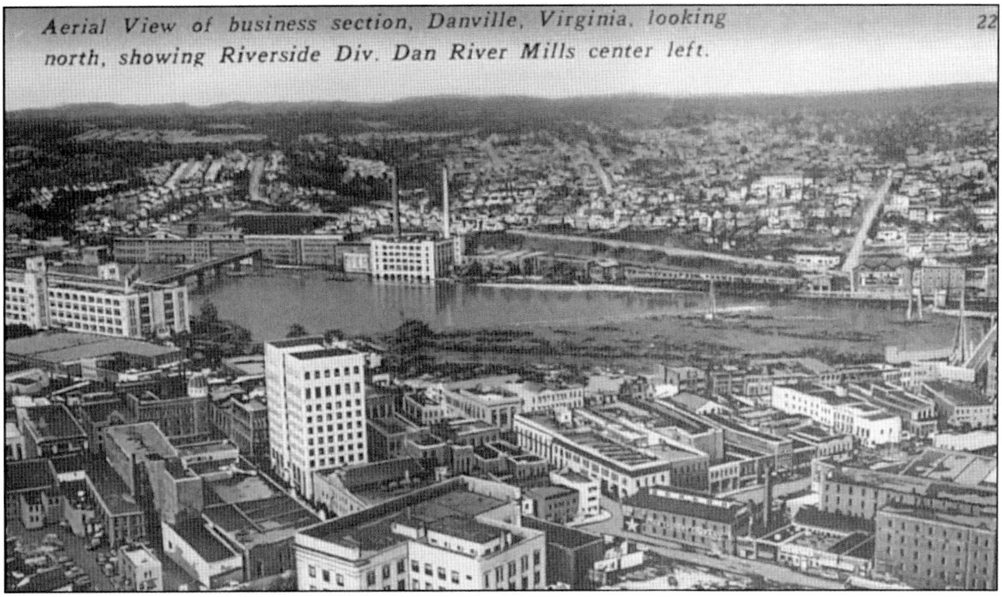

During and after the Depression, from 1930 to 1944, cards were printed on linen-type paper and the illustrations were hurriedly drawn and not very good. Looking closely at the paper one can see the pattern of threads showing through.

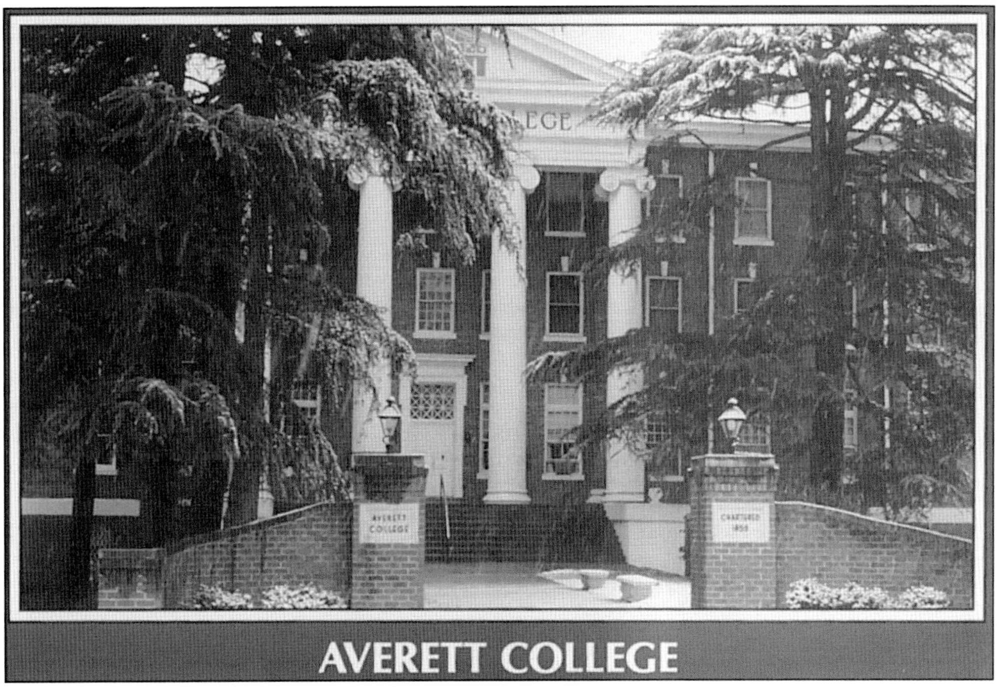

After World War II, color photography entered the postcard scene and "photochromes" dominated the cards that were produced, many for advertising purposes rather than scenic views, and many were published in the larger continental size. Postcards from the 1950s and 1960s have special value for today's collectors because they portray a world that doesn't exist anymore.

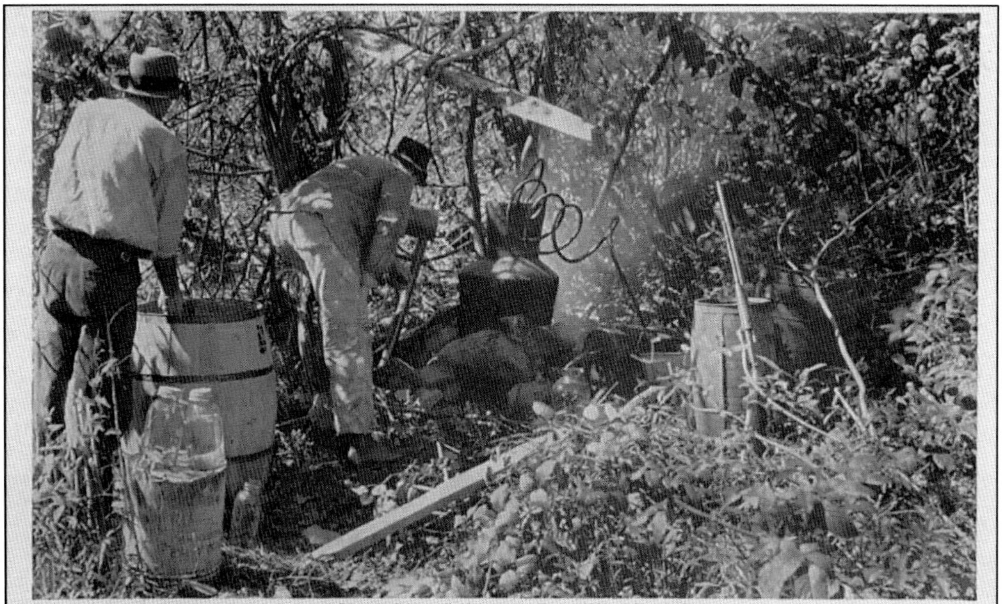

A Moonshine Still near Danville, Virginia

Danville, Virginia, holds an important place in the production of picture postcards in the past century. During the 1940s and 1950s, Robert H. Sanford Jr. owned and operated a company that produced black-and-white images of communities all over the South, not just of Danville. His Graycraft Card Company produced so many scenes from Southern communities that his cards today provide the core of many view card collections.

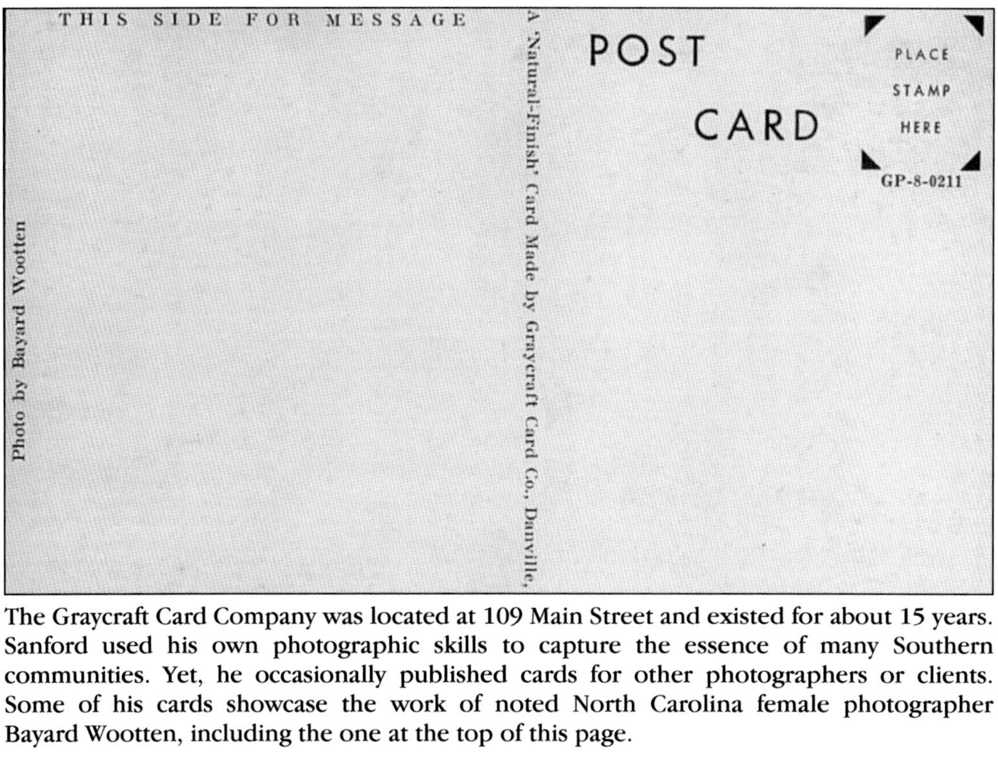

The Graycraft Card Company was located at 109 Main Street and existed for about 15 years. Sanford used his own photographic skills to capture the essence of many Southern communities. Yet, he occasionally published cards for other photographers or clients. Some of his cards showcase the work of noted North Carolina female photographer Bayard Wootten, including the one at the top of this page.

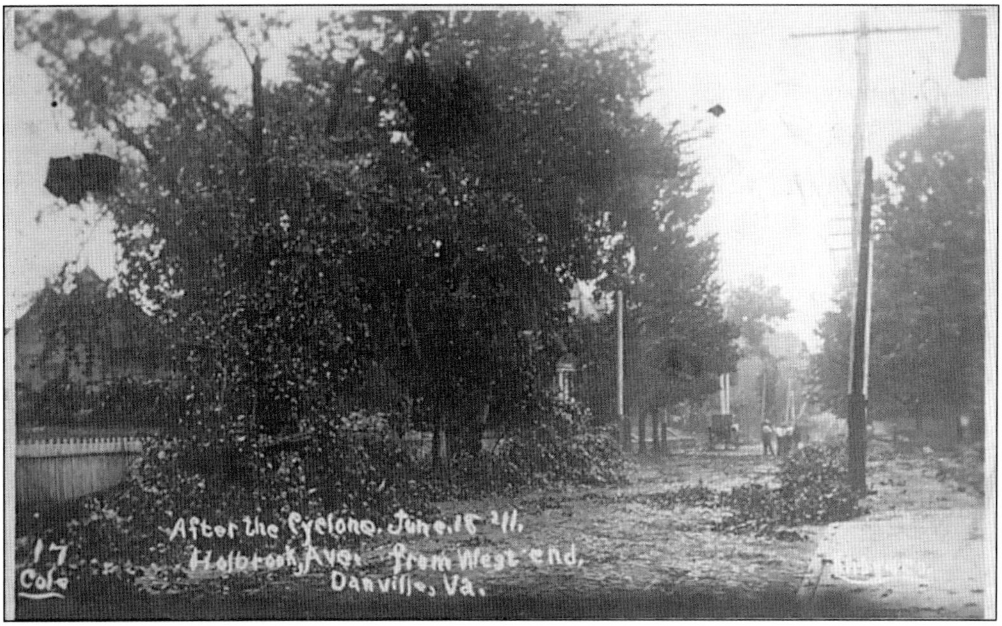

O.W. Cole was a local photographer who had a studio in the early 1900s at 317 Main Street. Cole published postcards of scenes that he himself had photographed and printed on postcard-stock paper. These unique "real photo" cards, or "photocards," have proved to be the most difficult to find (and often quite expensive) since only a few copies of each were made. Photocards frequently depict some kind of historic event that happened in a town.

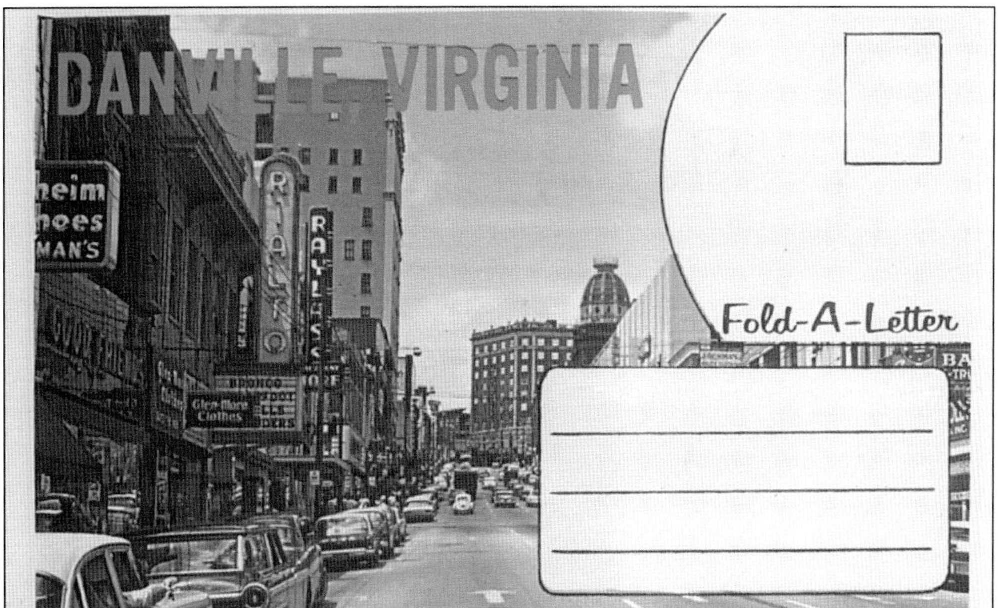

In the early 1960s Stavros Calos, a local photographer, issued several photochrome cards through his Piedmont Greeting Card Company. Calos also produced a unique fold-out card described as a Fold-a-Letter, which showed individual views around town on one side, yet provided a blank back for writing a long message.

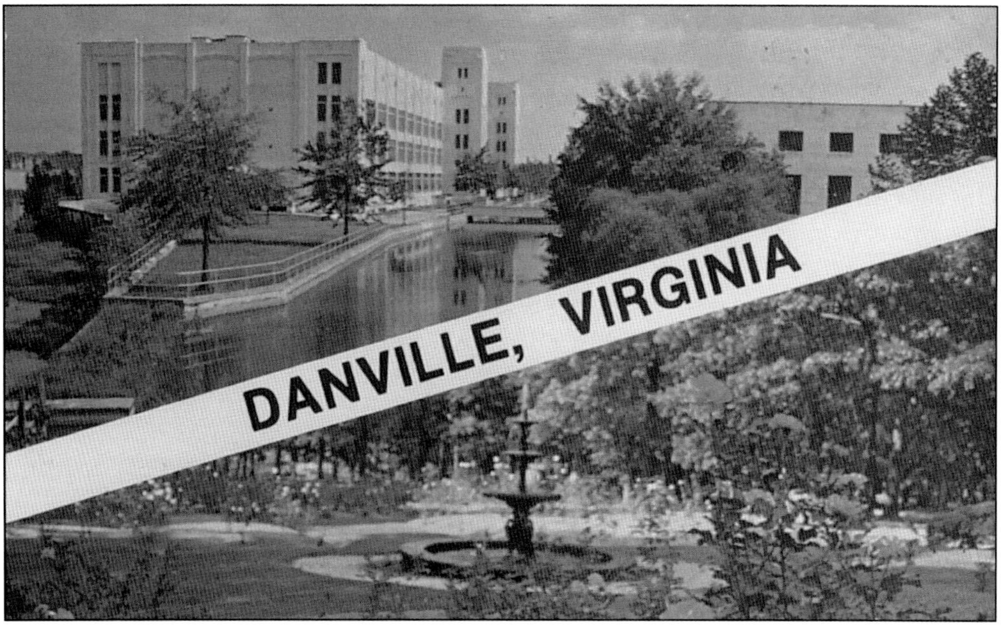

Henry Mitchell of Chatham, Virginia, for many years produced and distributed local postcards throughout Danville and the Piedmont. Since the 1950s other individuals and businesses in Danville have produced postcards to advertise their companies or products. Unfortunately for eager deltiologists, these later cards often prove difficult to acquire because many cards were tossed in the trash after the brief message had been read.

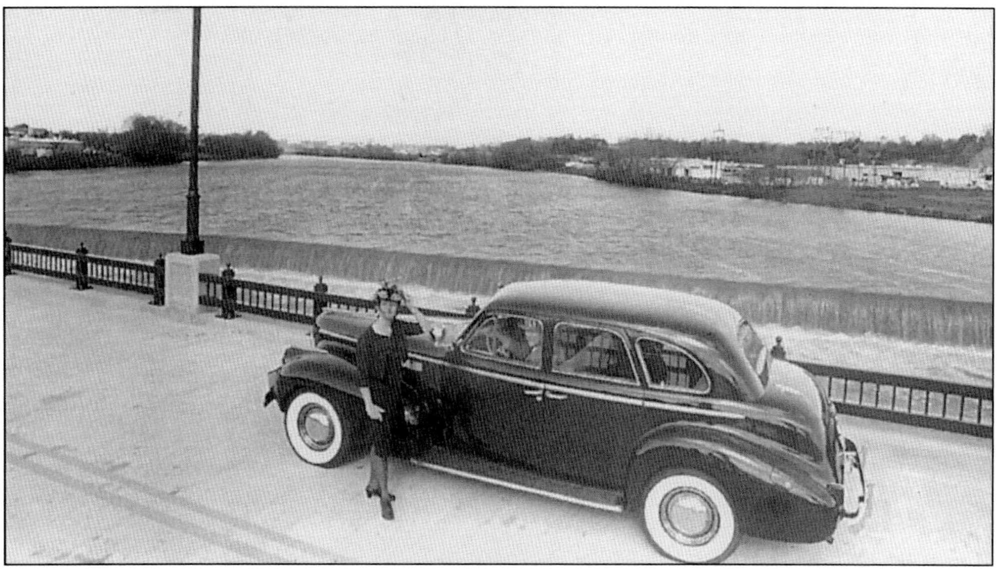

The most recent organization to publish Danville postcards is the City of Danville itself. A. Ray Griffin, city manager from 1992 to 1999, was intrigued by old postcard views of the downtown area. He was instrumental in the city's production of commemorative cards to showcase Danville and its tourist attractions. Griffin's first card featured the newly renovated Union Street Bridge with Susan Stilwell dressed as Lady Astor and Landon Wyatt sitting in his 1940 Buick.

Two

Bridges to Industry

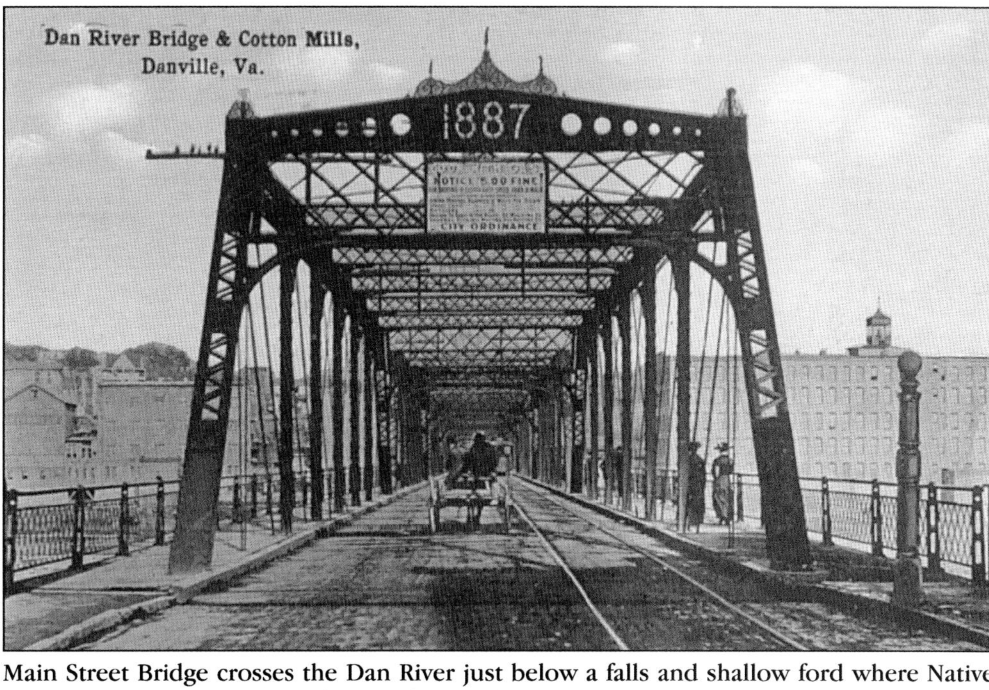

Main Street Bridge crosses the Dan River just below a falls and shallow ford where Native Americans once crossed on their trading path. Four bridges have been built on this same site. The first, a stone bridge, was washed away in the great flood of 1850. Tobacconist William T. Sutherlin bought the land and rights to build the second, a covered wooden bridge. The wooden bridge was torn down in 1887 and a modern steel structure was erected to span the river. Racing horses across the bridge was a problem for local police. This 1910 postcard shows that a notice was posted from the bridge that there would be a $5 fine for "driving at a faster rate of speed than a mule."

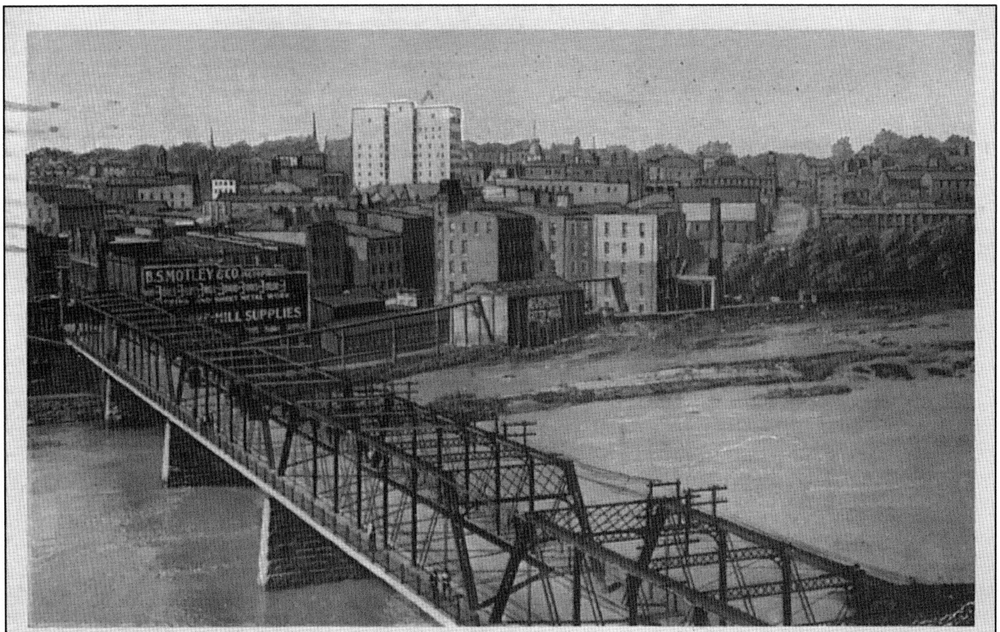

25. BIRD'S EYE VIEW FROM NORTH DANVILLE, VA

On June 30, 1927, the iron fireproof bridge caught fire and burned down. As workmen were making repairs on the bridge, a tar kettle ignited and set fire to the underpinnings of the bridge, totally destroying it. The burning of this fireproof bridge was recorded in Ripley's "Believe It or Not."

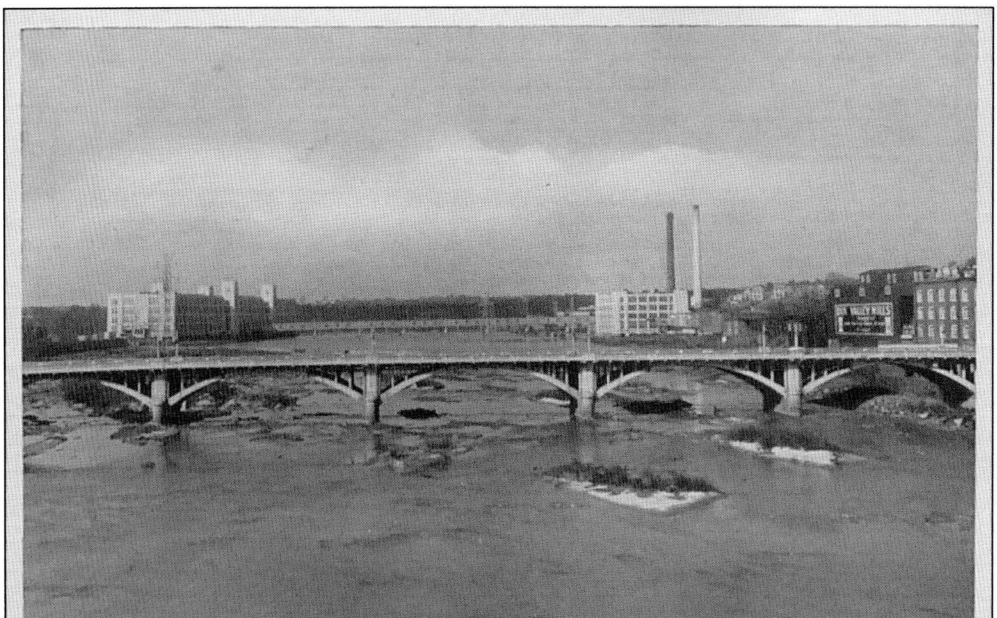

View from New Bridge over Dan River, Danville, Virginia

The iron bridge was replaced by an arched-span concrete bridge that was designed by noted engineer Daniel Luten. It was completed in 1928 and has survived many more years than its predecessors.

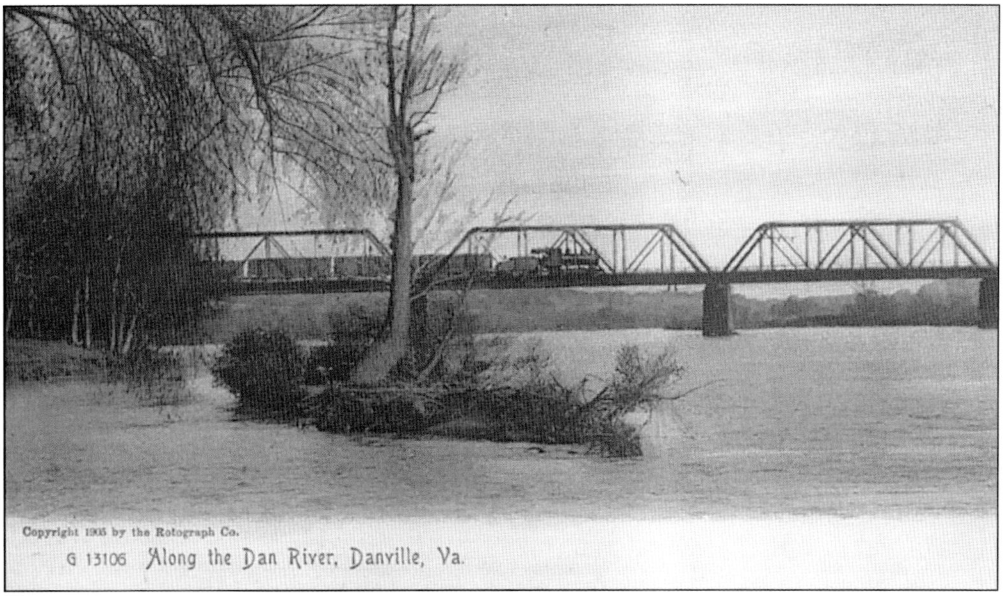

Due to the efforts of one man, Whitmell P. Tunstall, a train line was built through Danville instead of Milton, North Carolina, the alternate site. Tunstall believed that the railroad would bring growth and prosperity to the city. He succeeded but did not live to see the first train arrive in 1856.

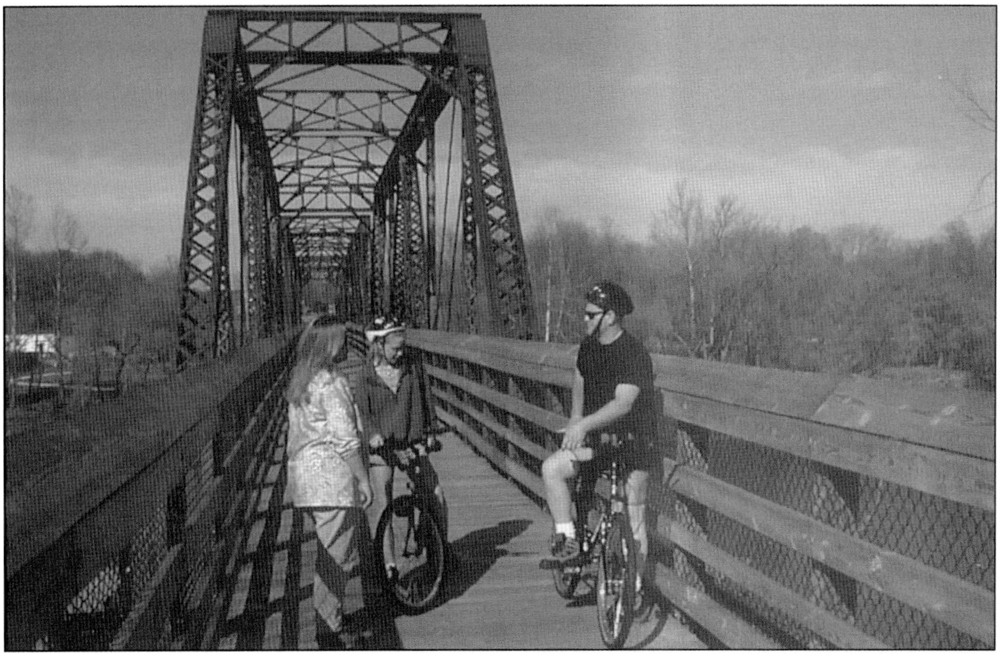

This tenth commemorative card published by the City of Danville shows the old iron truss railroad bridge as transformed into a part of the River Front Trail connecting the "Crossing at the Dan" to the Dan Daniel Memorial Park. Photographed by Dan Vaden in April 2000, this photochrome card features Kimberly Demont, Anna Rust, and Bobby Demont as they take advantage of the city's new pedestrian and bicycling trail.

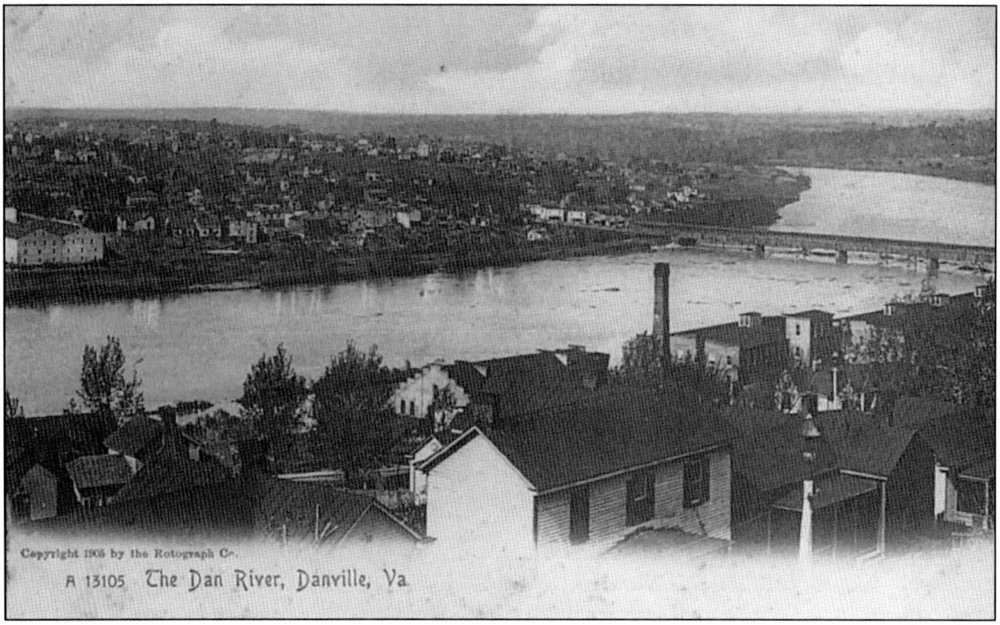

Even before the days of automobiles or trolley cars, people found it necessary to cross the Dan River for business or pleasure. To ease the growing traffic on Main Street Bridge, a second covered wooden bridge was constructed in 1879 just above the dam at Union Street.

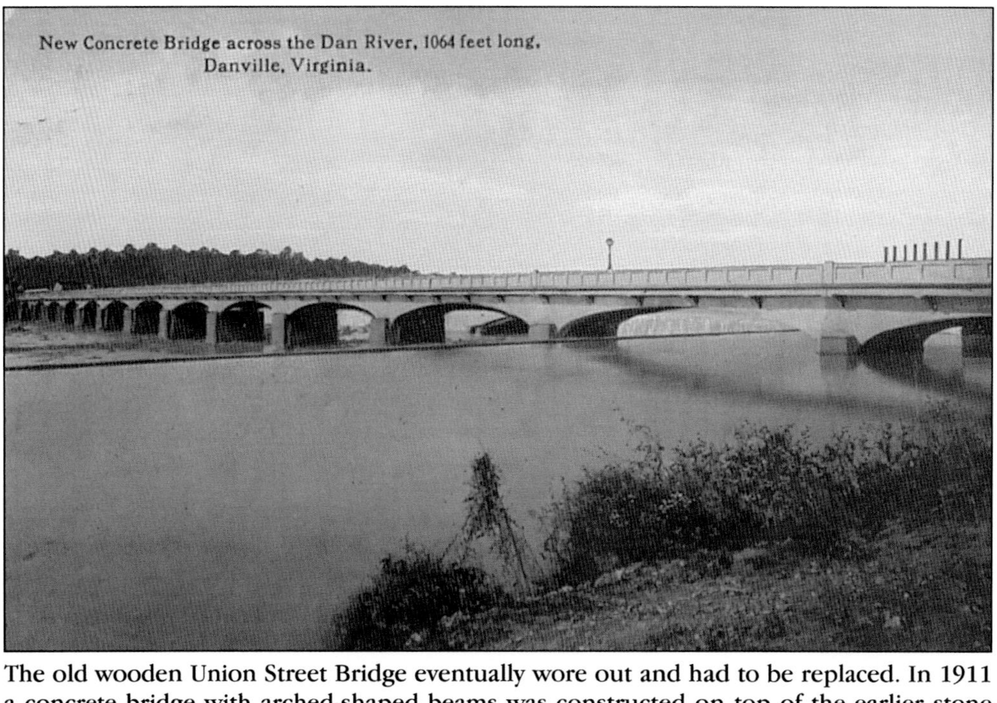

The old wooden Union Street Bridge eventually wore out and had to be replaced. In 1911 a concrete bridge with arched-shaped beams was constructed on top of the earlier stone piers. Union Street Bridge underwent extensive renovations in 1934 and again in 1994.

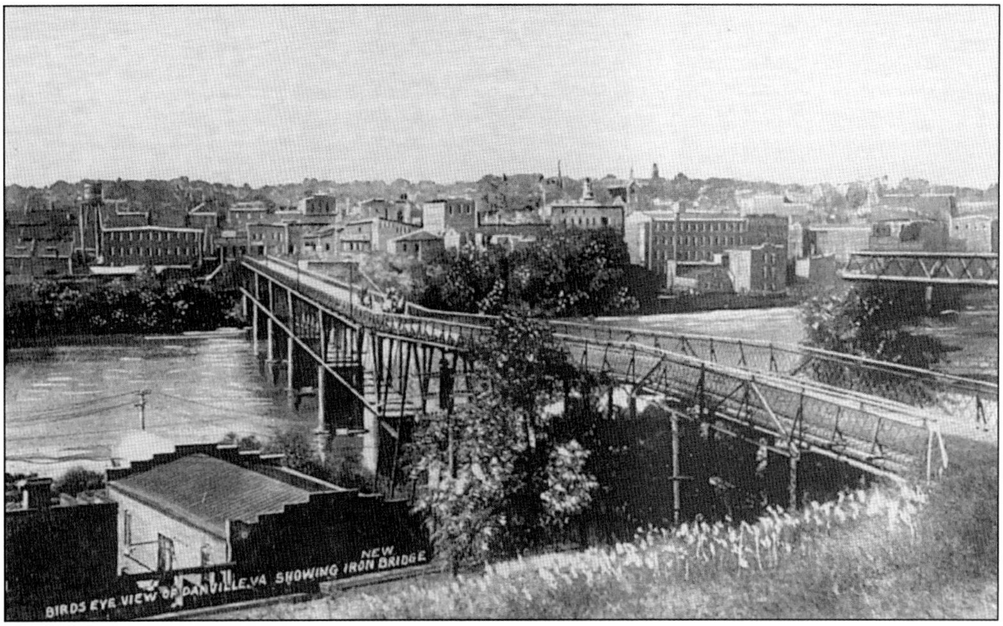

Some citizens of Danville objected to the city using noisy streetcars for public transportation. They feared that their horses and mules would be "spooked" by all the clanking sounds. A second iron bridge, the taller Worsham Street Bridge, was built solely for horse-drawn vehicles. This iron bridge was replaced in 1928 by a wide concrete span, the second of two bridges in town designed by Daniel Luten.

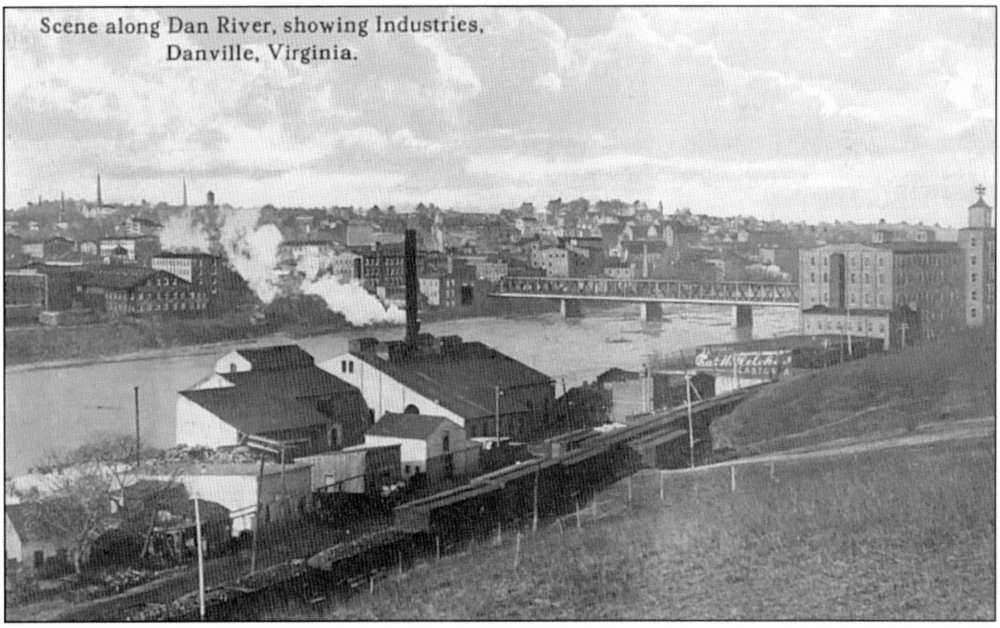

The Dan River has attracted industry to Danville since the town was first settled. This river has provided transportation as well as waterpower to many businesses that have been established on its banks.

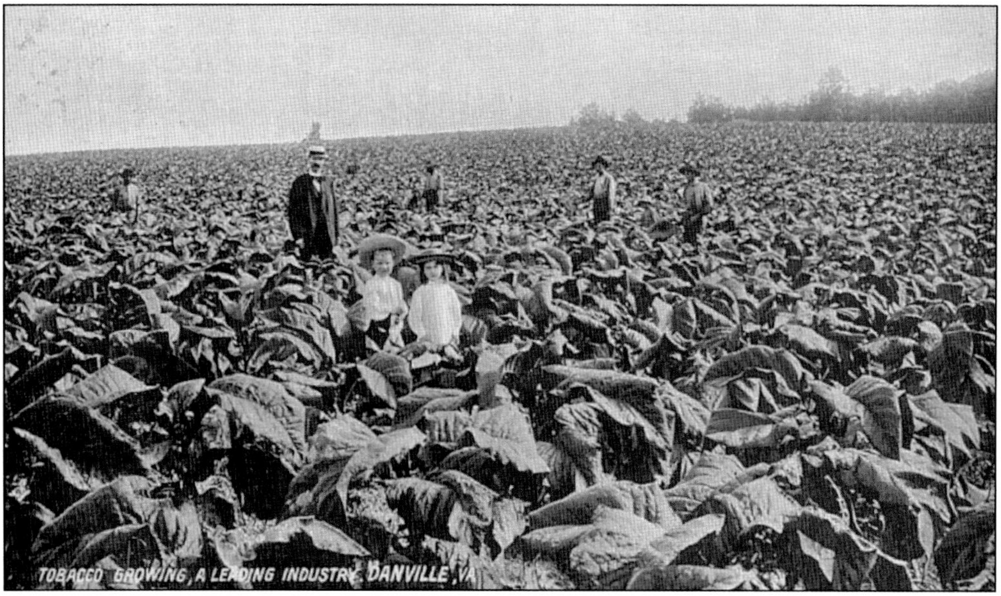

Tobacco is native to America and in fact was the country's first business. The red clay soil in and around White Oak Mountain north of Danville was discovered to produce the best grade of yellow leaf tobacco in the South. Tobacco brought more money to farmers than any other crop they could plant.

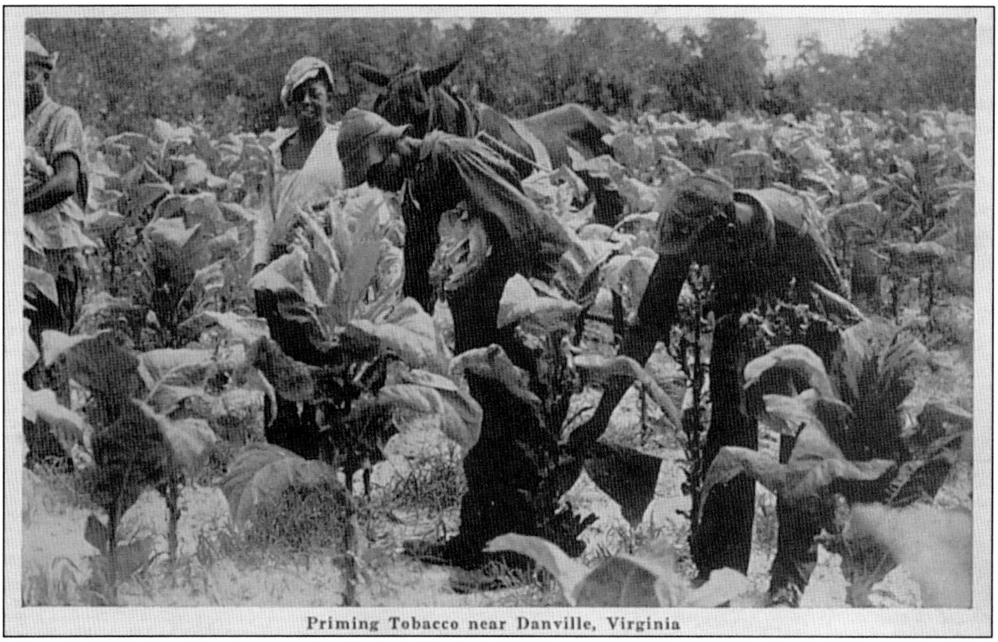

Tobacco leaves had to be pulled or primed from the stalks as soon as the plants began to ripen and then taken to special barns to be cured or dried out. North Carolina's Bayard Wootten photographed this 1940s view of local workers priming tobacco plants. Many of her original photographs are housed in the Photographic Archives of the University of North Carolina at Chapel Hill.

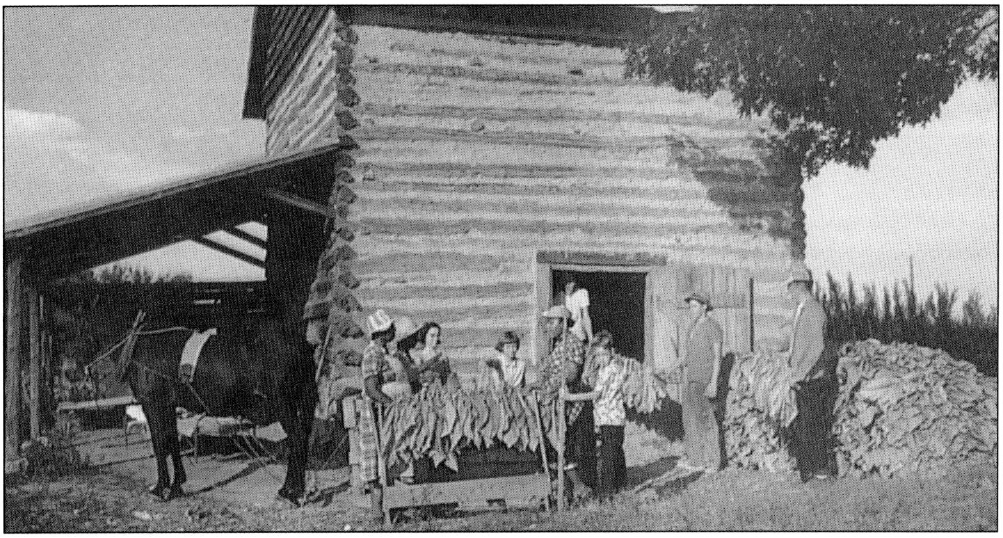

Brightleaf tobacco had its origins in the Piedmont areas of Virginia and North Carolina surrounding Danville. Tobacco leaves turn vibrant yellow when cured by quick exposure to dry heat inside the curing barns. Claimed to have been discovered by a slave of Abisha Slade of Caswell County, North Carolina, this process was nevertheless developed by the Slades and spread all over the South.

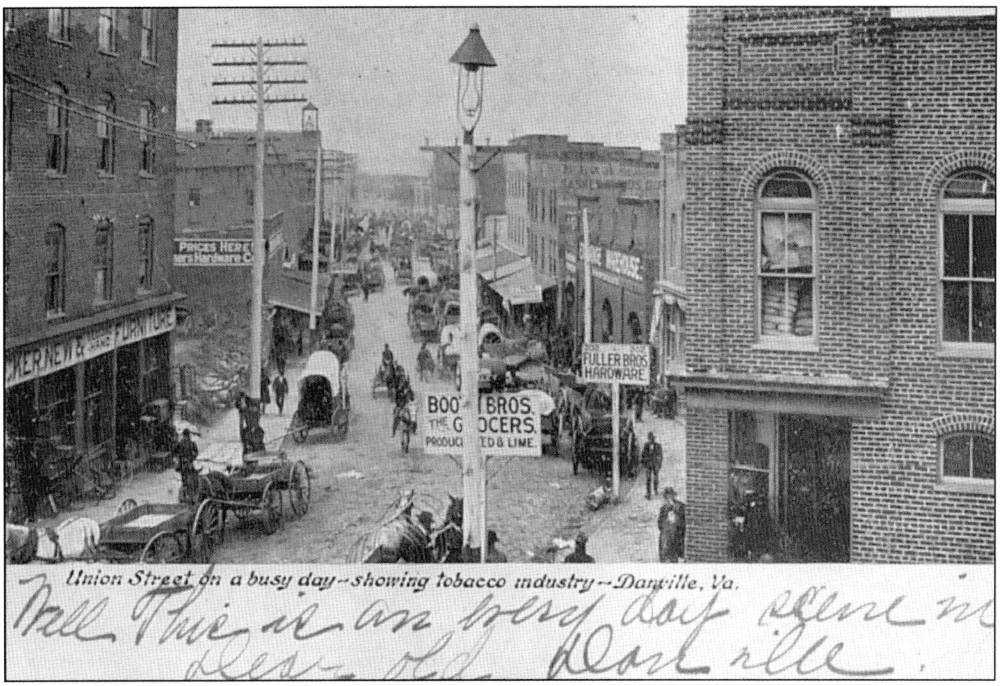

Every autumn farmers would bring bundles of tobacco by horse-drawn wagons to Danville, crossing the covered wooden bridges that led to numerous warehouses. Danville soon became the center of tobacco marketing and manufacturing in the South. Union Street, seen here in 1907, is today recognized for such businesses as the First State Bank on the left, and Abe Koplen Clothing Company and Beanie's Army Surplus on the right.

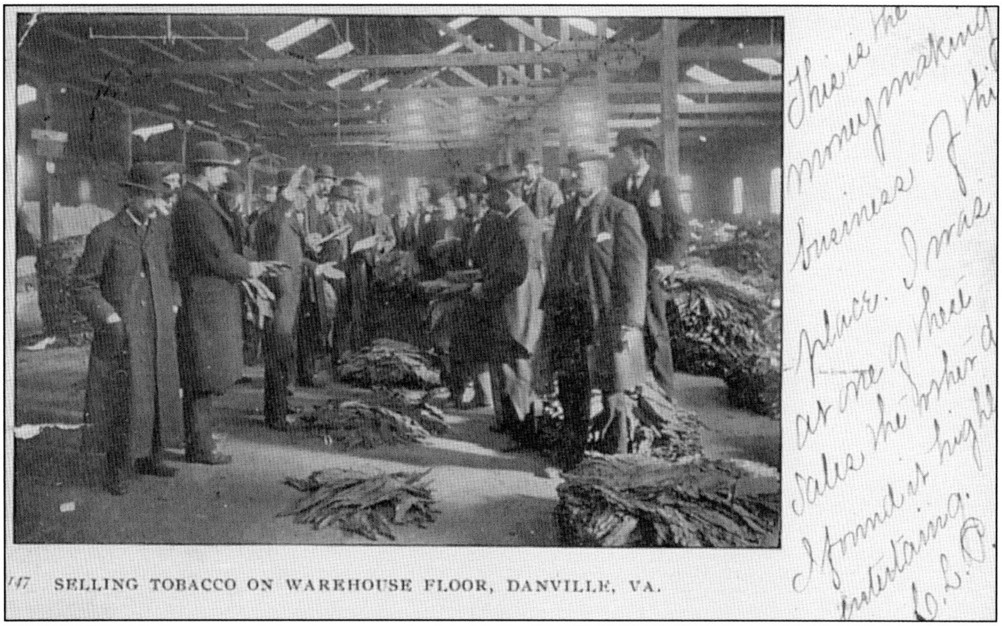

A revolutionary new auction system for selling tobacco was perfected in Danville in 1858 by Thomas D. Neal, a system that allowed buyers to inspect and bid on each individual pile of tobacco instead of making their purchases from samples. One of the more famous auctioneers of the late nineteenth century was Colonel Chiswell D. Langhorne, the father of Lady Nancy Astor and Irene Gibson, the "Gibson Girl."

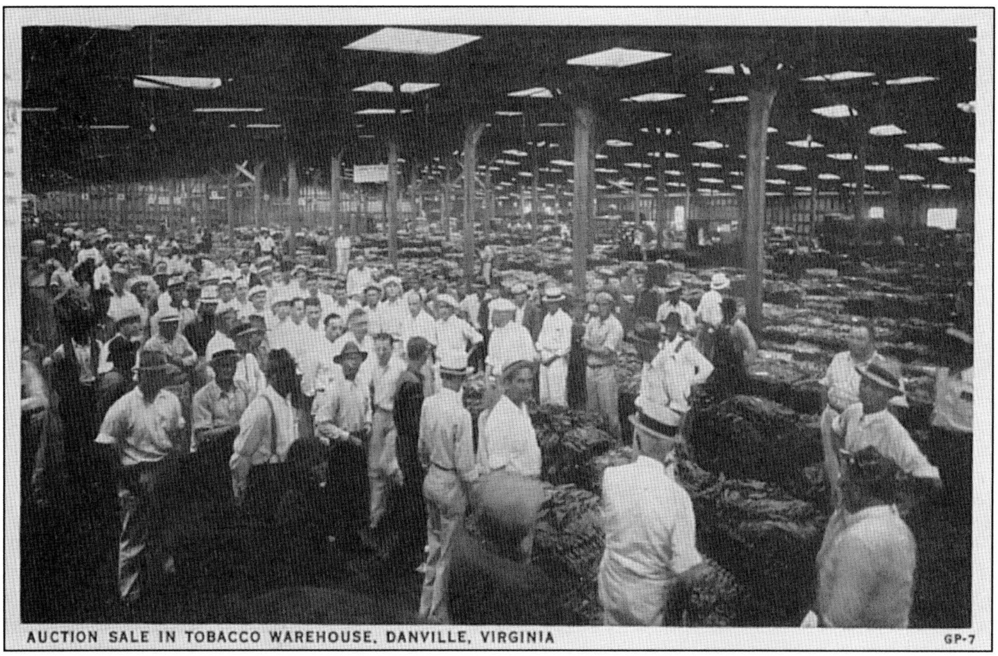

Totally unintelligible to the average listener, the songlike chant of tobacco auctioneers is captivating nonetheless. Bayard Wootten photographed this auction in Danville in the late 1930s, a scene quite typical of the cards produced by Graycraft Card Company.

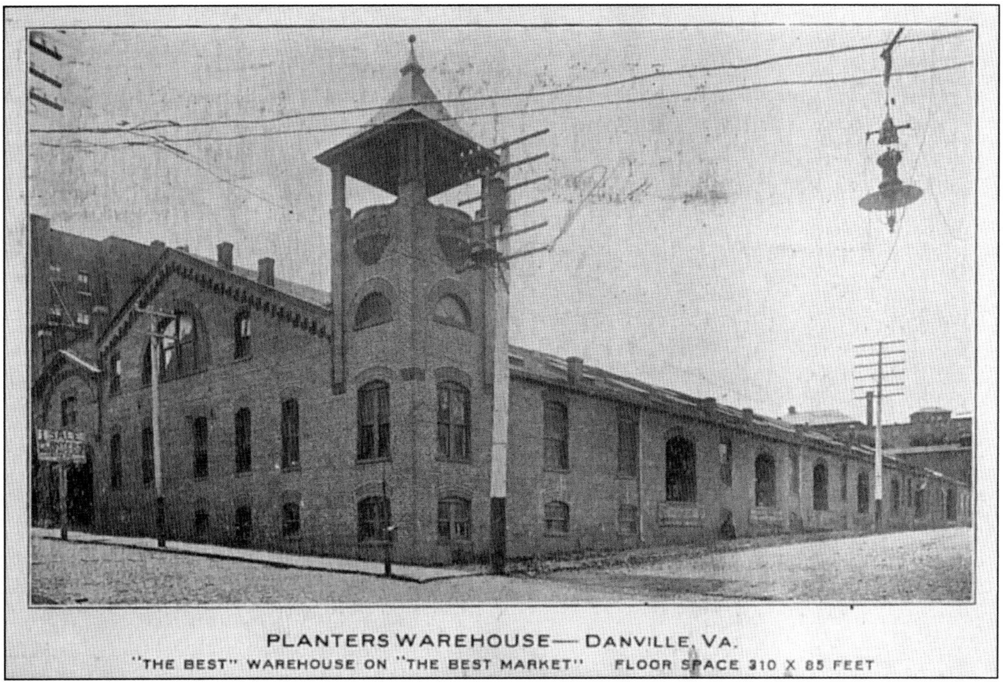

Planters Warehouse at the corner of Union and Spring Streets opened for business in 1869, the year that marked the beginning of the Danville Tobacco Association.

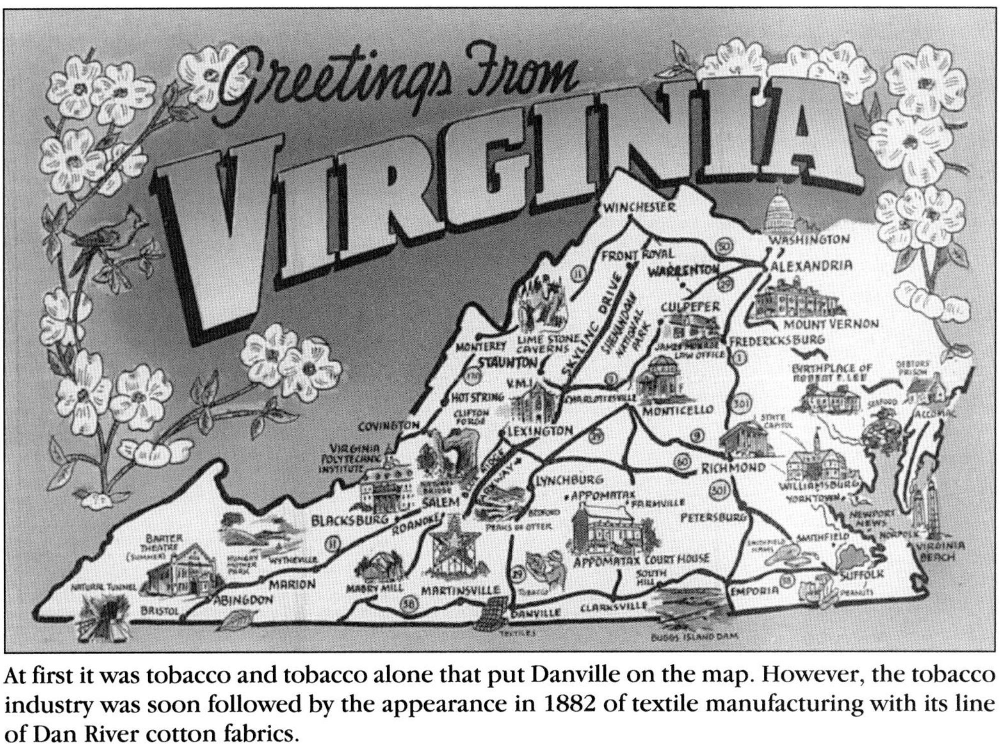

At first it was tobacco and tobacco alone that put Danville on the map. However, the tobacco industry was soon followed by the appearance in 1882 of textile manufacturing with its line of Dan River cotton fabrics.

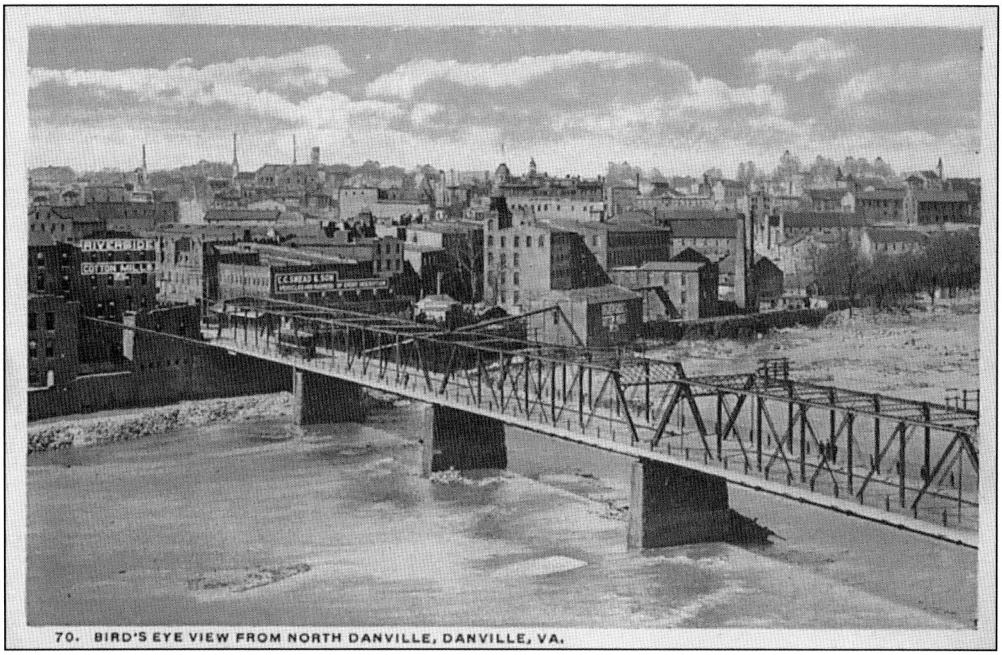

The cotton industry was brought to Danville by a group of six local businessmen, a group that included Thomas B. Fitzgerald, who was elected the first president of the Riverside Cotton Mills. Riverside was chartered in July 1882, opening its business at Mill No. 1 beside the Main Street Bridge.

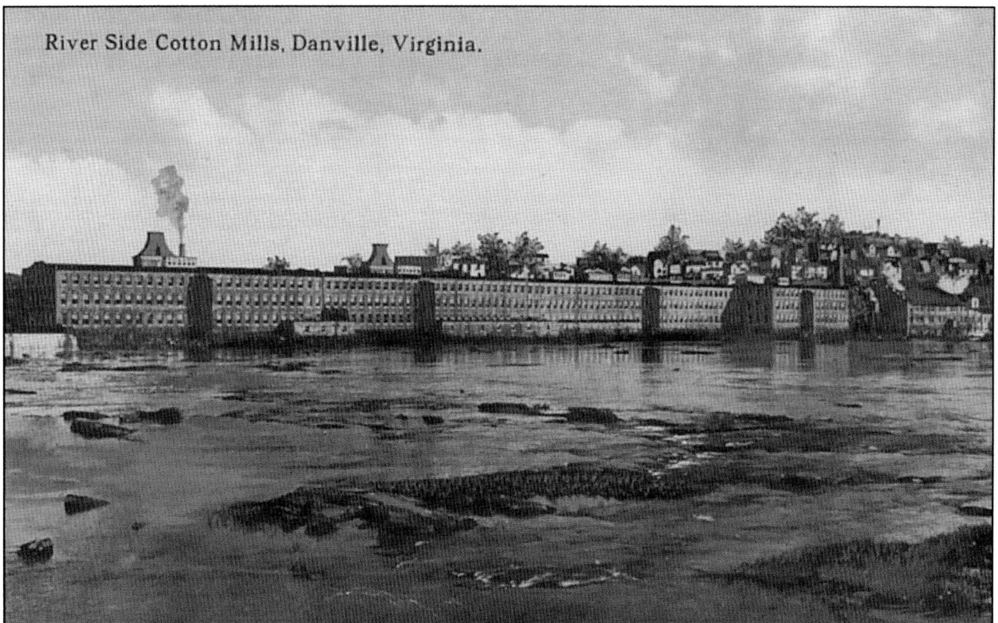

Riverside Cotton Mills expanded its business to the north side of the river with the addition of the Long Mill, or Mills No. 2, 3, 5, and 7. The company began production as a manufacturer of 27-inch-wide plaid fabrics.

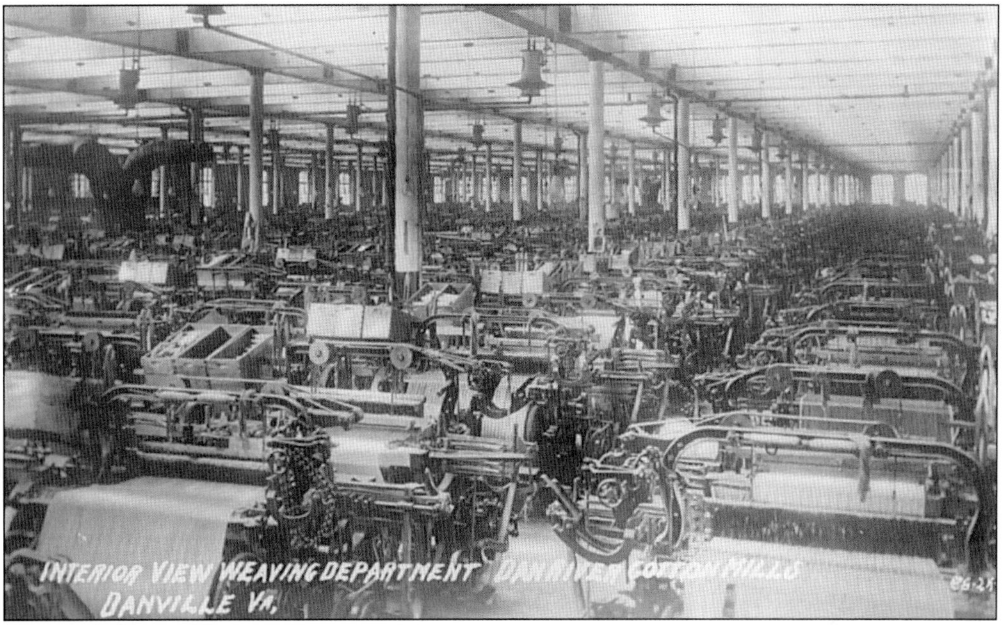

This interior view of Riverside Cotton Mills depicts the machinery used in the weaving department around 1910. Card collectors place higher value on interior scenes of businesses because fewer were published than external views, and fewer still showed people inside at work.

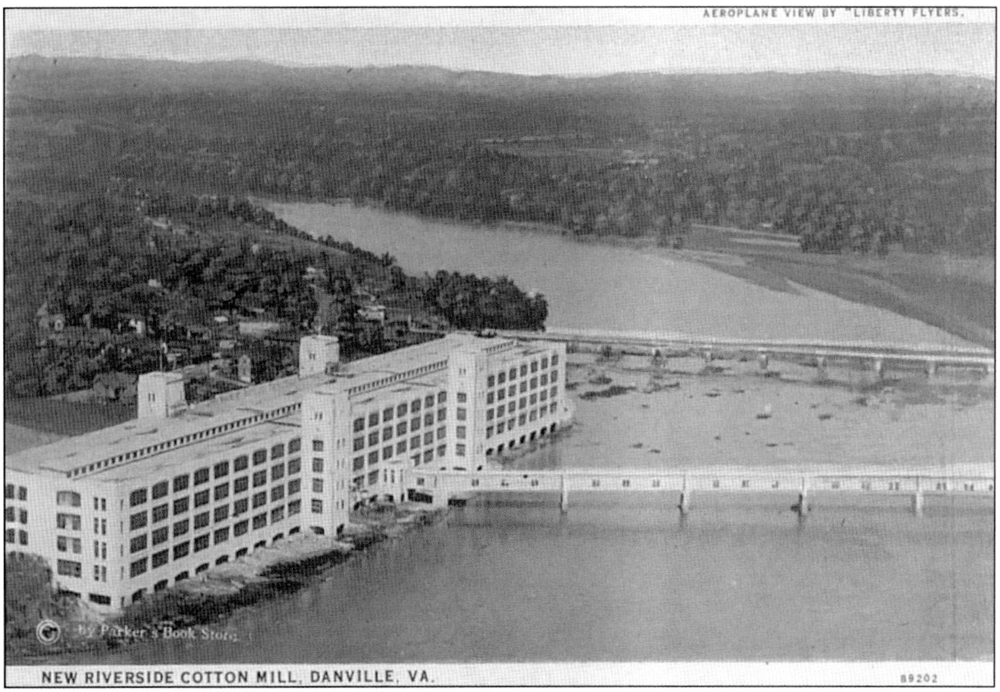

Constructed in 1921 of reinforced concrete, Mill No. 8 was situated beside the Roanoke Navigation Company's canal on the south side of the Dan River. Memorial and Riverside Drives did not exist at this time.

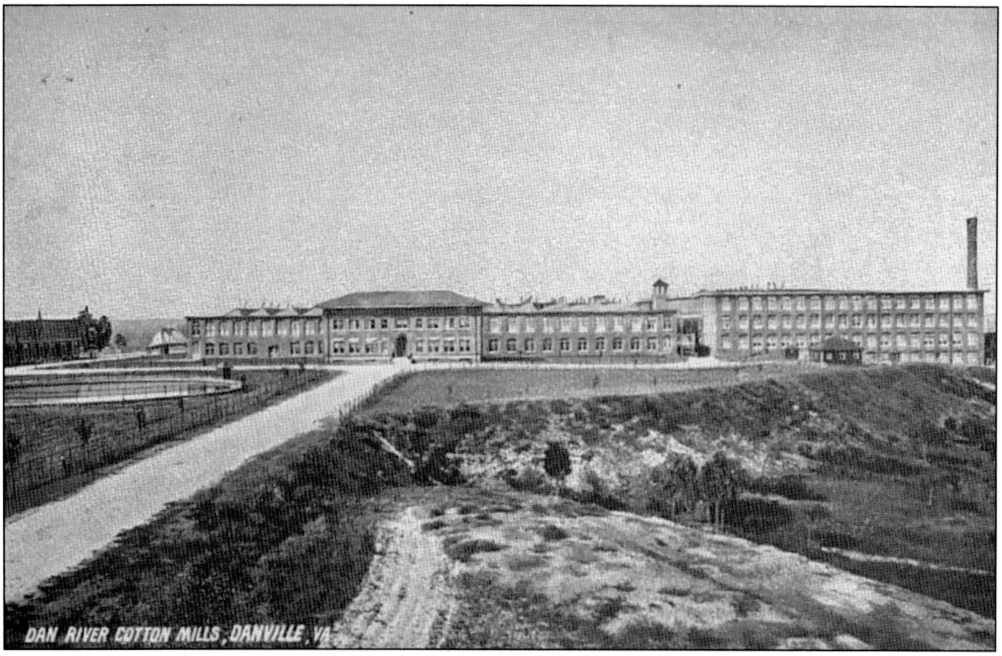

The cotton mill owners eventually acquired 1,100 more acres on the south side of town for expansion of their fast-growing industry. On top of mill buildings at both ends of town, electric signs welcomed travelers to the "Home of Dan River Fabrics."

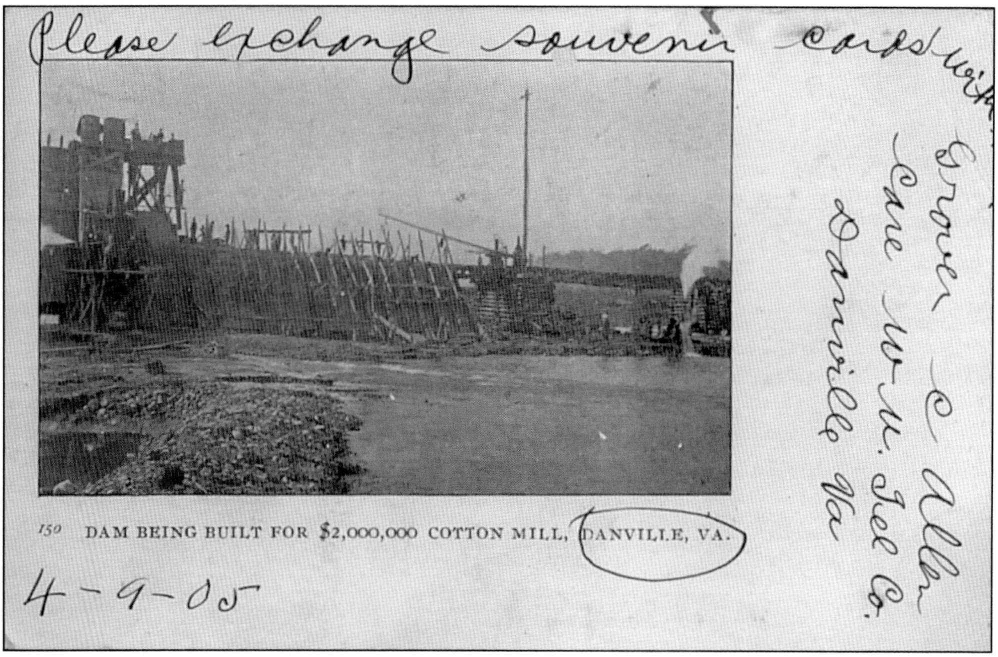

One of the early postcards of Danville, dated 1905, shows the construction of the dam at Schoolfield, just beyond Ballou Park. The sender of this card was obviously eager to swap with someone in order to enlarge his personal collection of picture postcards.

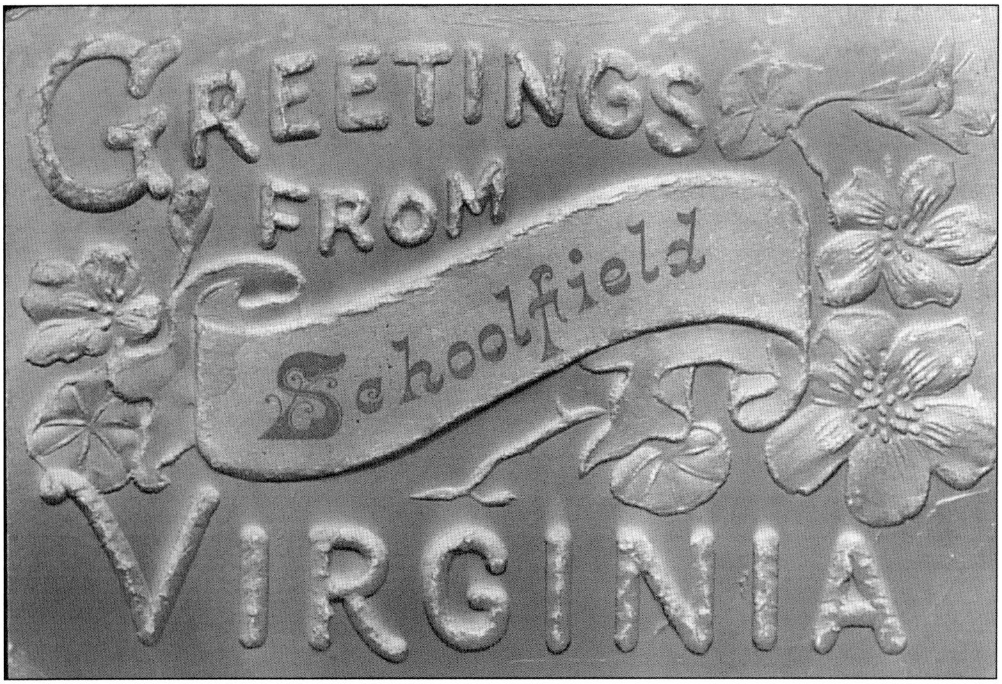

This embossed greeting card is a rare one, coming from the independent town of Schoolfield. Called Schoolfield after the prominence of that family's involvement with the mill, the company provided housing nearby for many of its workers. The village of Schoolfield gradually surrounded the textile giant.

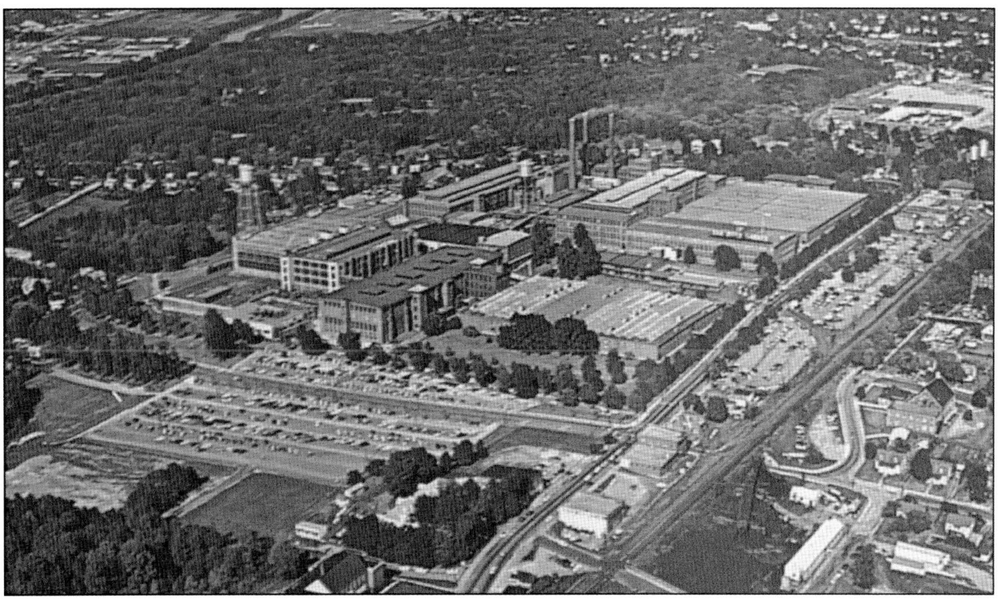

The town of Schoolfield was annexed by the City of Danville in July 1951. Stavros Calos photographed this aerial view of the cotton mills in the late 1950s, about the time that Dan River produced its successful WRINKL-SHED with DRI-DON fabric, and sold the first 100% cotton wash-and-wear dress shirts for men.

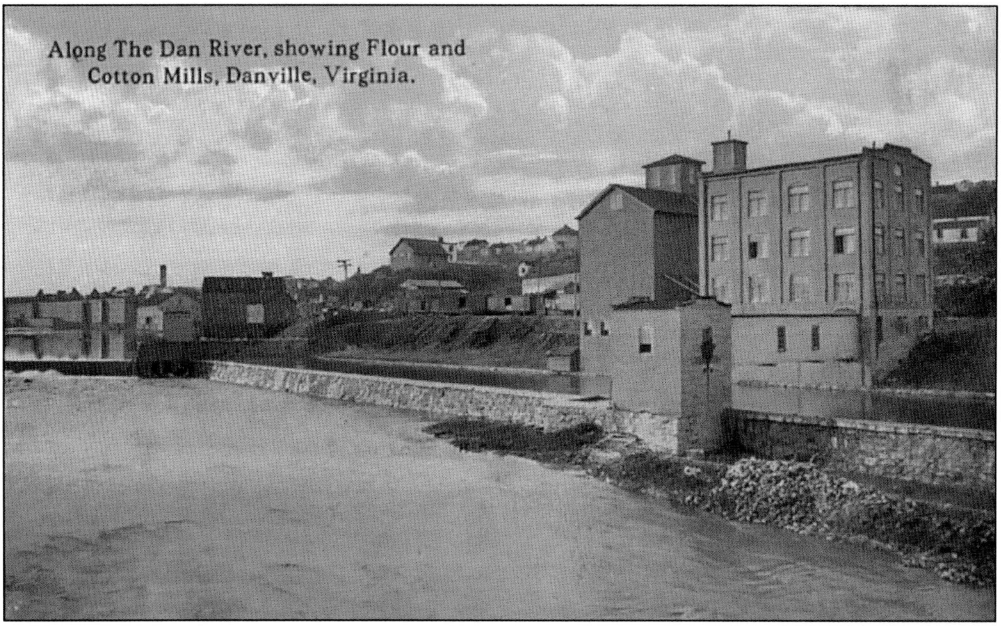

Another business to make use of waterpower from the Dan River, the Dan Valley Flour Mills opened in 1893 on the north side of the river. It was one of the largest in the South, producing flour with the brand names "Dan Valley" and "Oak Ridge."

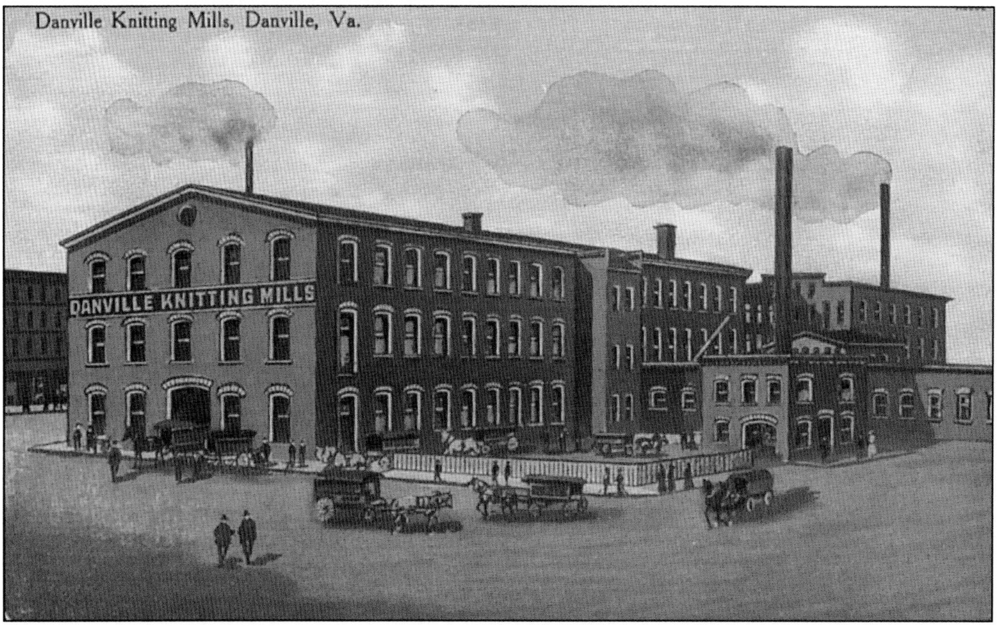

The Danville Knitting Mills at 515–525 Lynn Street (later Durham Hosiery) opened for business in 1889, offering various styles of hosiery for men, women, and children. This mill closed in the late 1990s.

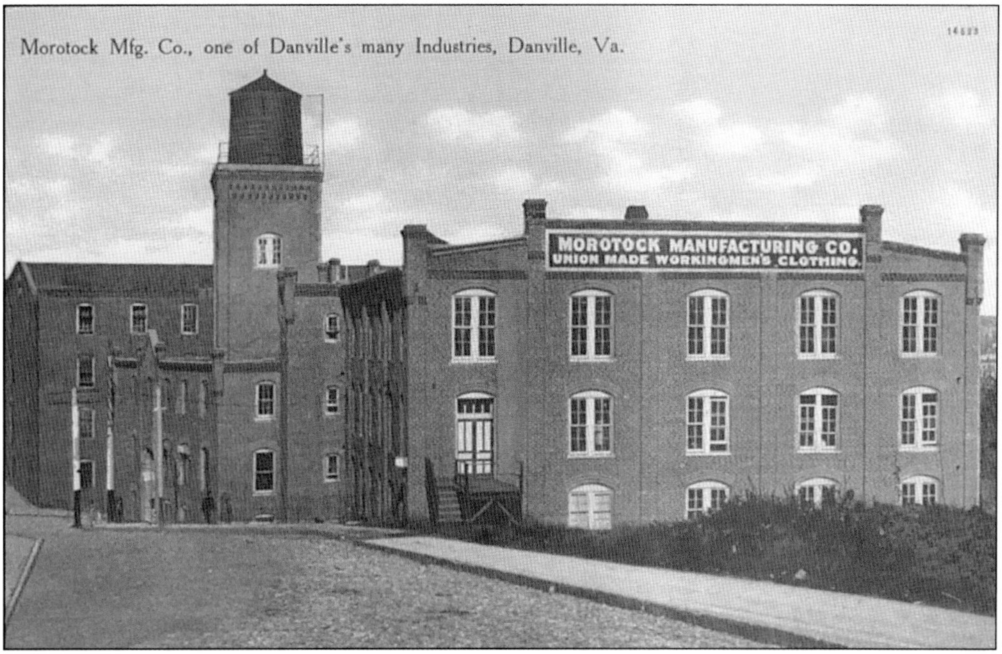

The Morotock Manufacturing Company at 100 North Floyd Street opened its textile business for the manufacture of overalls. Constructed around 1900 by a local architectural firm, Deitrick & Pearson, the intricate brickwork of the building is typical of the construction practices of the time.

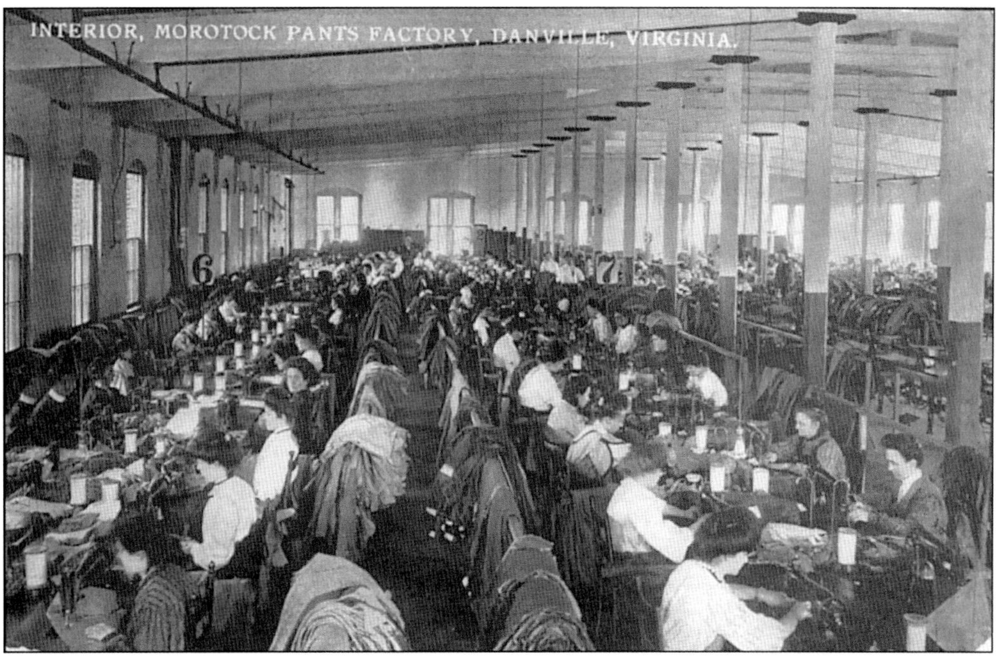

This unique interior view card from around 1912 shows laborers at work inside the Morotock factory. The overalls they stitched were sold under such brand names as Chief, Elk High Back, New South, or Bandana.

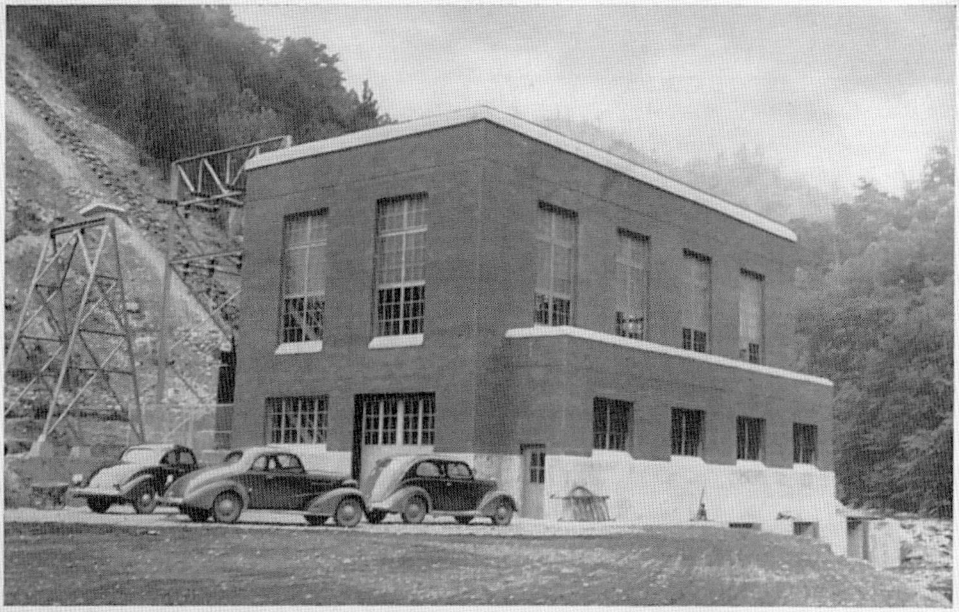

City of Danville Pinnacles Hydro-Electric Power Plant

The use of electricity by the citizens of Danville grew at such a fast pace that it was necessary to build a hydroelectric station outside of town to furnish the needed power. By 1938 a power plant was constructed at the Pinnacles of the Dan in Patrick County, Virginia, 82 miles from Danville.

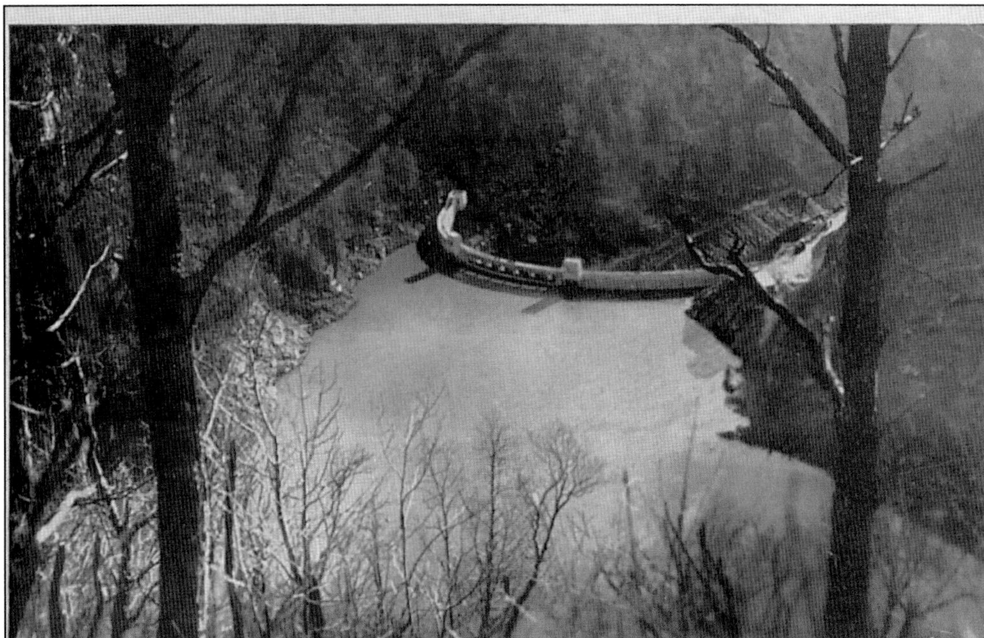

Townes Diversion Dam and Reservoir from Rim of Dan River Gorge

The Townes Diversion Dam at the Pinnacles is 3,000 feet above sea level, 113 feet high, and 575 feet long.

Three

MAIN STREET

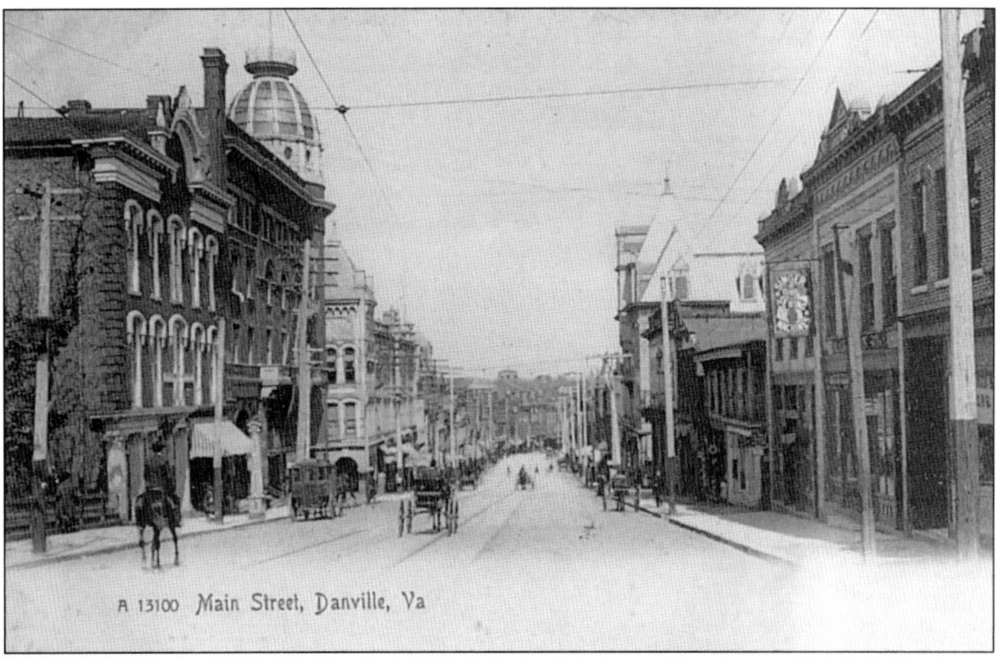

Before the advent of the automobile, this 1905 view of Main Street shows a stagecoach stopped in front of the Burton Hotel on its probable northerly run over the turnpike to Chatham and Lynchburg, Virginia.

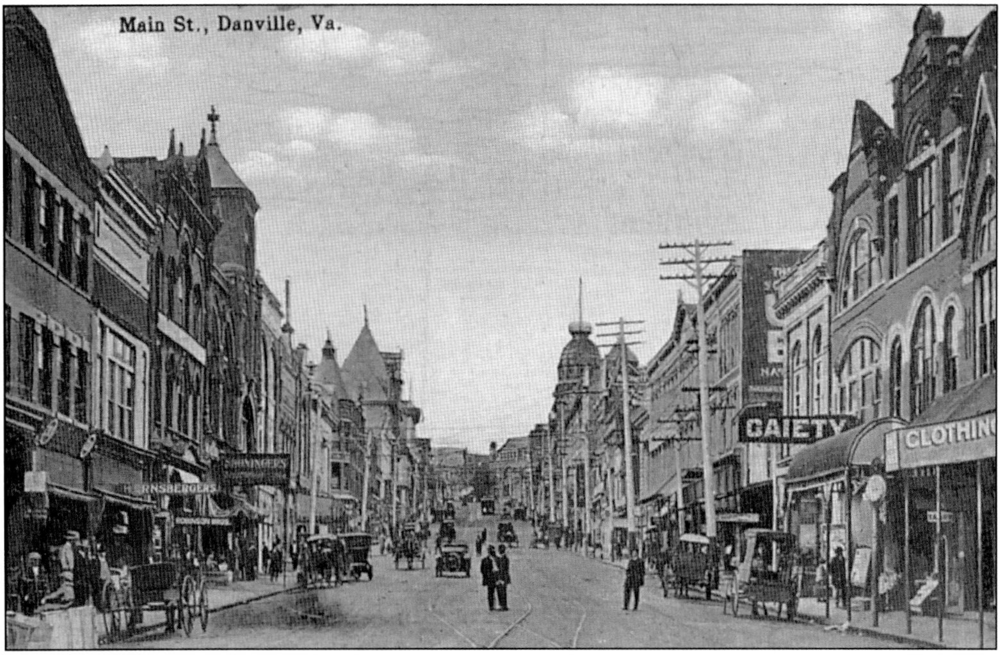

Main Street welcomed Danville's first automobile in the year 1908. People still used horses, carriages, streetcars, or trains for travel, or they walked. The Gaiety Theater on the right was one of Danville's early vaudeville theaters.

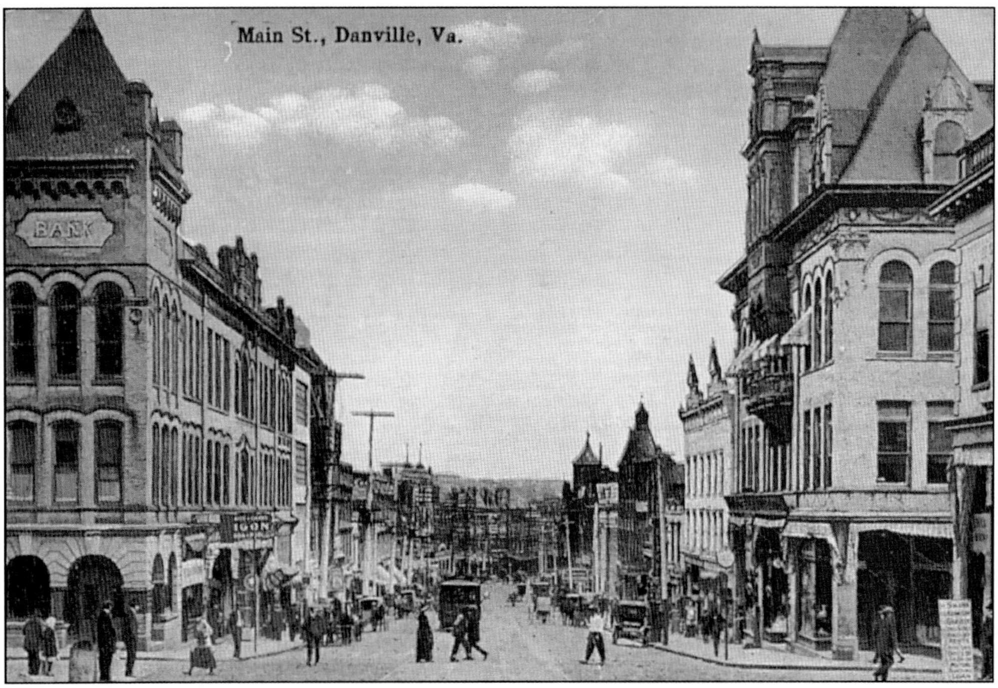

This 1914 view of Main Street at the corner of Union shows the Masonic Temple on the right and the Dudley Building on the left. Many elegant brick buildings lined the street all the way down to the bridge. The last two blocks were demolished in 1973.

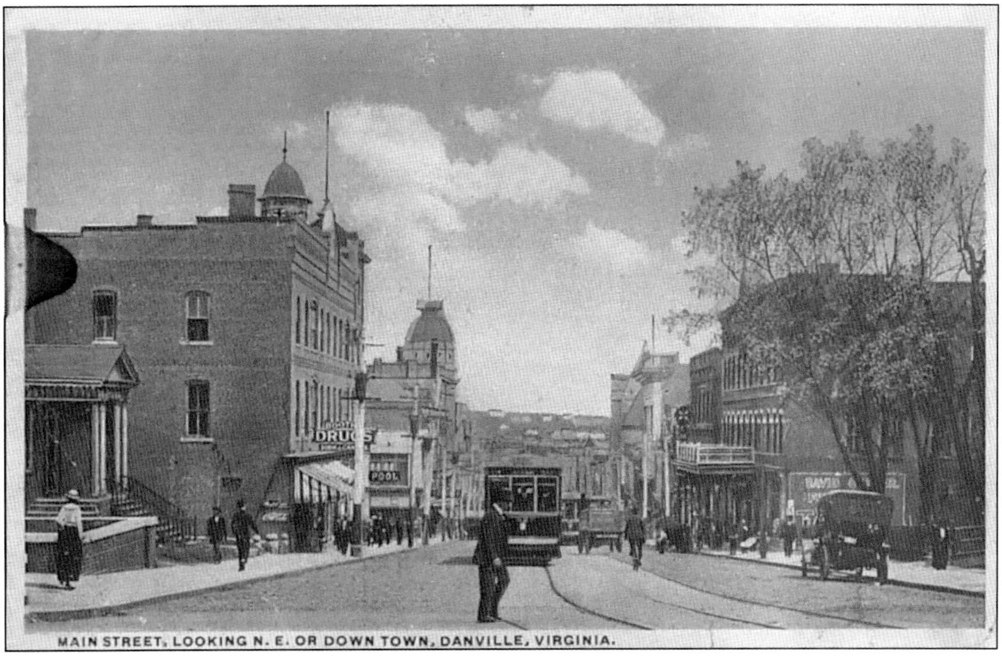

Danville's Opera House or Academy of Music was located at 541 Main Street, on the right side of the street in this 1919 card. Later the home of the Virginia Theater, in 1936 this was the first movie house in town to show a film on a Sunday.

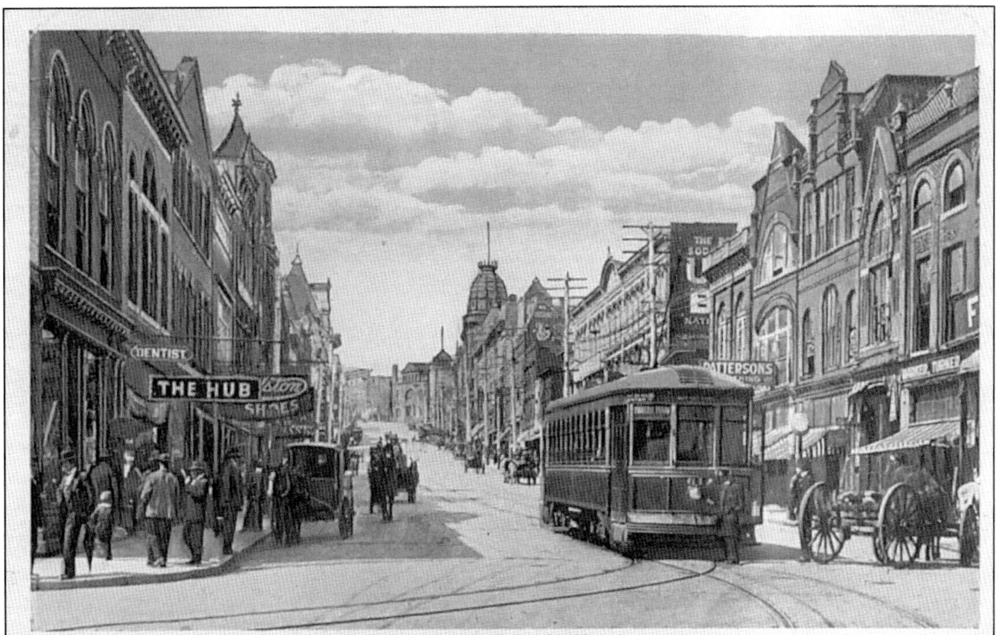

At 319 Main Street near the corner of Craghead stood the men's department store known as The Hub, which was advertised in 1912 as the "Clothiers, Where Fashion Revolves." Electric streetcars were the main form of public transportation from 1888 until 1938, when they were replaced by motor buses.

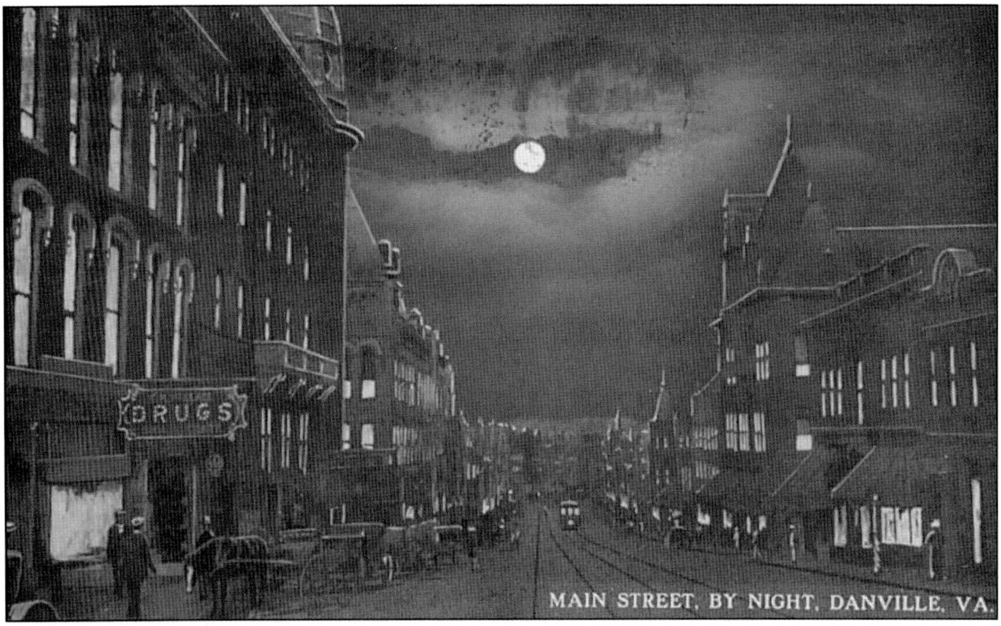

Night scenes on postcards can occasionally be found. Sometimes one can even locate a matching card with the same view shown in daylight. In comparing the cards, one sees that the publisher used the identical negative and simply altered the coloring or maybe forgot to change the direction of the shadows if a moon was added in the sky.

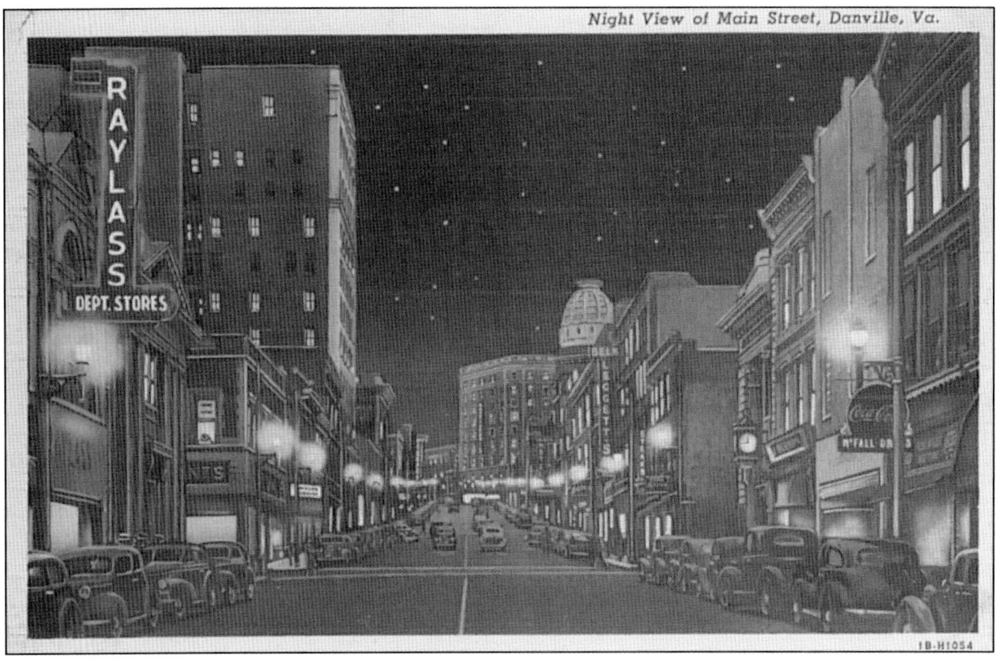

Even in the dark one can identify J. Berman's store for men's fashions and Belk-Leggett's department store (which opened in 1920 and moved to Piedmont Mall in 1984). Leggett's had a very popular basement section for those looking for the best bargains in town. Rayless Department Store stands across from McFall's Drug Store.

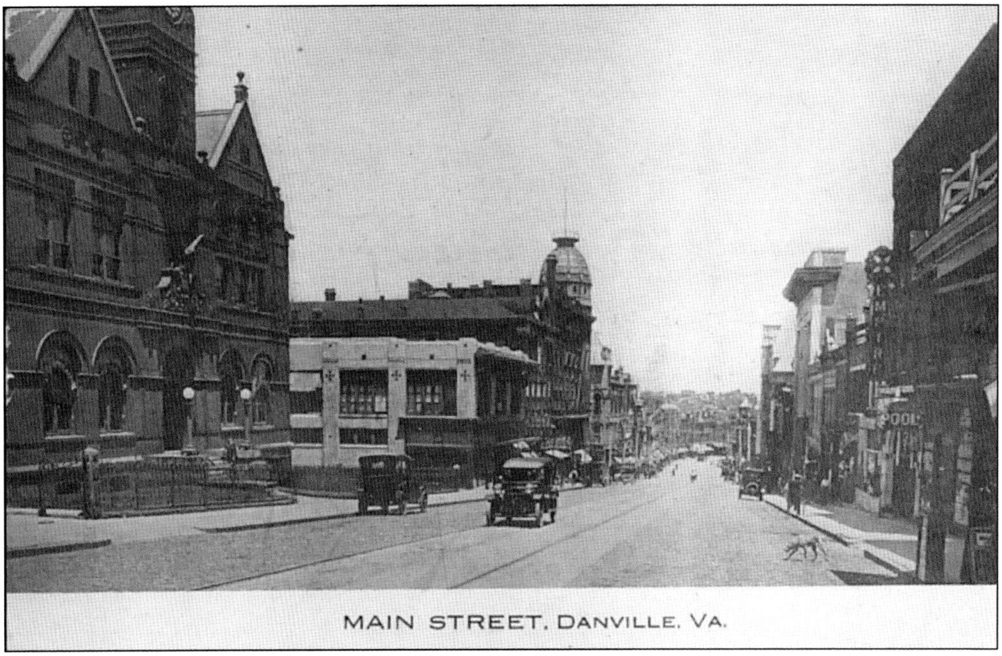

In this 1920s view, the Arcade Building at 520 Main Street stood downhill from the post office. Many people remember as children the anxiety of walking upstairs into this early "mini-mall" to visit Drs. Sam or E. Budge Kent, dentists.

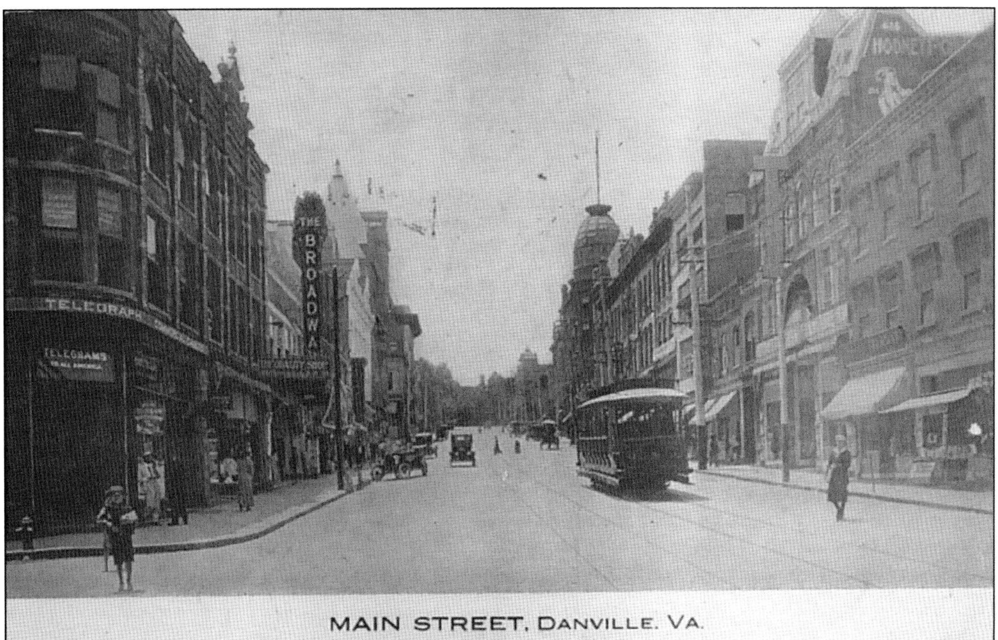

The Broadway Theater at 329 Main Street was one of the most popular movie houses in town at the turn of the twentieth century. It burned in later years and reopened as the Lea Theater

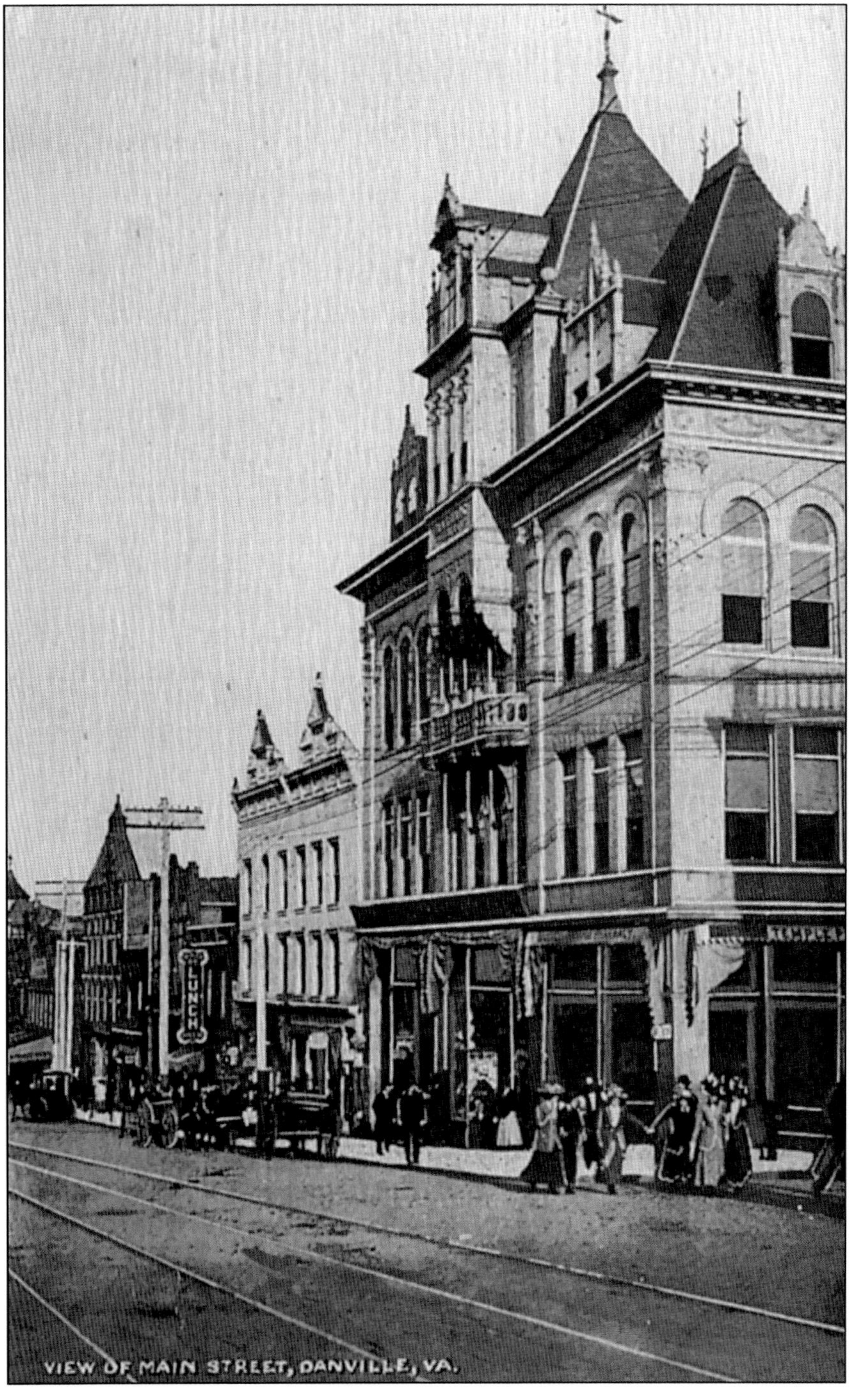

This 1909 postcard shows a view rarely seen of the right side of lower Main Street. The four-story Masonic Temple was built in 1901, yet burned to the ground when a fire broke out in 1920 that consumed nearly the entire block. Jacob's Drug Store, Woolworth's, Parker's Book Store, the Broadway Theater, Z.V. Johnson's Department Store, and other businesses were also destroyed by this disastrous fire.

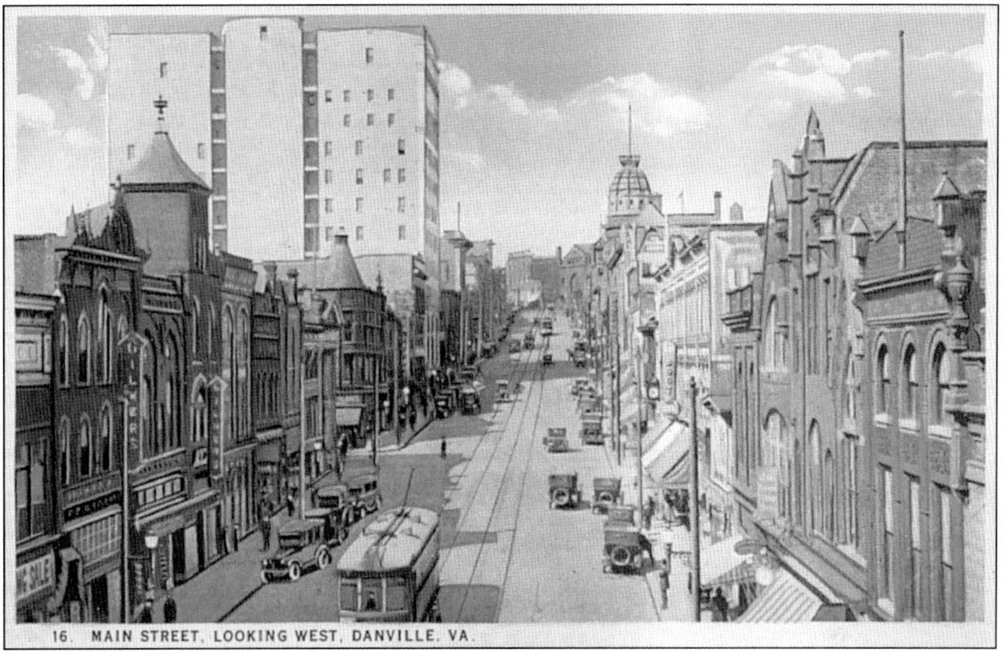

It is interesting to see subtle changes made in the course of a few brief years. The city's first "skyscraper" was built in 1922, the third building on the same site known as the Masonic Temple. Lower down on the left two businesses feature towers at the tops of their buildings.

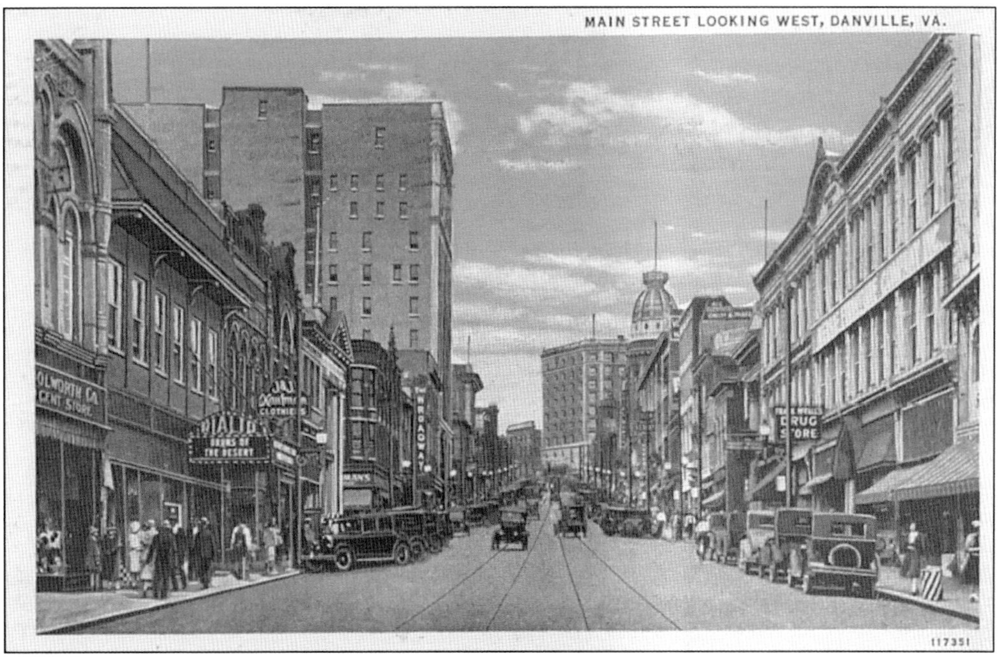

By 1926 the Municipal Building at the top of the hill was replaced by the newer Hotel Danville (the second skyscraper) and the towers were removed from the buildings on the left. One can clearly see the location of Woolworth's, J. & J. Kaufman Clothier's, and the Rialto and Broadway Theaters.

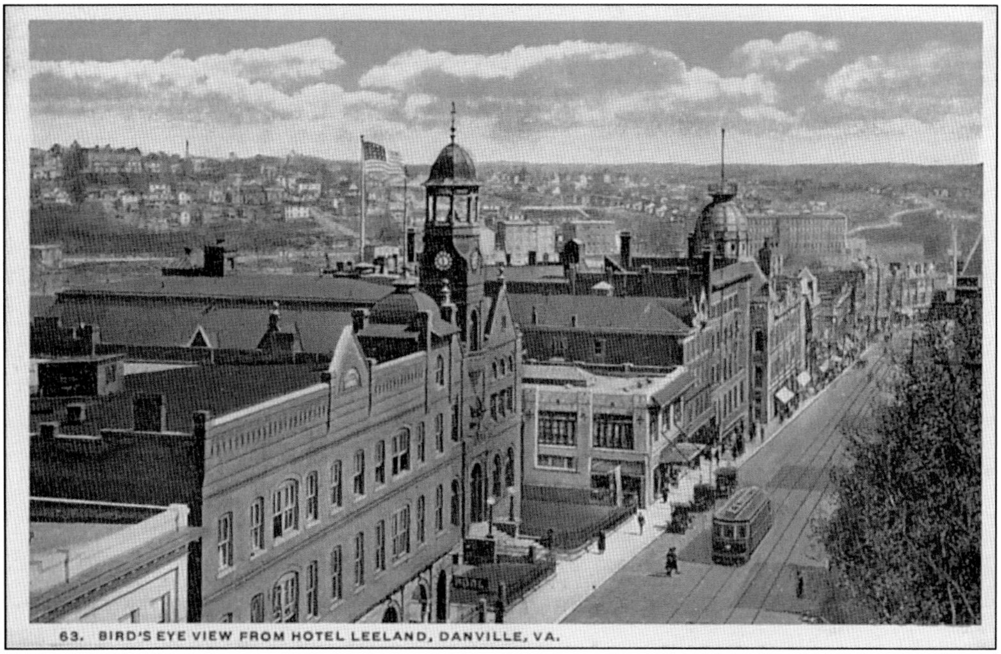

The Curt Teich Company of Chicago published many Danville postcards at the request of shops like Parker's Book Store (in the white building at the far left). J.F. Parker was responsible for ordering many Danville postcards from Teich, finding it a challenge to provide enough variety for the public who constantly demanded new views.

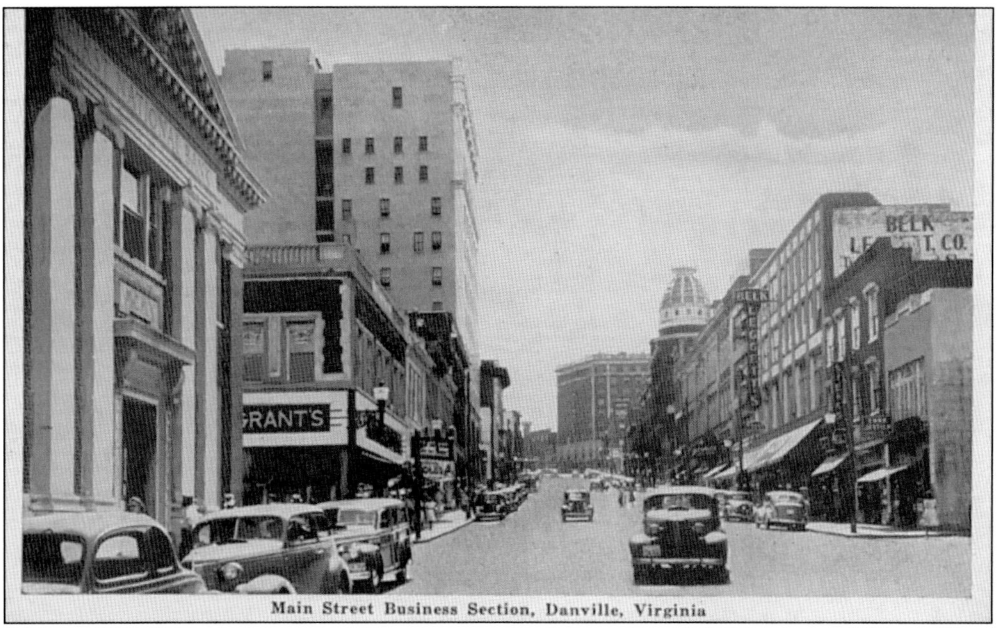

Main Street was wide enough to continue two-way traffic through the 1940s. The First National Bank on the left of this scene was founded in 1872 as the Planters National Bank. This bank has undergone numerous name changes including First & Merchants National Bank, SOVRAN National Bank, NationsBank, and currently the Bank of America.

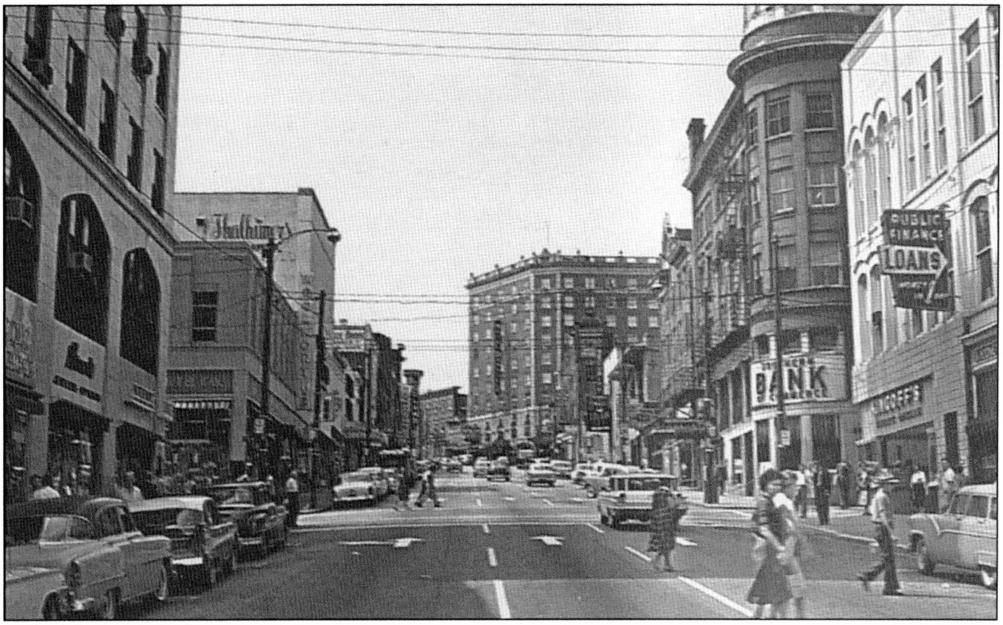

In 1952 traffic along Main Street was altered to a one-way pattern. The number of individual cars owned by citizens grew at a swift rate during the prosperous years of the 1950s, especially when gasoline cost only 29¢ per gallon. In 1988 Main Street again opened to two-way traffic as numerous downtown stores relocated to the Piedmont Mall.

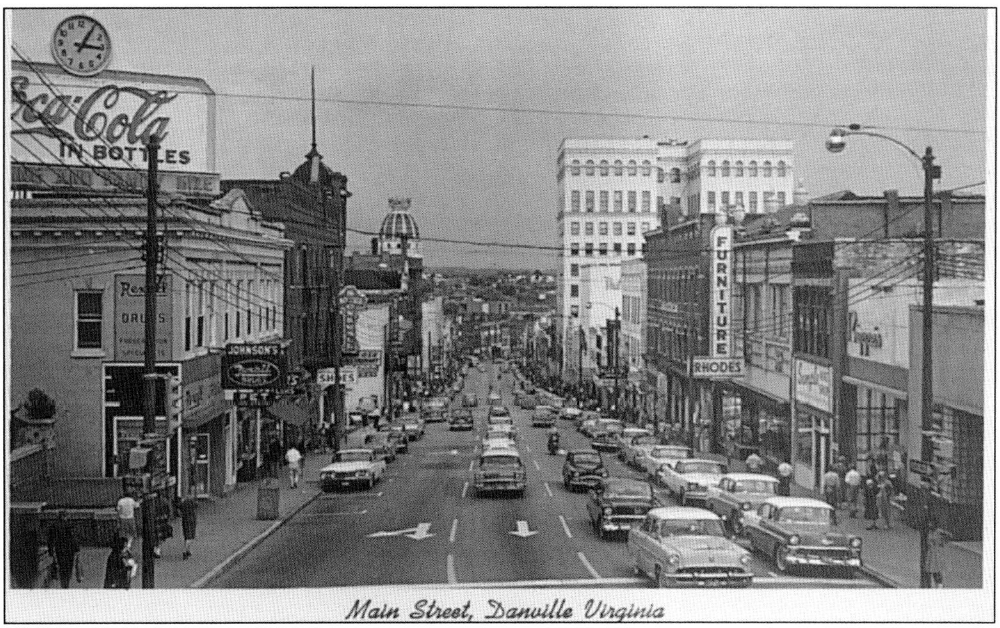

The size of cars definitely reflected the prosperity of the 1950s, as did bright colors and chrome trimming. Billboards like Coca-Cola's adorned buildings as well as roadsides. Rhodes Furniture Store at 549 Main Street (now occupied by Clement & Wheatley Law Offices) and Rippe's (a fashionable ladies' clothing store that opened in 1907) at 559 Main Street can be seen on the right.

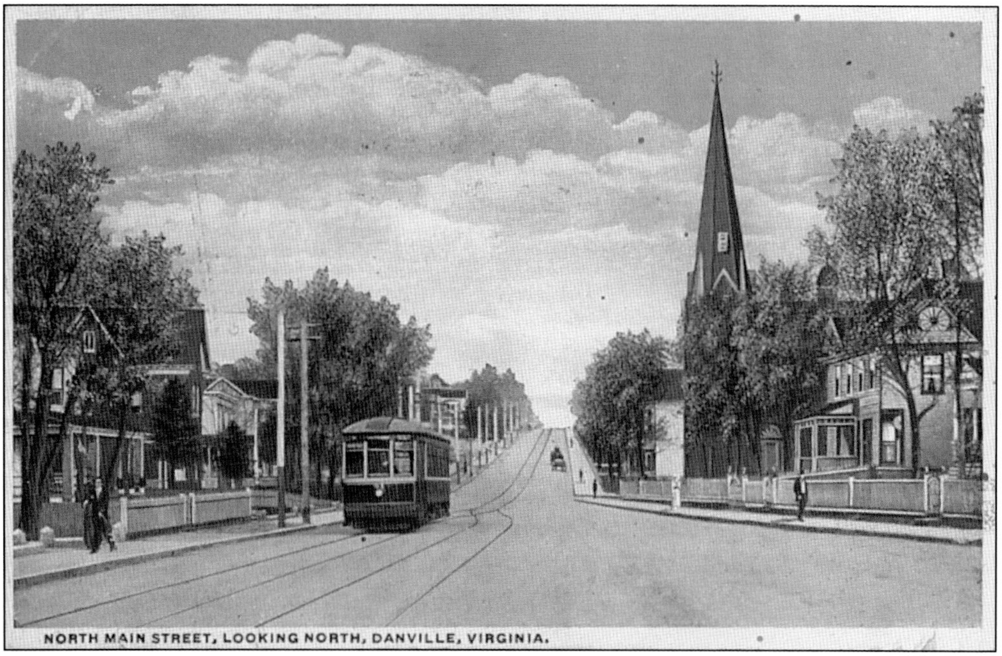

Main Street continues through the entire length of the city and across the river becomes North Main Street. North Danville, once an independent town called Neapolis, was annexed by Danville in 1896. Some years later two schools were built a few blocks up this street: Woodrow Wilson Junior High (1926) at Benefield Avenue and William F. Grasty Elementary (1935) on New Street.

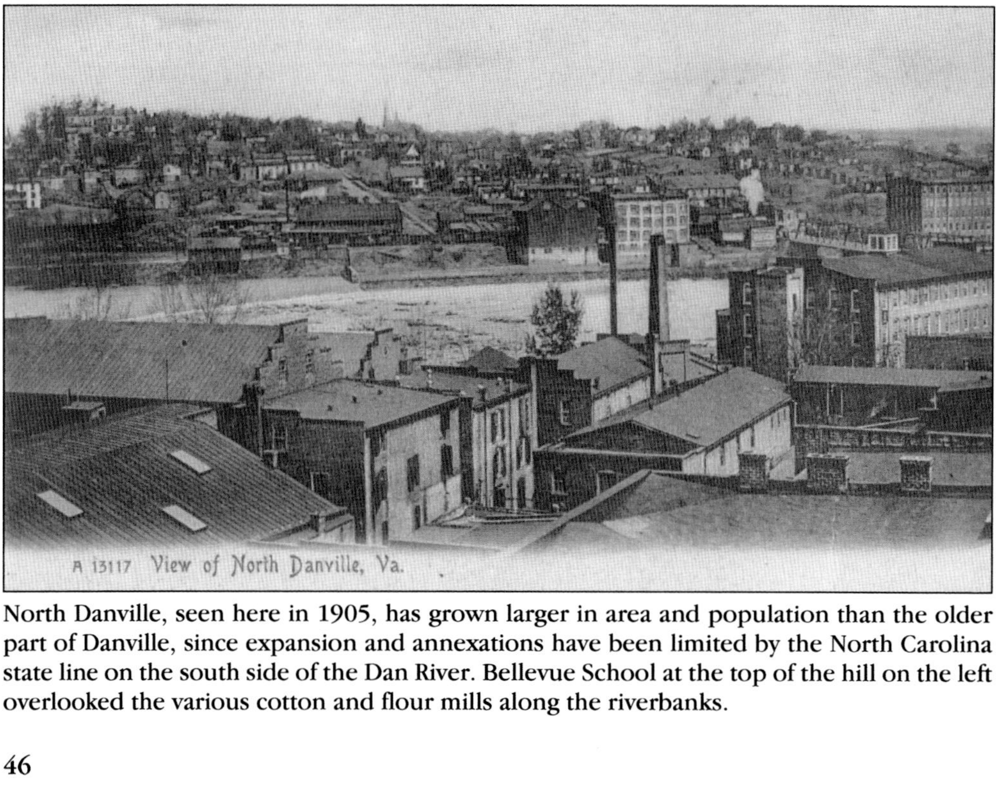

North Danville, seen here in 1905, has grown larger in area and population than the older part of Danville, since expansion and annexations have been limited by the North Carolina state line on the south side of the Dan River. Bellevue School at the top of the hill on the left overlooked the various cotton and flour mills along the riverbanks.

Four

HEART OF THE CITY

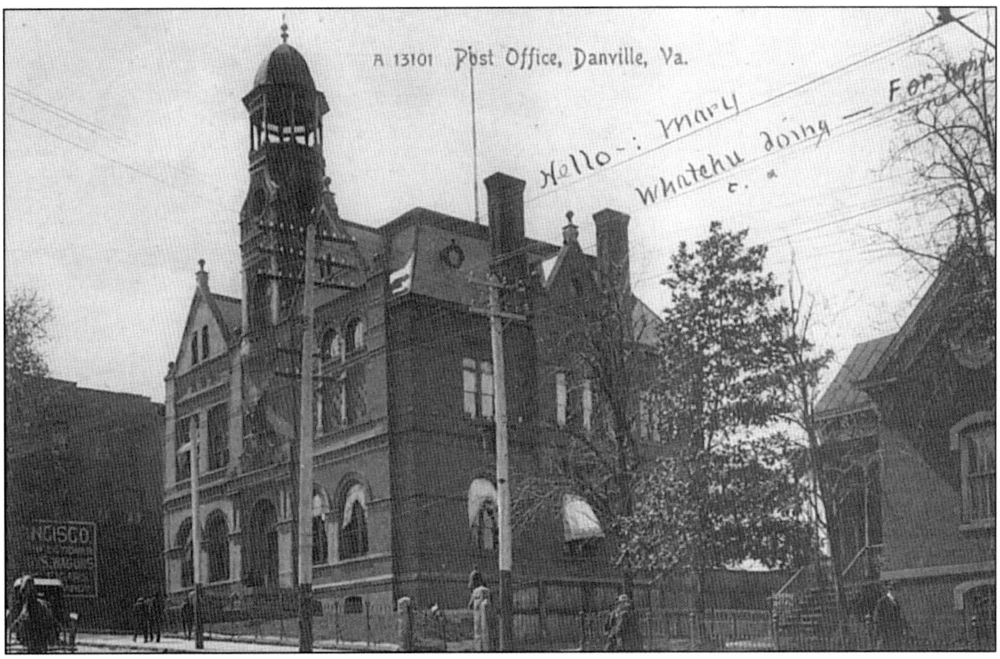

The United States Court and Post Office at 530 Main Street (where First Citizens Bank now stands) was completed in 1883. One value of this 1907 postcard is that it shows family residences that once lined the upper blocks of Main Street. The small brick house on the right was the home of banker William F. Cheek.

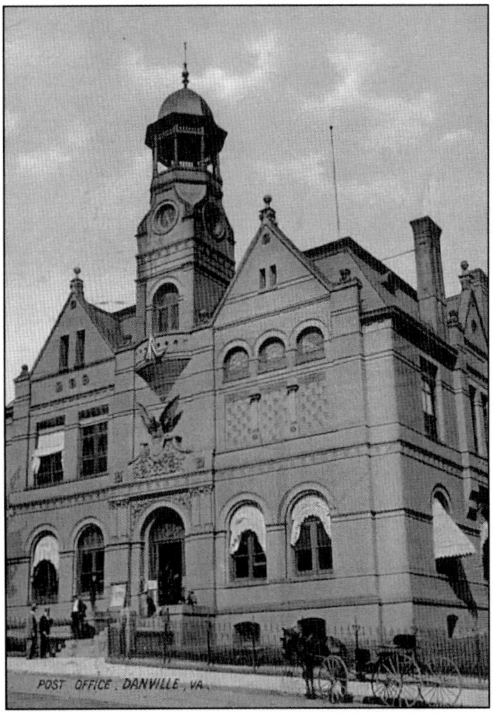

Designed by James G. Hill in the style of the Bureau of Engraving and Printing in Washington, D.C., the post office was torn down in the 1930s when a larger building was erected further up the same street.

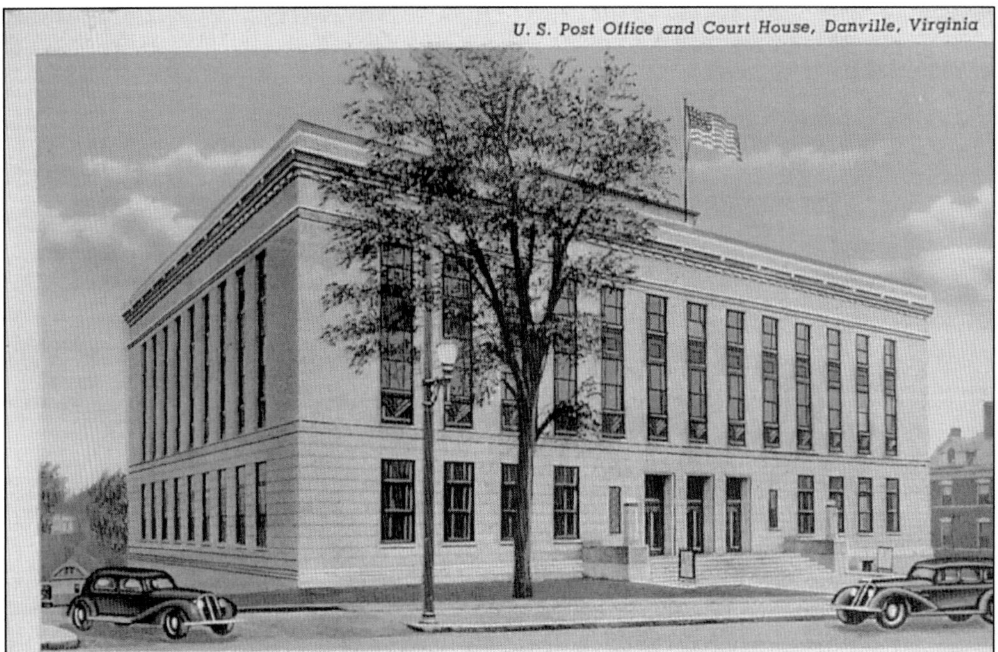

The Danville Post Office at 700 Main Street was erected in 1932 in the Art Deco style frequently used by architect J. Bryant Heard for commercial downtown buildings. The federal post office and courthouse has served the city well for decades, but will be expanded with a newer facility late in the year 2000 that will be located across the river near the mall.

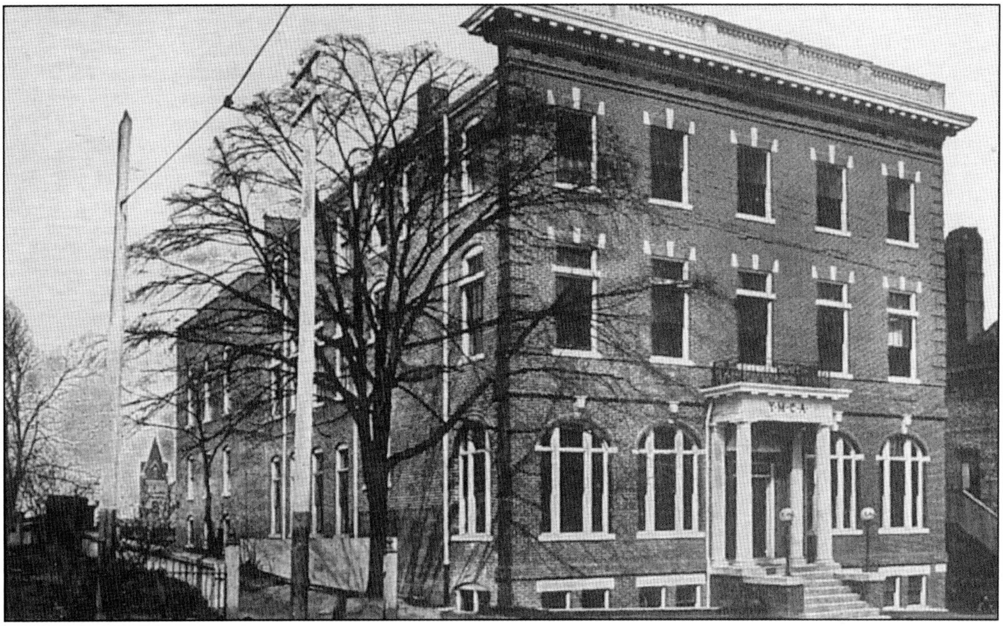

The Danville Young Men's Christian Association was established in 1907 at 616 Main Street and served the menfolk of Danville for 62 years at that site. It was razed in 1969, the year that man (Neil Armstrong) first set foot on the moon.

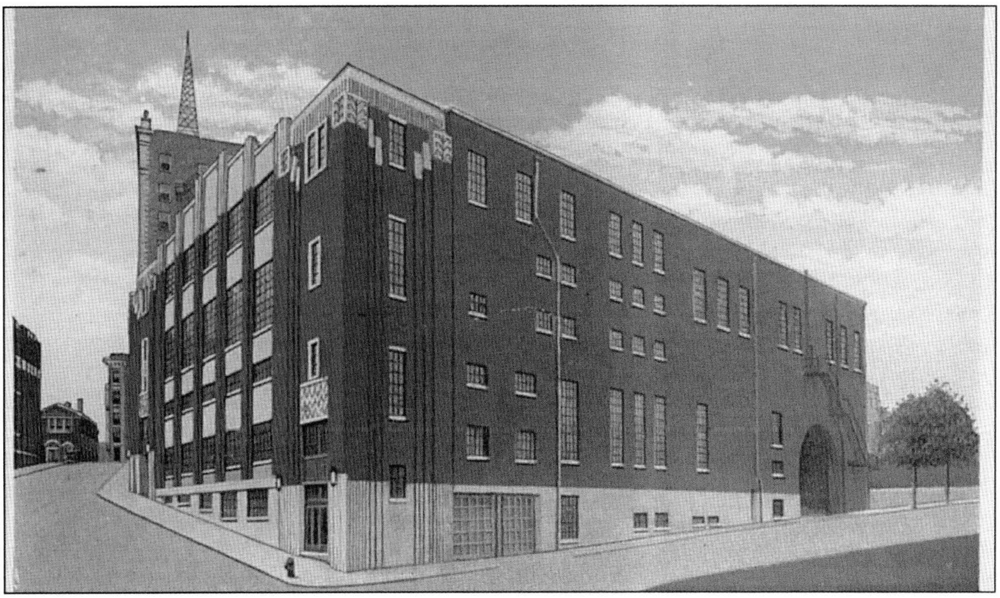

Danville's former city armory on Floyd Street was built around 1931 in the popular Art Deco style of the day. For many years Anne Boyer's dance recitals were performed in its auditorium, where Martha Fowlkes and Meredith Gravely were featured soloists. At the top of the hill beside the armory, the home of John M. Johnston can be seen. Built in 1860, the upper part of the residence was used to house the Bank of Danville. In April 1865 the gold reserves of the Confederacy were stored in this bank for the ten days that Danville was actively involved in the Civil War.

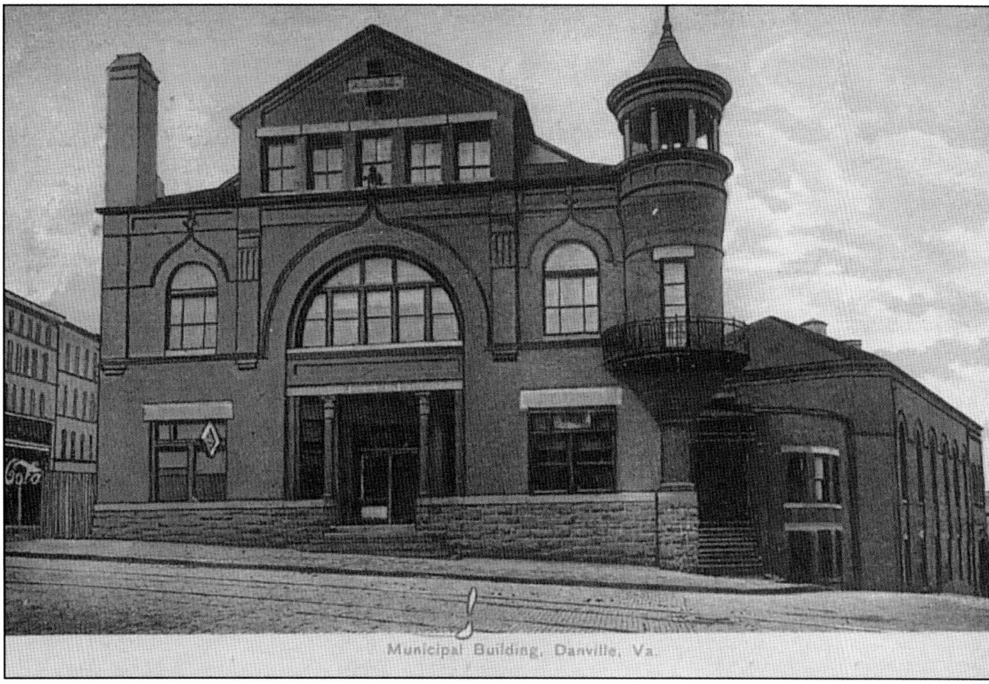

The Municipal Building stood from 1890 to 1926 at the corner of Main and Floyd Streets, with the City Market located behind the building. A terra cotta bull's head still overlooks the entry to the market area. James H. Fitzgerald, a cousin of T.B. Fitzgerald, is credited with the construction of this building.

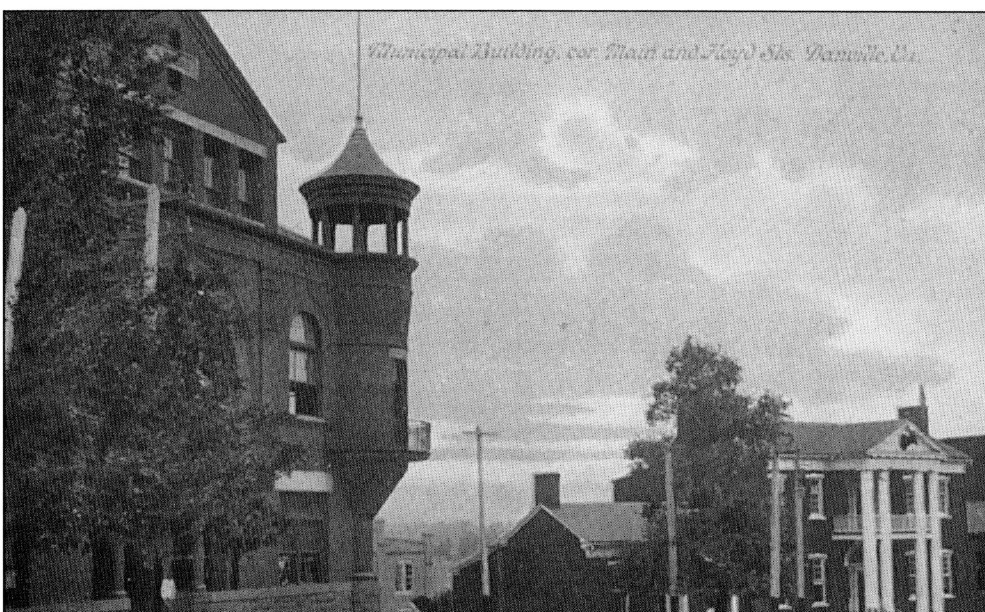

Across Floyd Street from the Municipal Building stood the home of James Lanier, Danville's first mayor. Built in 1839, Lanier used the lower wing of the house as the office of the Farmers' Bank of Virginia, where he served as cashier.

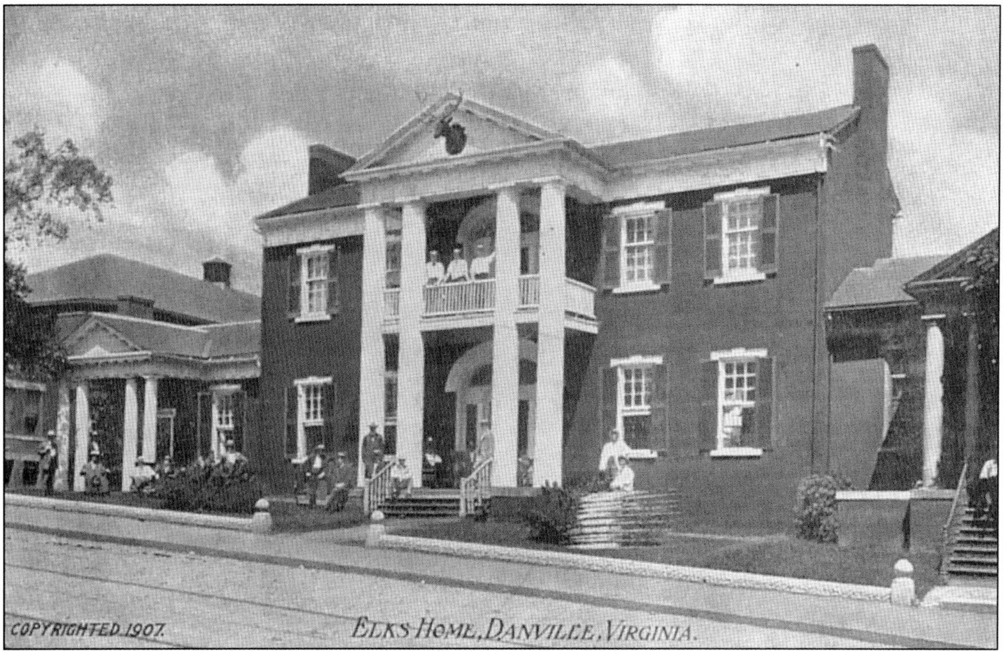

In 1906 the Danville Lodge No. 227 of the Benevolent and Protective Order of Elks bought this Federal-style brick house and used it for their members for several years before constructing a newer and larger building.

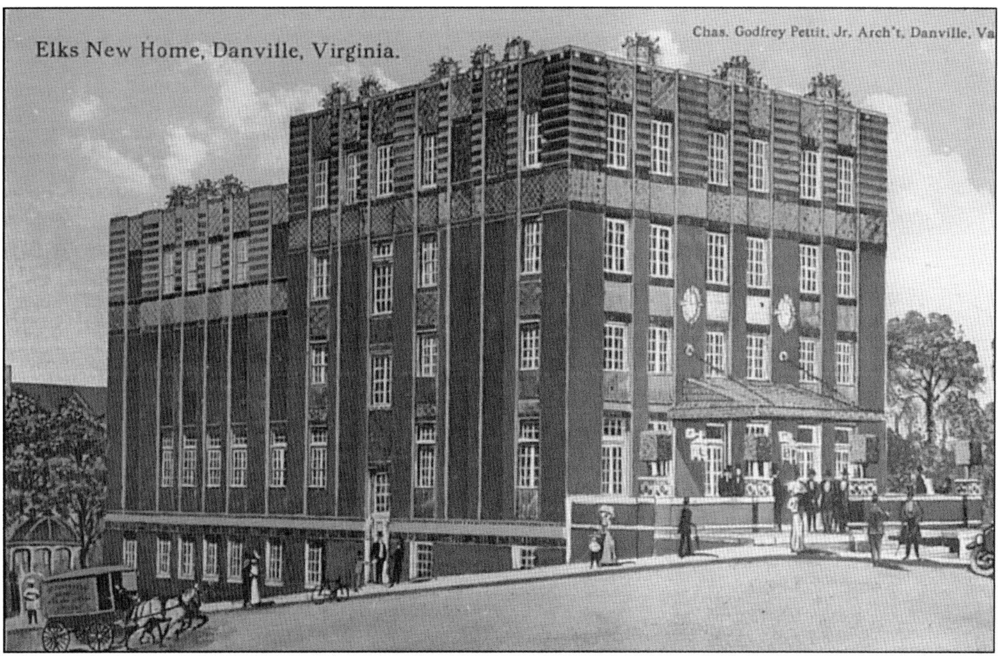

The lodge has played an important part in the history of Danville since its founding in 1892. This new Elks Home built by the noted Danville architect, Charles G. Pettit Jr., was opened to members in 1913.

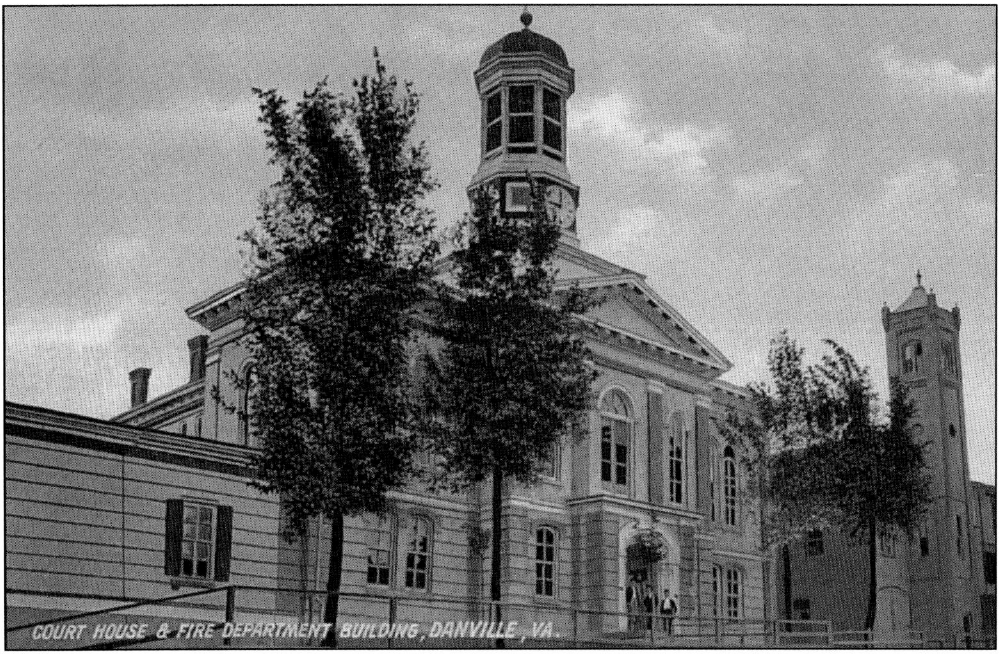

Danville's Court House on Patton Street, resplendent with an octagonal clock tower, was built in 1873. It stood on the site of the current Municipal Building. This original court house inspired the 1999 annex to the 1975 Court and Jail Complex. The only fire station on the south side of town sat beside this court house.

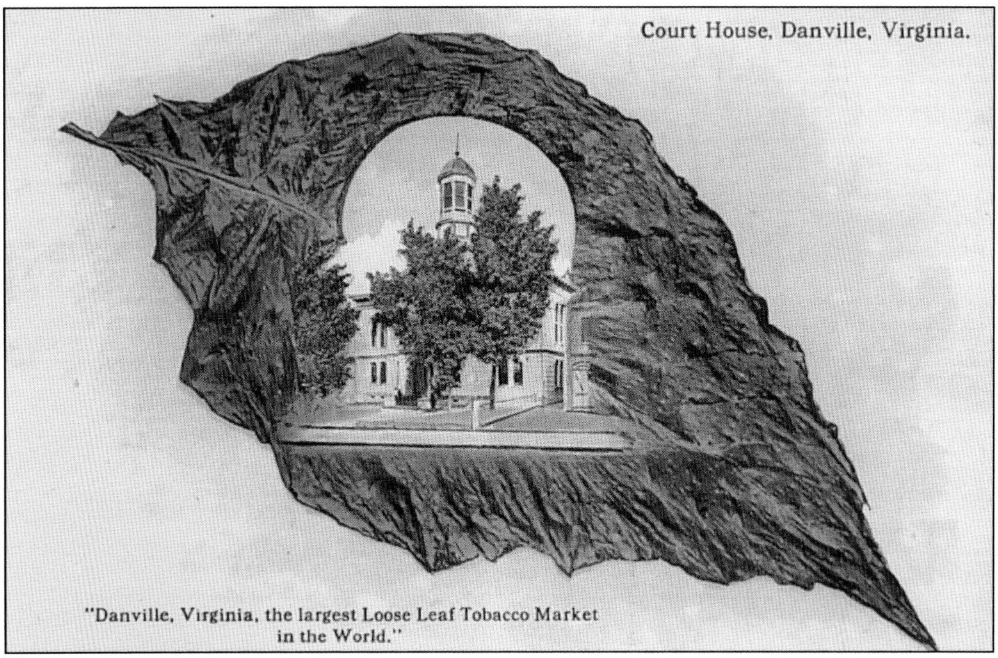

One hard-to-find postcard shows a view of the old Court House framed by a single tobacco leaf. This building was torn down in 1926 and the site was used for the current Municipal Building.

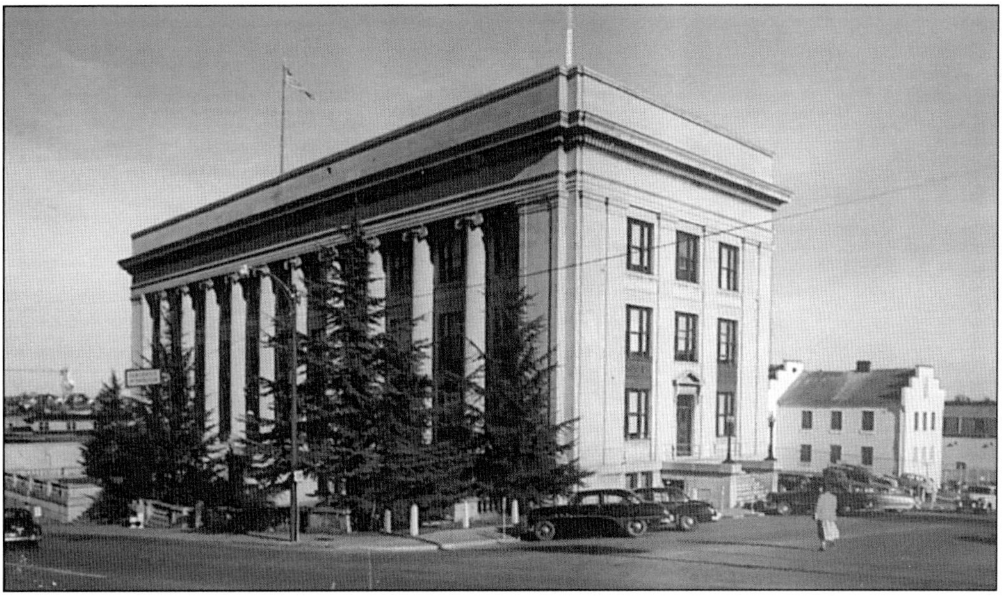

A combined Municipal Building and Court House was erected in 1927 at the corner of Patton and Court Streets and designed by local architect, J. Bryant Heard. For many years the city school system and other organizations have used this facility for their offices.

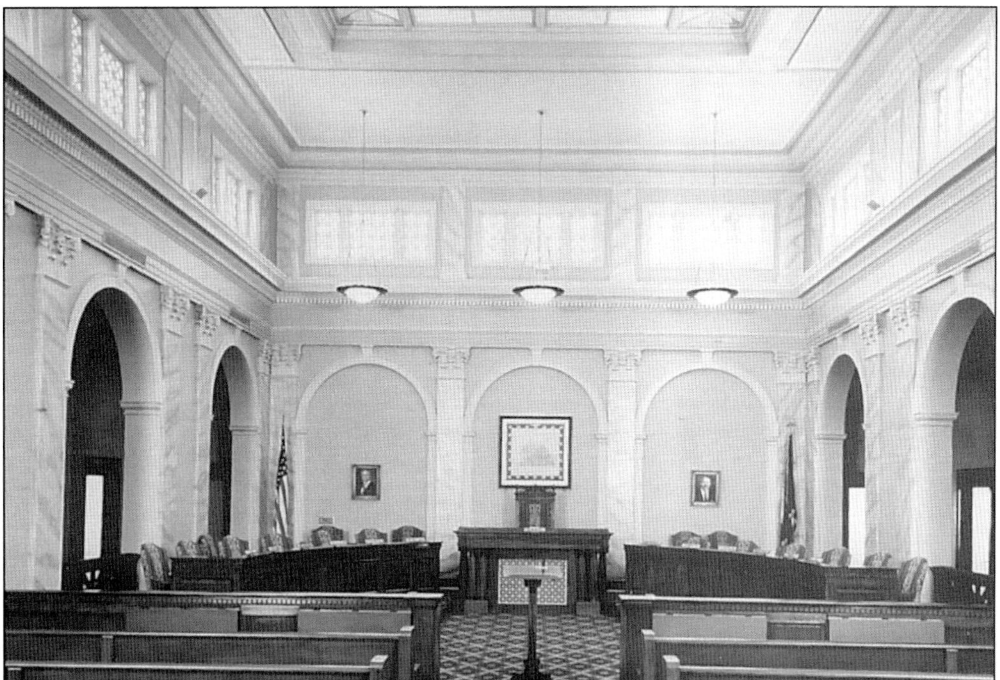

Photographed in 1996 by Joseph Romeo for the City of Danville, this commemorative card features the inside of the Corporation or Circuit Court, which has been used for years as the City Council Chambers, after its latest renovation during the tenure of City Manager A. Ray Griffin.

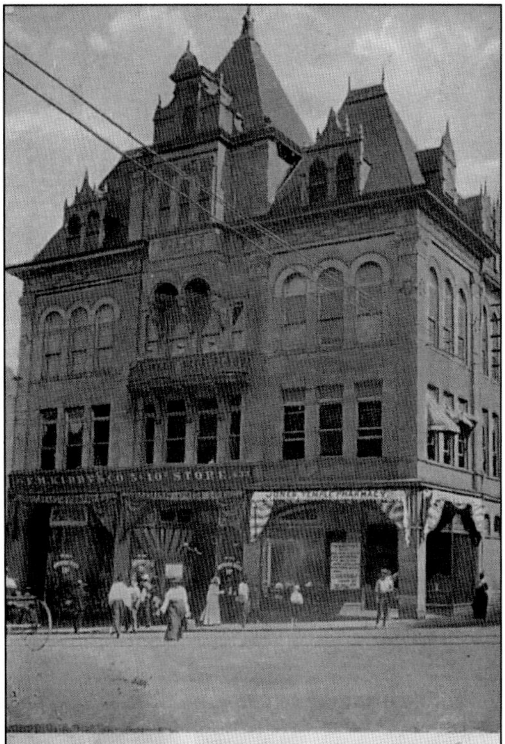

Masonic Temple. Main St. Danville, Va.

The F.M. Kirby Company in the second Masonic Temple, built in 1901, was one of the first "ten-cent" stores to come to Danville. Literally, nothing sold for more than a dime, and the chain store (later Woolworth's) offered staple goods, novelties, and bric-a-brac. Seventeen years later the Masonic Temple burned to the ground, along with many other stores on that city block.

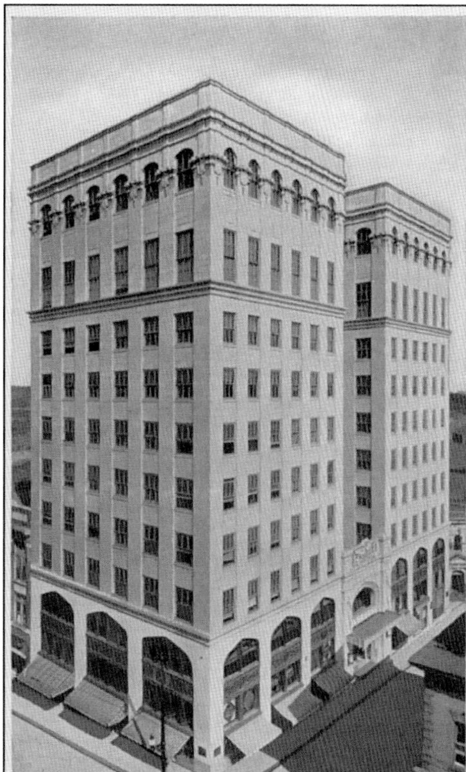

The Masonic Temple Building, Danville, Virginia

By 1922 a new, 11-story temple was constructed and was one of only two "skyscrapers" in town. It is a well-known city landmark. Brown's Jewelers and Patterson's Drug Store occupied offices on the ground floor. Fond memories include (Virginia) Poteat's Beauty Parlor in the basement and the Edwardian brass control box that gracious elevator operators still use to manually transport people from the ballroom on the top floor to the basement.

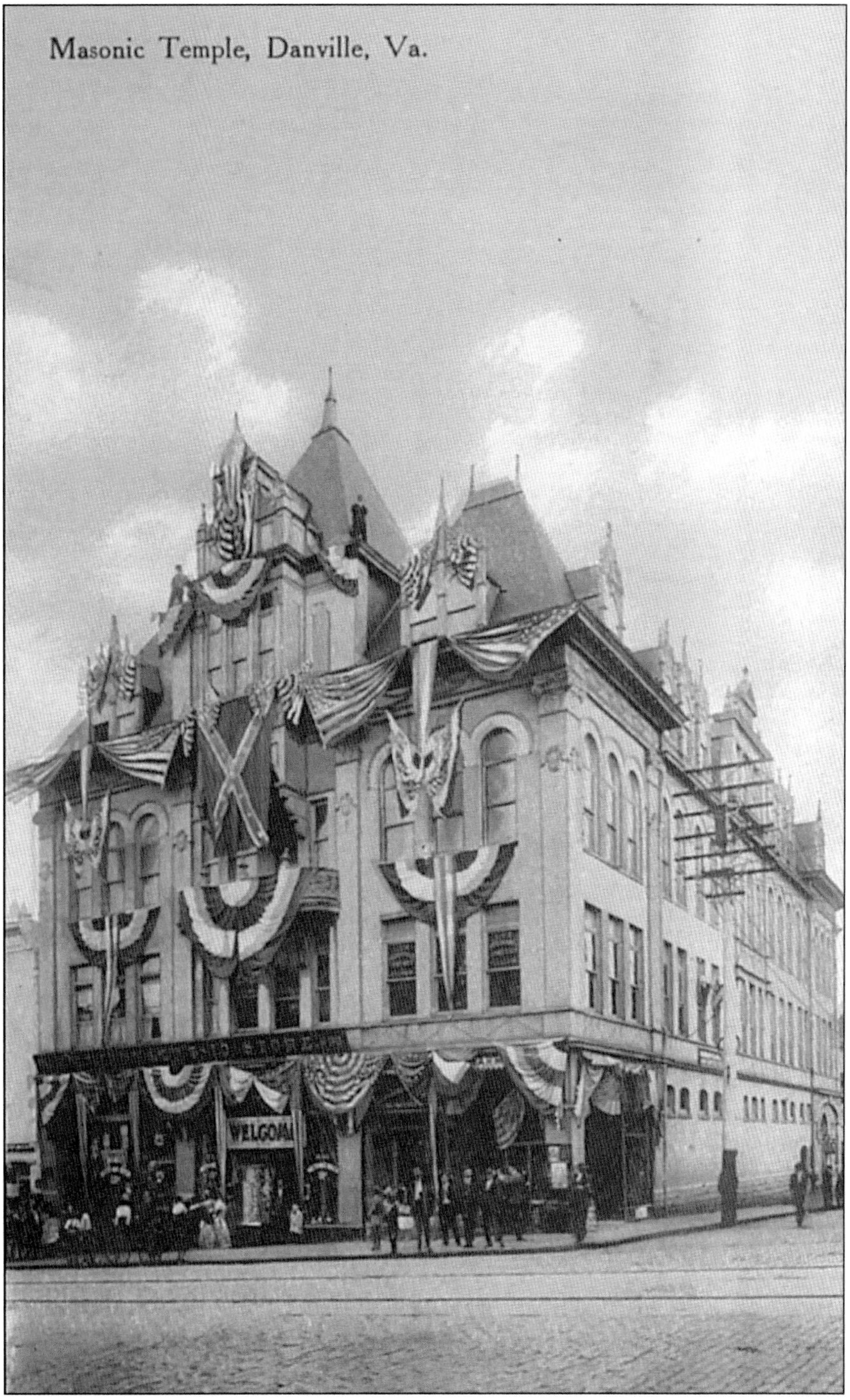

This card, dating somewhere between 1907 (it has a divided back) and 1914 (the end of German postcard printing in the United States), presents a puzzle. What does the bunting represent? Who was being welcomed to town? It is possible that the October 1909 statewide reunion of Confederate Veterans that was held in Danville is the solution.

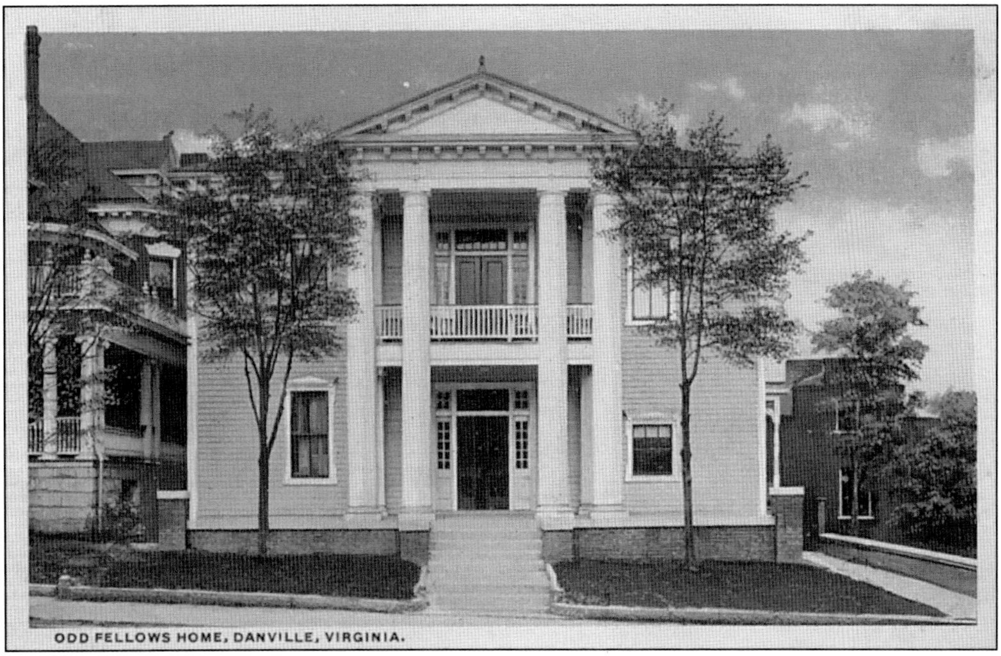

Reverend George W. Dame, minister of the Episcopal Church of the Epiphany, helped found the Bethesda Lodge No. 57 of the Independent Order of Odd Fellows in 1847. In 1913 the Lodge purchased this house at 630 Main Street, which had belonged to a Dr. Koontz and stood next door to the residence of Dr. C.W. Pritchett. The Lodge met in this building until 1919, when they sold the property to Dr. Pritchett.

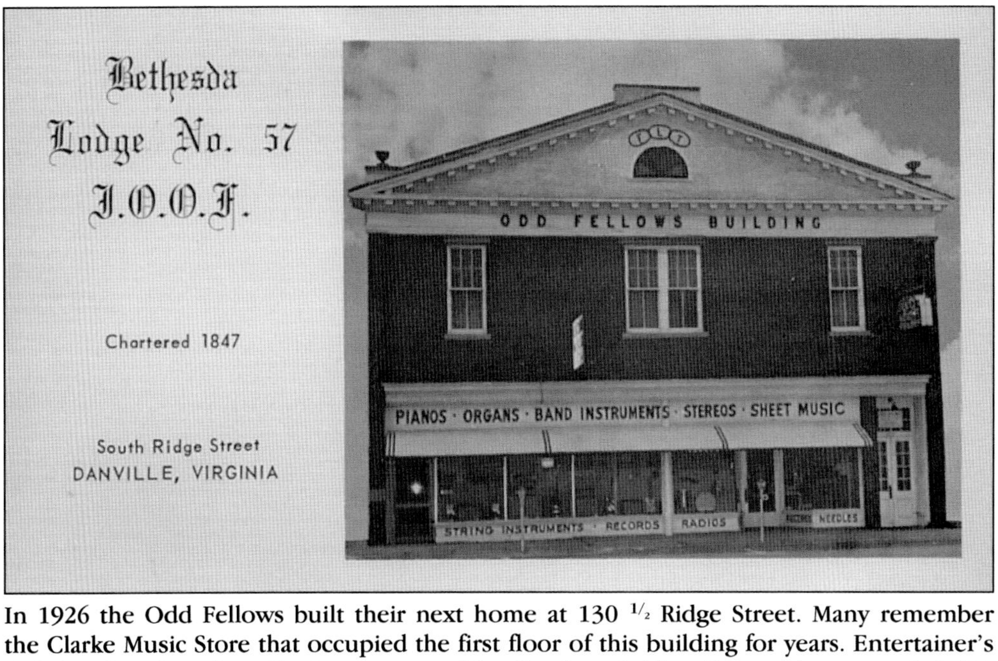

In 1926 the Odd Fellows built their next home at 130 $^{1}/_{2}$ Ridge Street. Many remember the Clarke Music Store that occupied the first floor of this building for years. Entertainer's Delight, the charming gift shop operated by Sarah and Allen Bryant, has occupied this site since 1985.

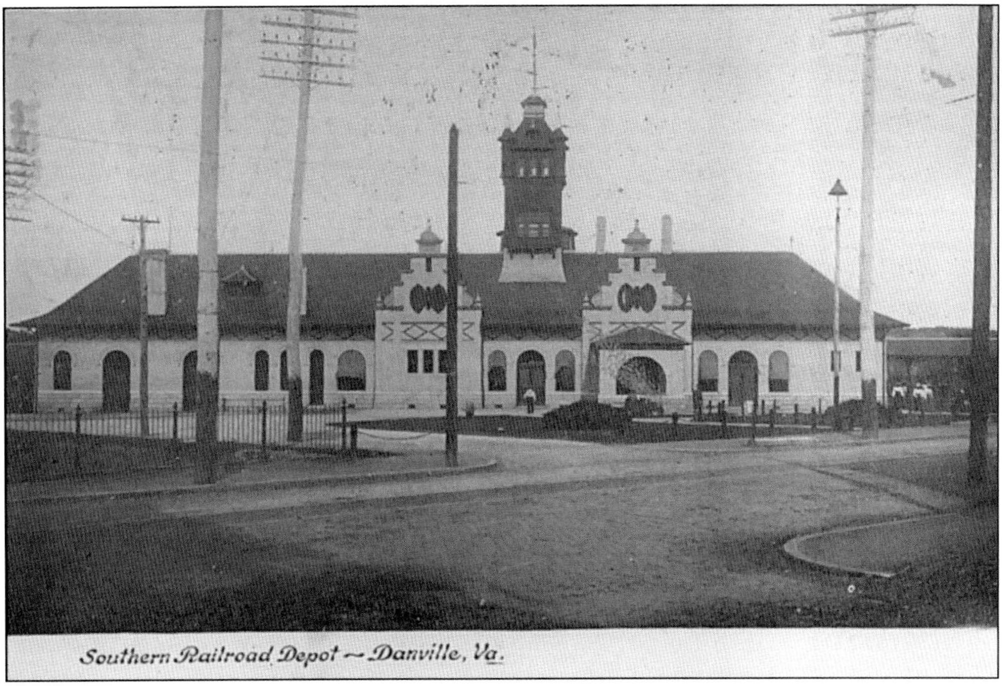

Danville's train depot was constructed in 1899 by the Southern Railway System. Designed by Frank Milburn and built by R.B. Graham, the station was physically moved from an adjacent lot in 1915 to its current site.

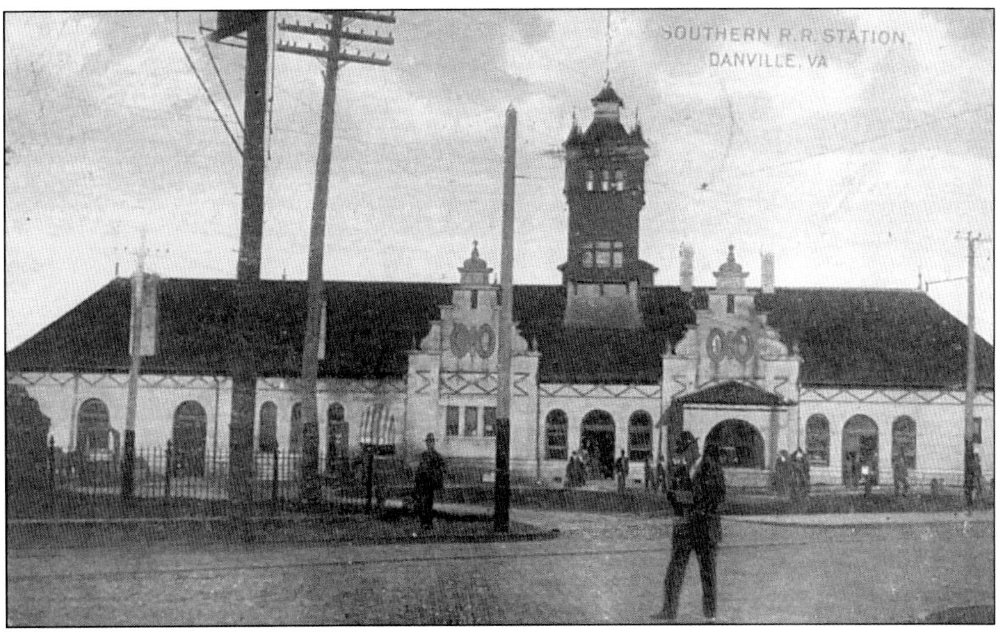

The center tower was damaged in a fire that swept throughout the depot in 1922, destroying all but the outer walls of the station. Instead of pulling these walls down, Southern Railway decided to reconstruct the inside of the building as before, leaving Danville with a treasure from its past.

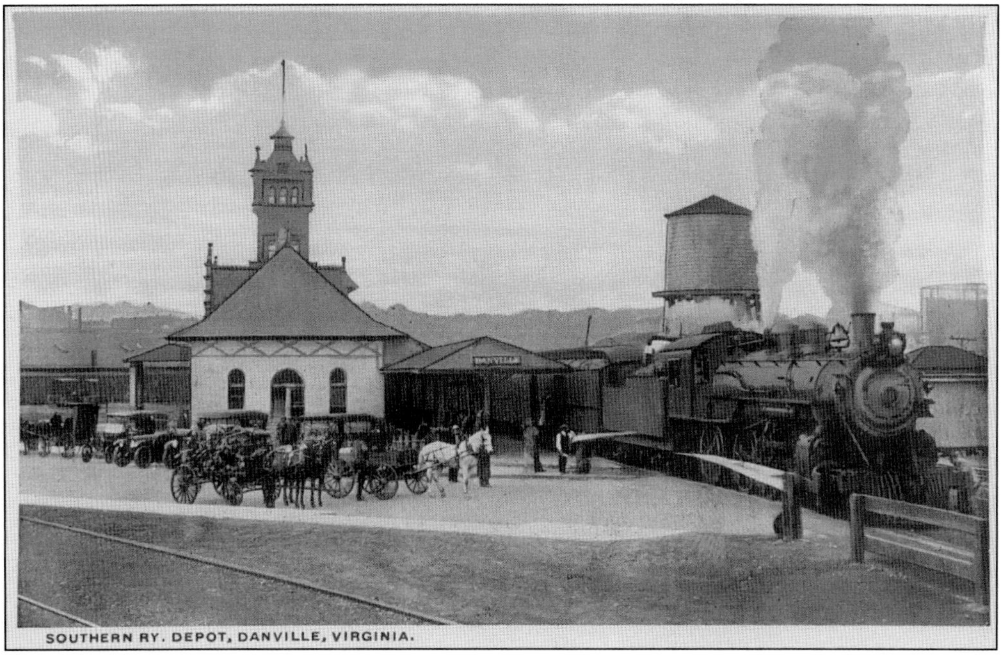

This Curt Teich postcard is extremely rare in that it represents almost every mode of transportation in the early 1920s. It is the type of card sought after by deltiologists who collect railroad scenes, train stations, or cards with automobiles and horse-drawn carriages together. It is particularly rare in depicting an engine stopped beside the depot.

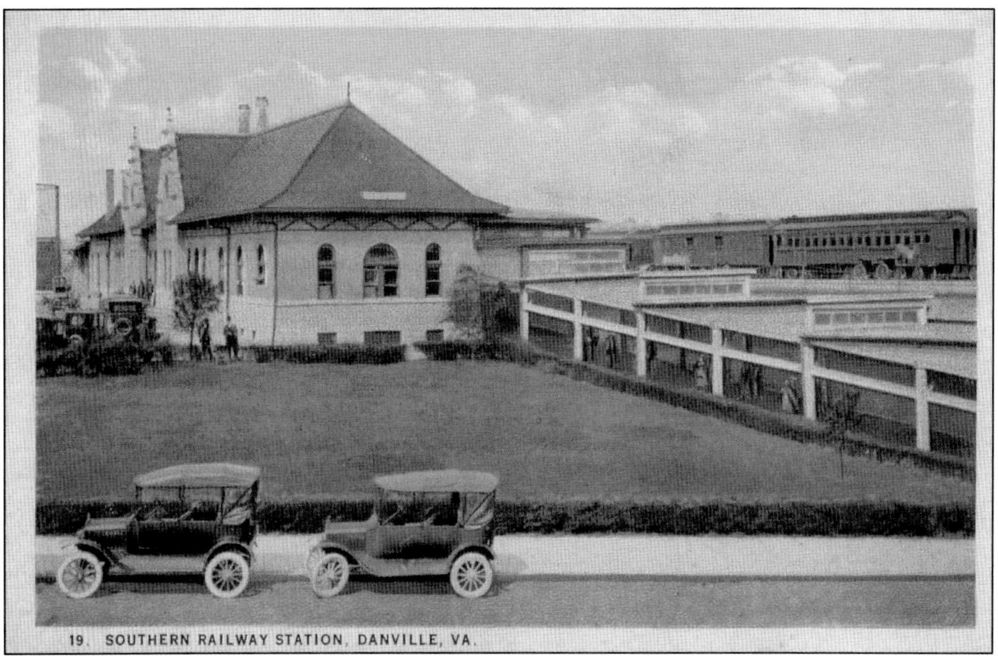

A similar card also by the Teich Company shows a different side view of the Danville railroad station with a train stopped on the tracks. These two cards are more highly prized than cards showing an empty station with no kind of traffic or people in transit.

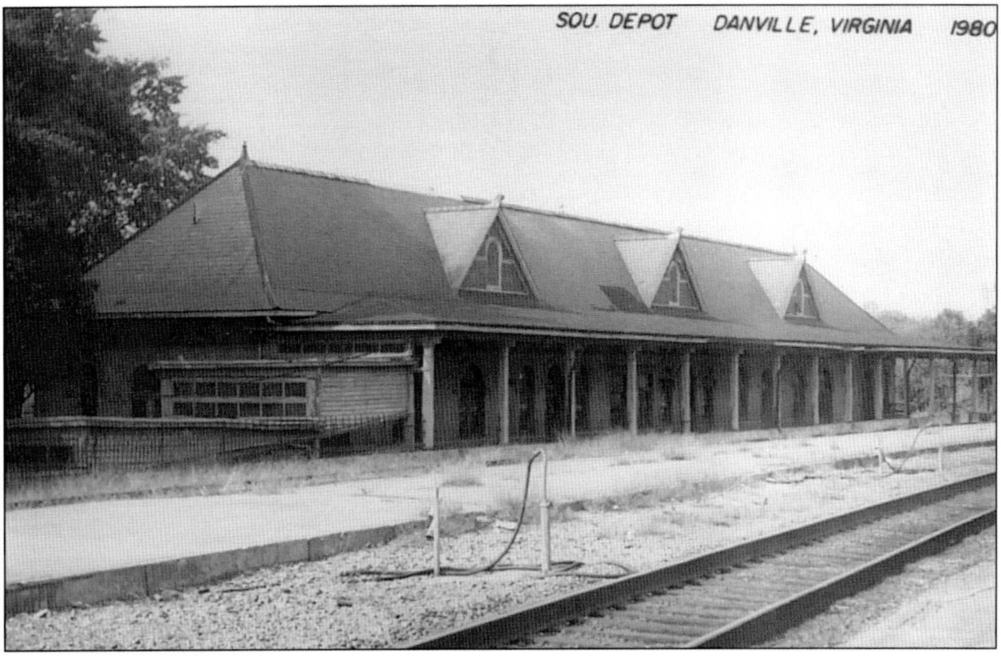

In 1980 an unidentified photographer toured the South and recorded scenes of local train stations. This photocard shows the back of the station, the part that passengers see when traveling through Danville. It is exciting for the historian to find a photograph taken from this angle.

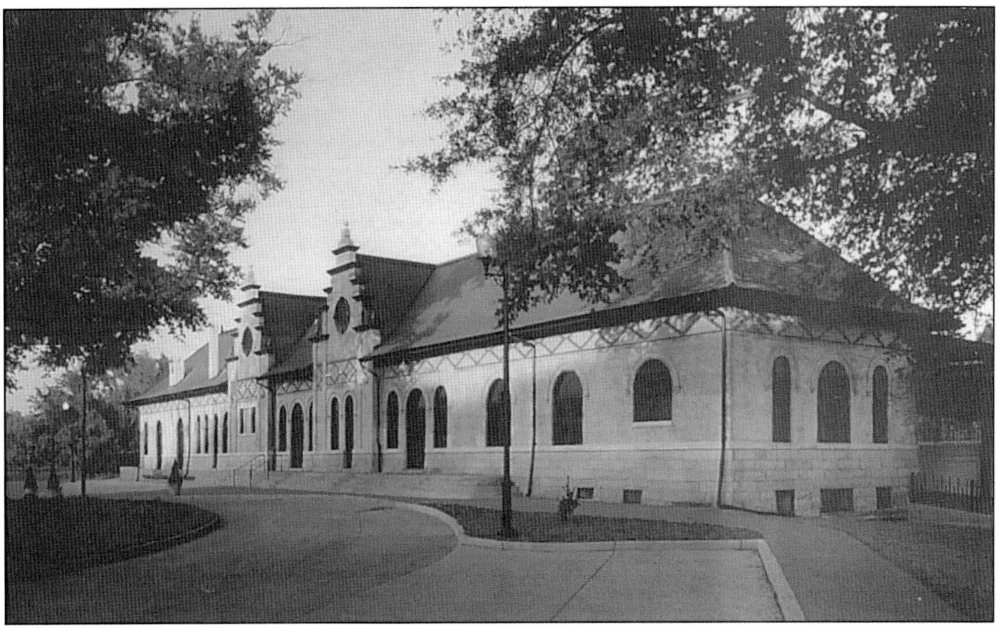

Danville's railroad station at 677 Craghead Street was renovated in 1994–1995 and is currently used for Amtrak service and for the Danville Science Center. Photographed by Compson Studios, this is the fourth of ten commemorative postcards published by the City of Danville.

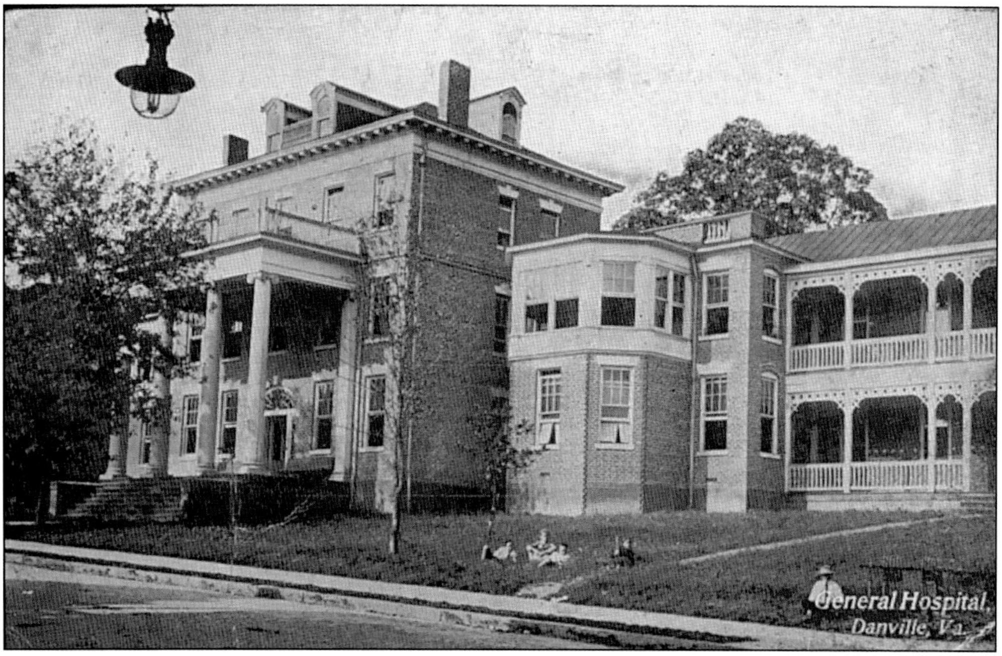

The Ladies Benevolent Society of Danville was founded in 1884 by a group of local women who strove to provide a "Home for the Sick." Using a building offered by the Danville Female Academy at the corner of Jefferson and Loyal Streets, the Danville General Hospital came into being.

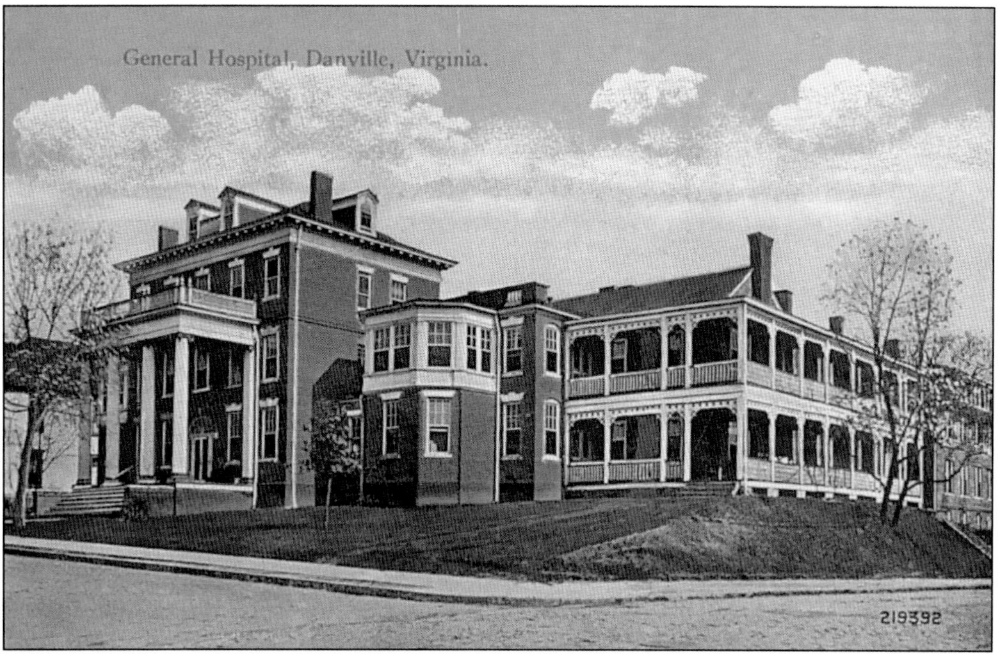

By 1898 a wing was added to the hospital that provided rooms for the training of medical personnel, and the first school of nursing was created. This hospital served Danville well until it was replaced in 1926 by a newer and larger building on South Main Street.

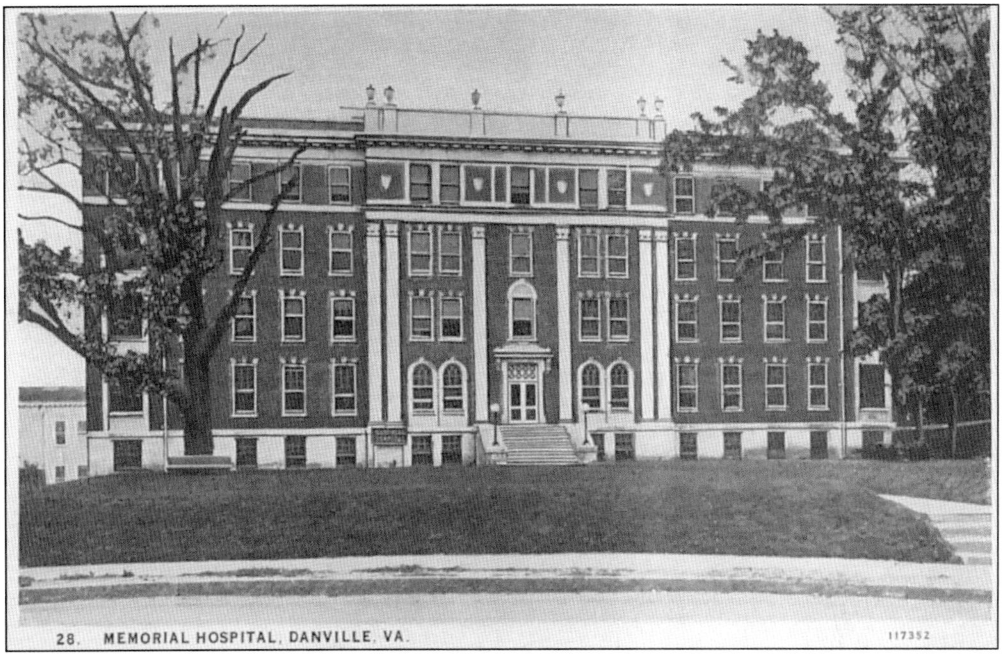

Memorial Hospital at 142 South Main Street was completed in 1926, a gift from and in honor of John Edward Hughes, a local tobacconist who left in his will $250,000 for its construction plus funds for the creation of the Hughes Memorial School for orphans at 1501 Franklin Turnpike.

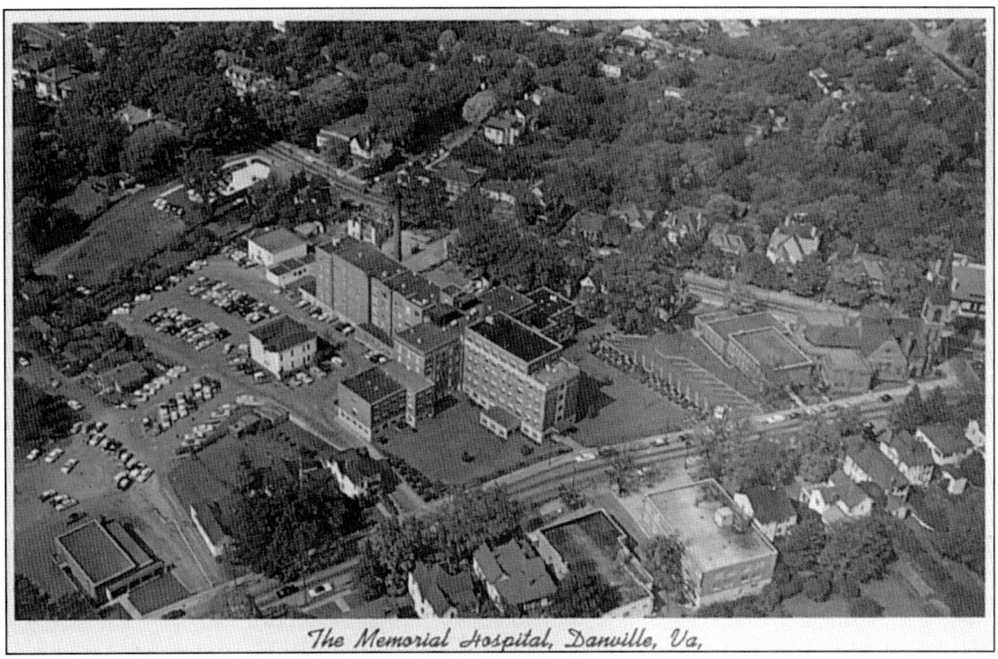

This hospital has expanded many times to accommodate the medical needs of the people of the community, but in this aerial view one can still locate the central building bequeathed by Hughes. It is currently known as the Danville Regional Medical Center.

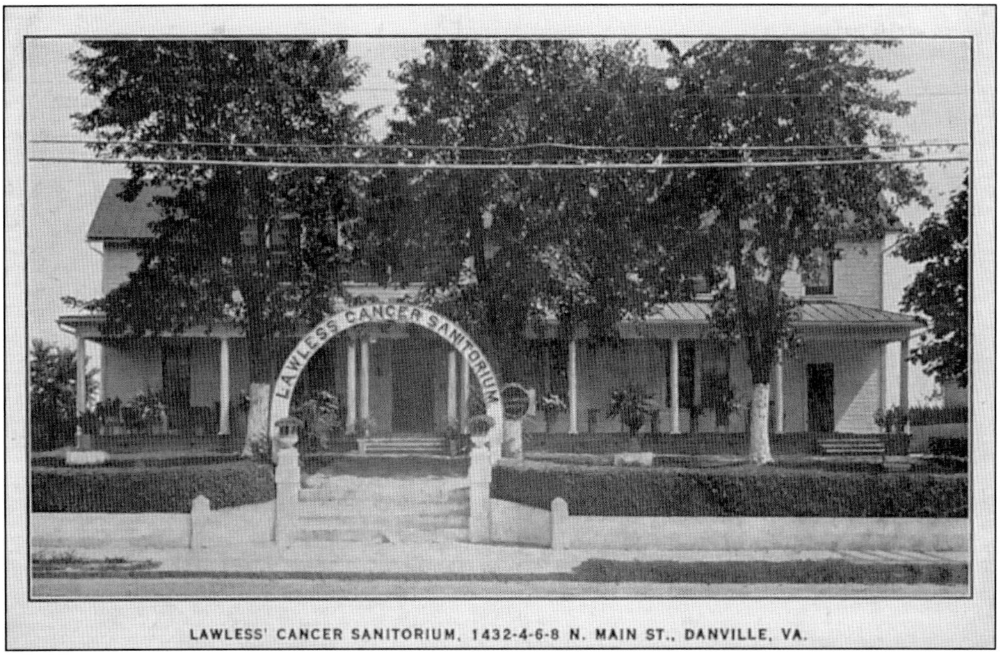

Over the years Danville has offered medical services to its citizens through a variety of clinics and hospitals including Hilltop Sanitorium for the treatment of tuberculosis, the Lawless Cancer Sanitorium, the Community, Providence, and Winslow Hospitals.

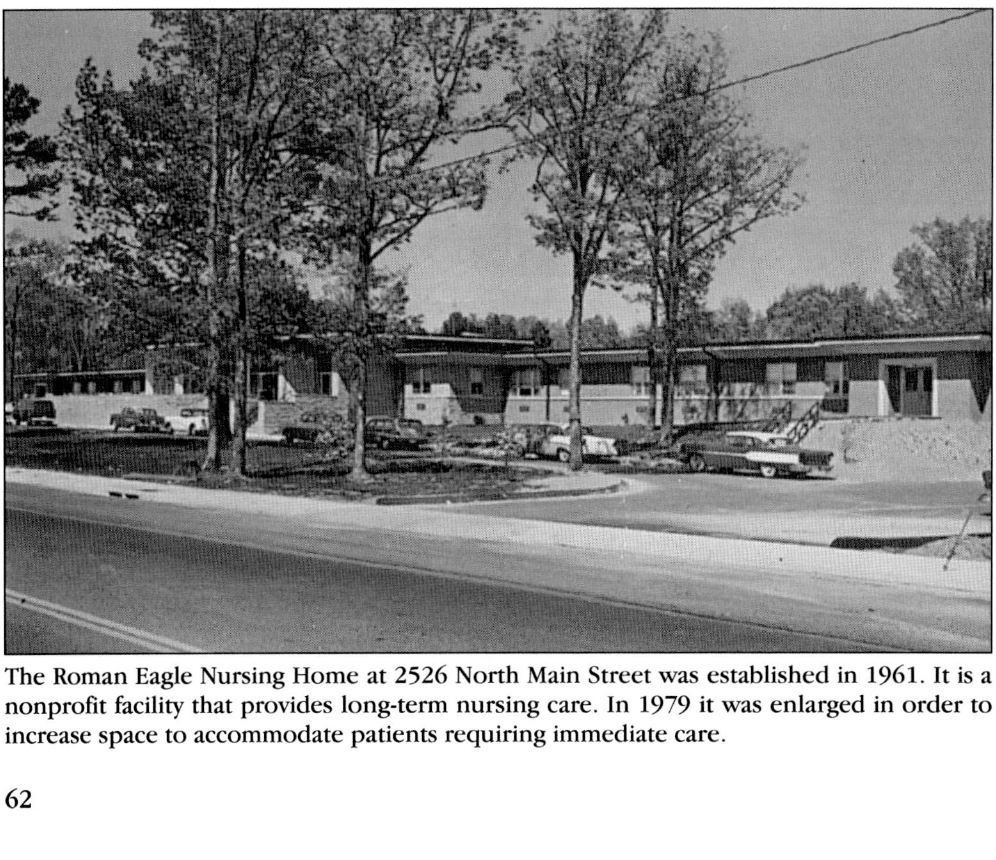

The Roman Eagle Nursing Home at 2526 North Main Street was established in 1961. It is a nonprofit facility that provides long-term nursing care. In 1979 it was enlarged in order to increase space to accommodate patients requiring immediate care.

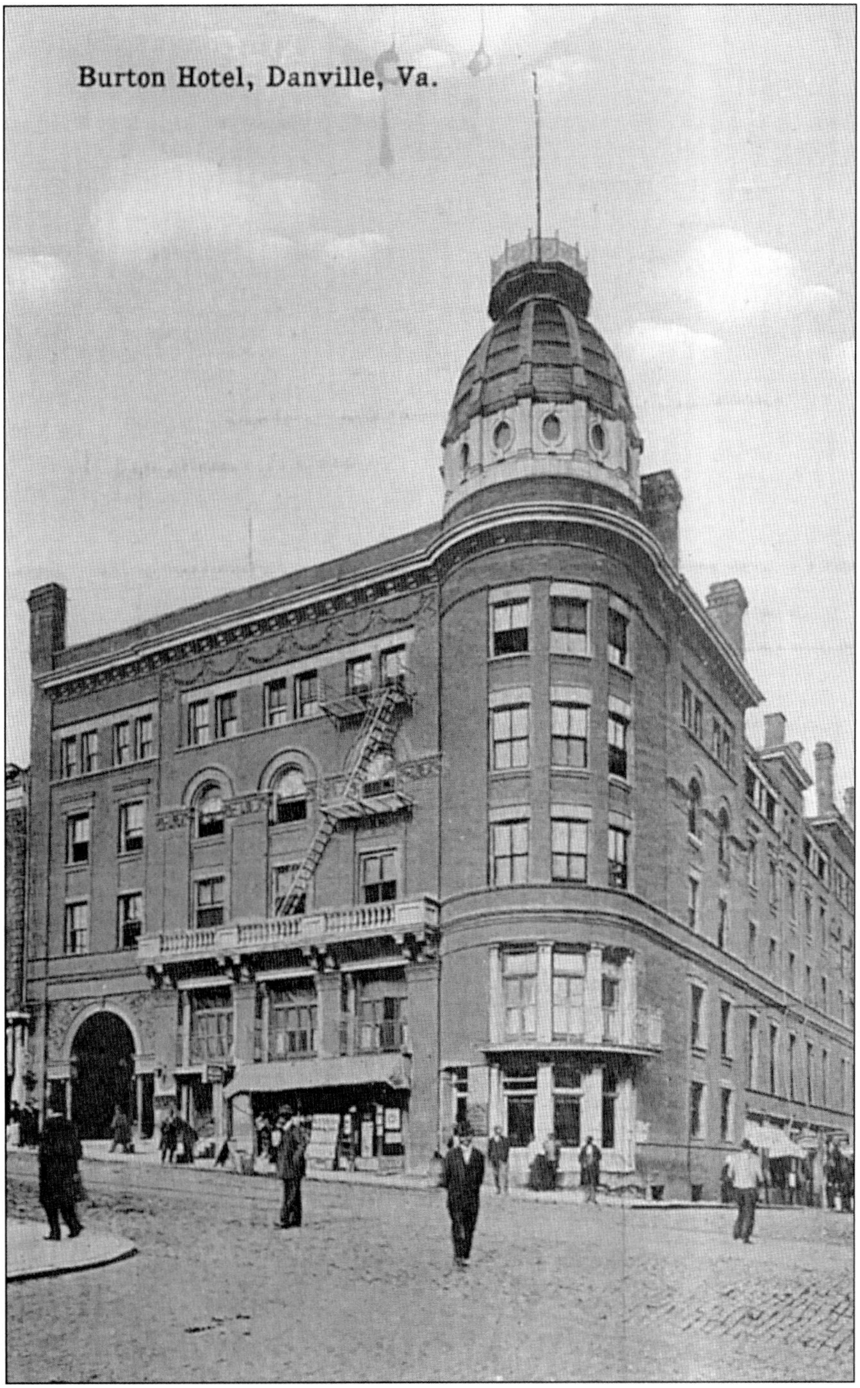

Hotel Burton was built in 1891 at the corner of Main and Union Streets. Elegant in its day, the Burton even had a special "ladies' entrance," where females might enter and go up unseen to the Ladies' Parlor on the mezzanine floor. The Burton was replaced in 1962 by the Downtowner Motor Inn, the same year that the "Twist" changed the dance world forever and virtually brought an end to popular ballroom dancing.

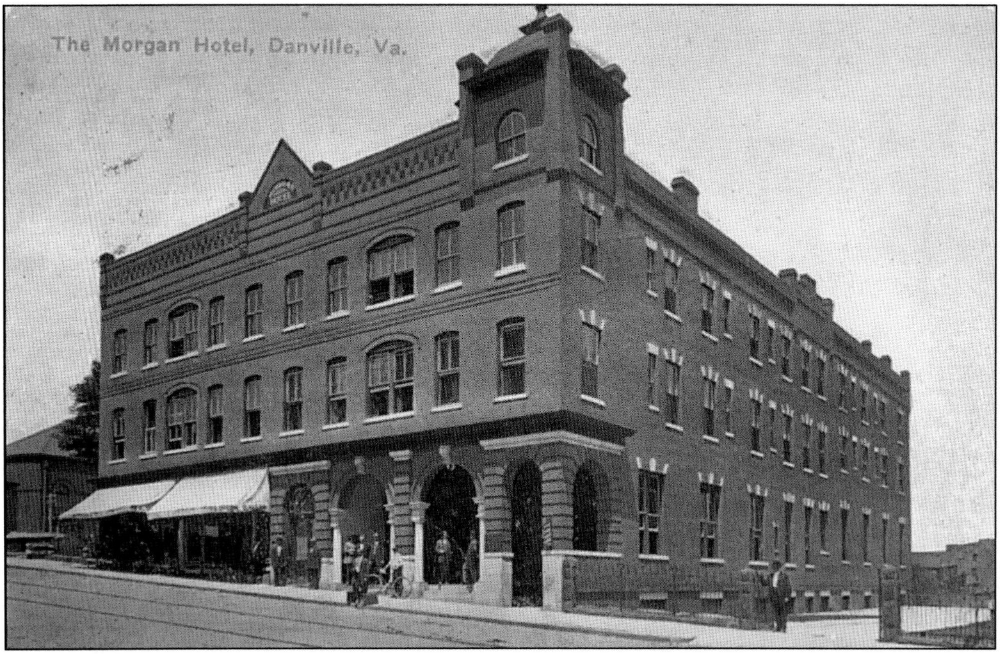

The Morgan Hotel stood at 542 Main Street near the top of the hill from 1907 until it was demolished in 1982. At one time renamed the Stonewall Jackson, the hotel boasted a large painting of Jackson that now hangs in the Danville Museum of Fine Arts and History.

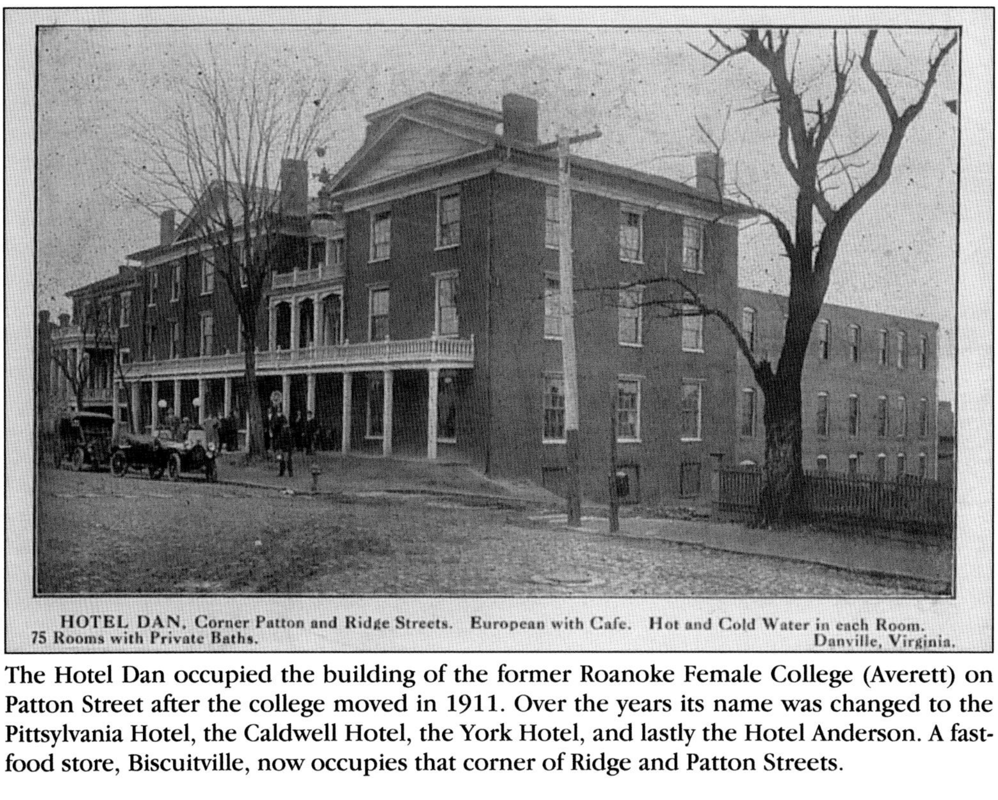

The Hotel Dan occupied the building of the former Roanoke Female College (Averett) on Patton Street after the college moved in 1911. Over the years its name was changed to the Pittsylvania Hotel, the Caldwell Hotel, the York Hotel, and lastly the Hotel Anderson. A fast-food store, Biscuitville, now occupies that corner of Ridge and Patton Streets.

Catering to traveling salesmen, the Hotel Leeland opened its doors in 1915. Built by K.C. and E.C. Arey, local businessmen, the Leeland was advertised as having an elevator, and a telephone in each room. The Strand Theater was located inside the Leeland, though it had a short life of only seven months. The proscenium can still be seen in the back of Hiles Gift Shop at 607 Main.

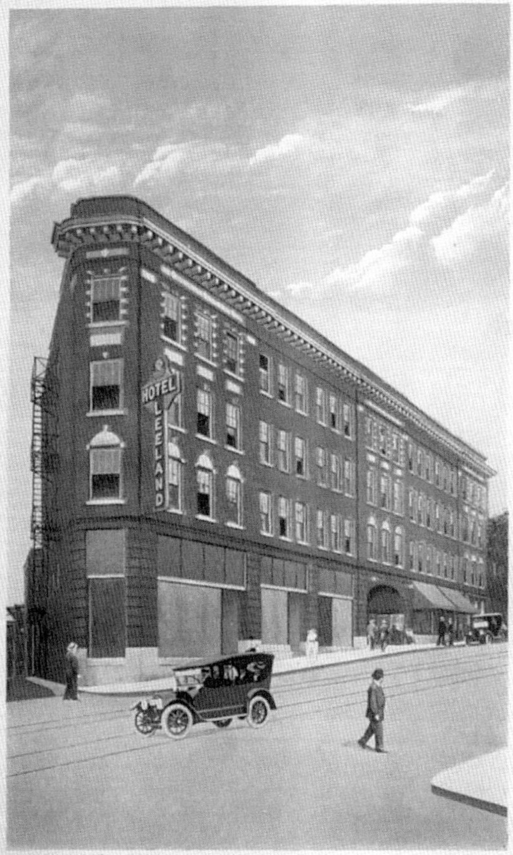

NEW HOTEL LEELAND, DANVILLE, VIRGINIA.

There was little copyright protection for the early postcard photographer. Companies borrowed freely from competitors and frequently altered the negatives. This view card shows that the hotel was stretched to double its size, and people and vehicles were painted in to enhance the scene of the Hotel Leeland.

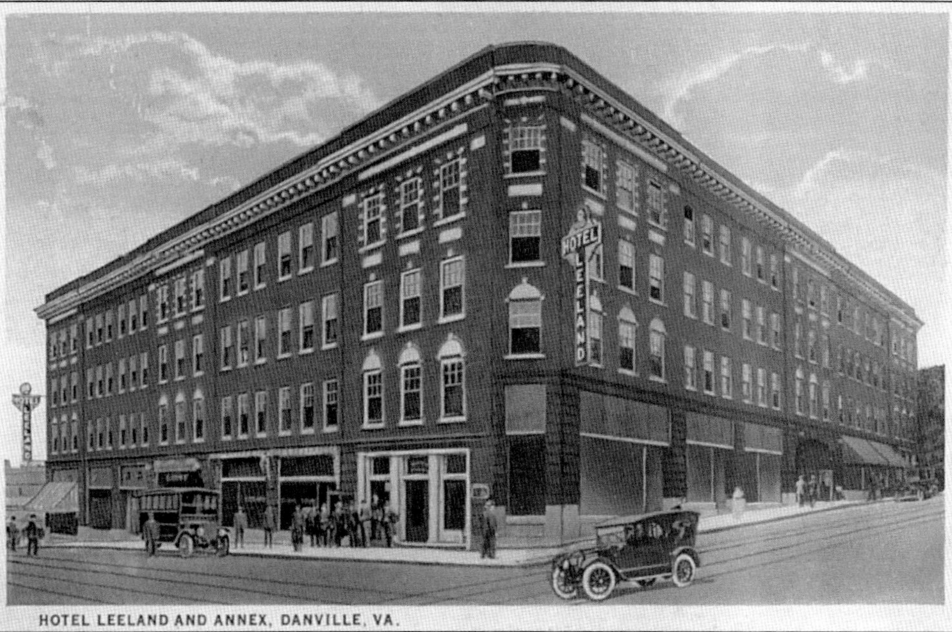

HOTEL LEELAND AND ANNEX, DANVILLE, VA.

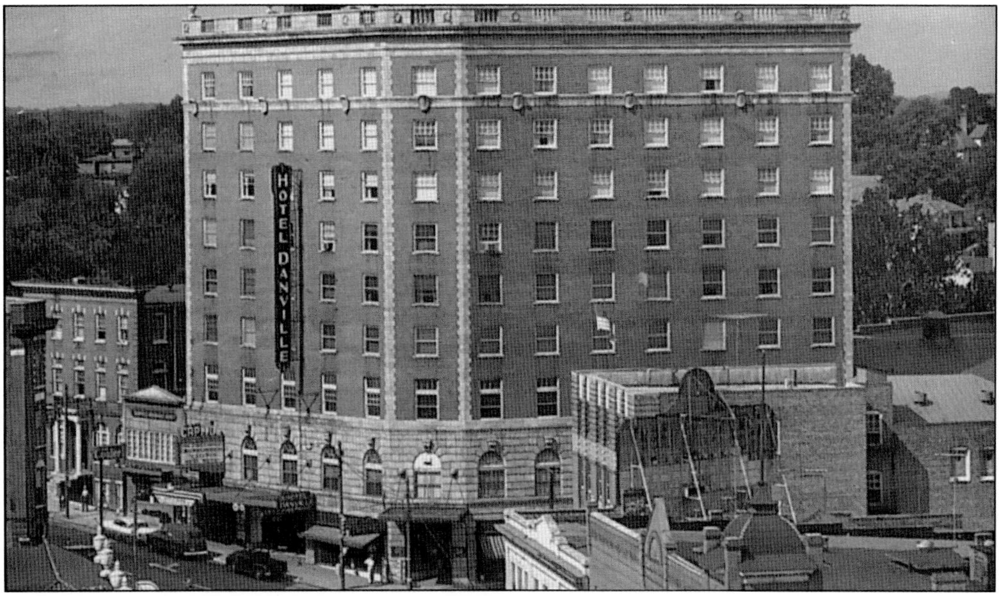

Hotel Danville was built in 1927 on the site of the former city Municipal Building. Clements and Parker, a home furnishings store, occupied the basement and part of the ground floor until the 1970s. The Capital Theater, managed by Charlie Abercrombie, was the finest movie theater in town from the 1930s to the 1960s and showed only first-run films. During the Depression the Capital charged a quarter for adults and a dime for children under 16.

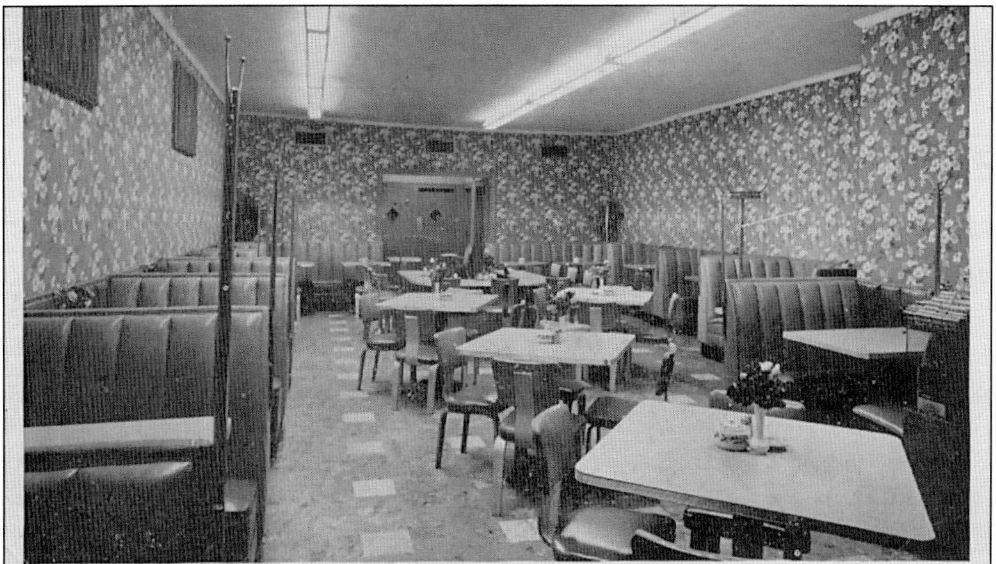

The Cavalier Restaurant at 612 Main Street, situated between Hotel Danville and the YMCA, was owned and operated by George Gantsoudes from 1951 to 1963. Serving three meals a day, this restaurant catered to downtown workers, to hotel guests, and to young couples who attended the movie theater next door. Also associated with the Golden Nugget and Busy Bee restaurants, Gantsoudes was a founder of the Saint Peter's Greek Orthodox Church on Jefferson Avenue.

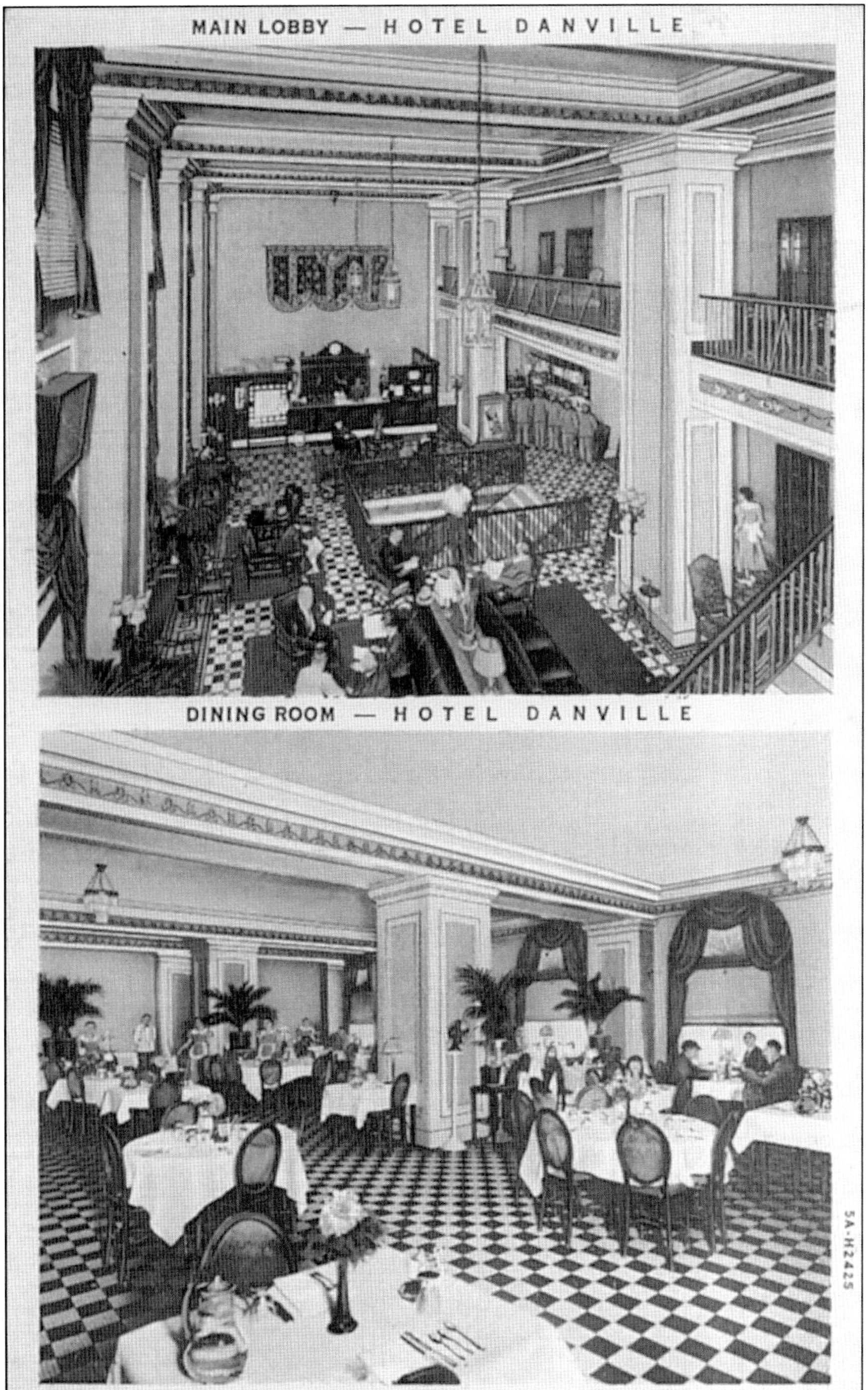

Hotel Danville featured an impressive marble lobby with an elegant stairway leading up to its large dining room. Many local organizations held dinners, dances, and meetings in the grand ballroom, which could hold a capacity crowd of 225 people. The hotel closed in 1975, when it was converted into apartments for the elderly.

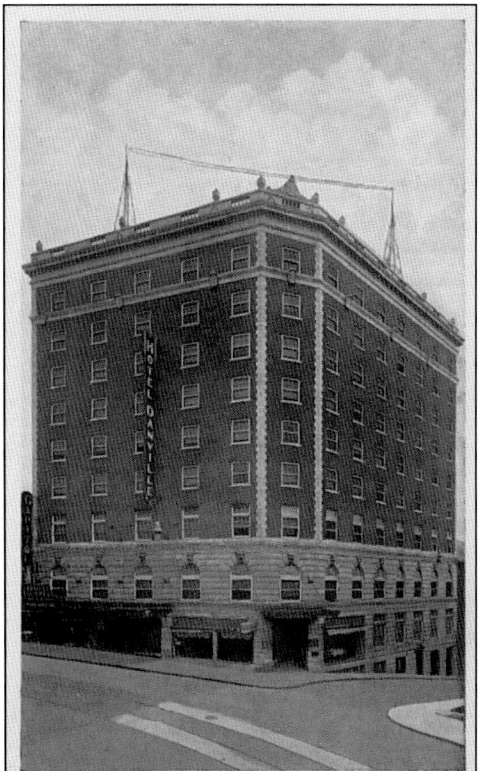

Hotel Danville, Danville, Virginia

The original antenna for WBTM radio station was stretched between two towers on the top of Hotel Danville. The first radio station in town, WBTM began broadcasting in 1930. The call letters WBTM were chosen from two of Danville's epithets: World's Best Tobacco Market and World's Biggest Textile Mills.

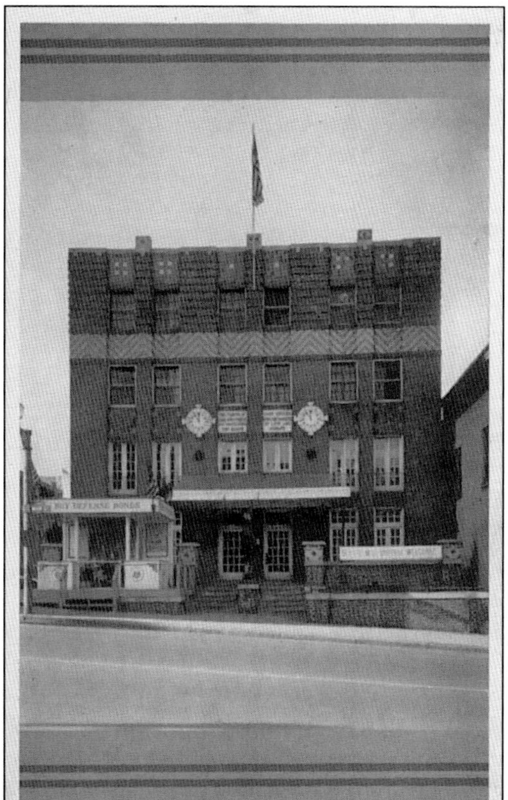

Elk's Home, Danville, Virginia

Everyone in town was involved with the war efforts during the 1940s. WBTM built and operated the "Little Treasury House" next door to their station in front of the Elk's Club on Main Street. Many citizens participated in money-raising events to contribute to the speedy end of World War II.

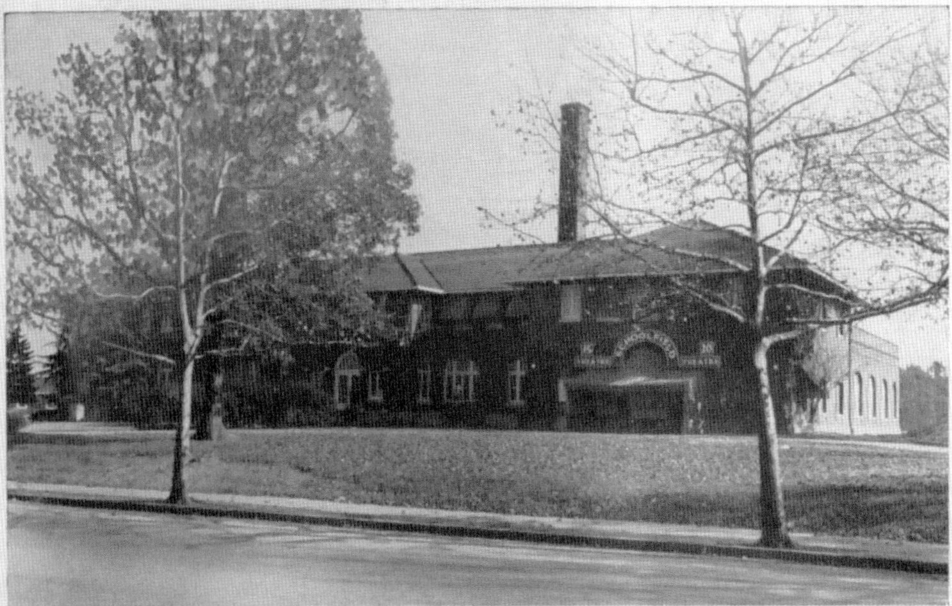

Schoolfield Theatre and Y. M. C. A. Building, Schoolfield, Virginia

The movie theater at the Schoolfield "Y" was run by Leonard Lea for folks who lived in the area near the cotton mill. Remembered particularly for Saturday afternoon double-feature westerns, the Schoolfield Theater, in 1944, charged 30¢ for adults and 18¢ for children, and moviegoers could stay all day if they wished.

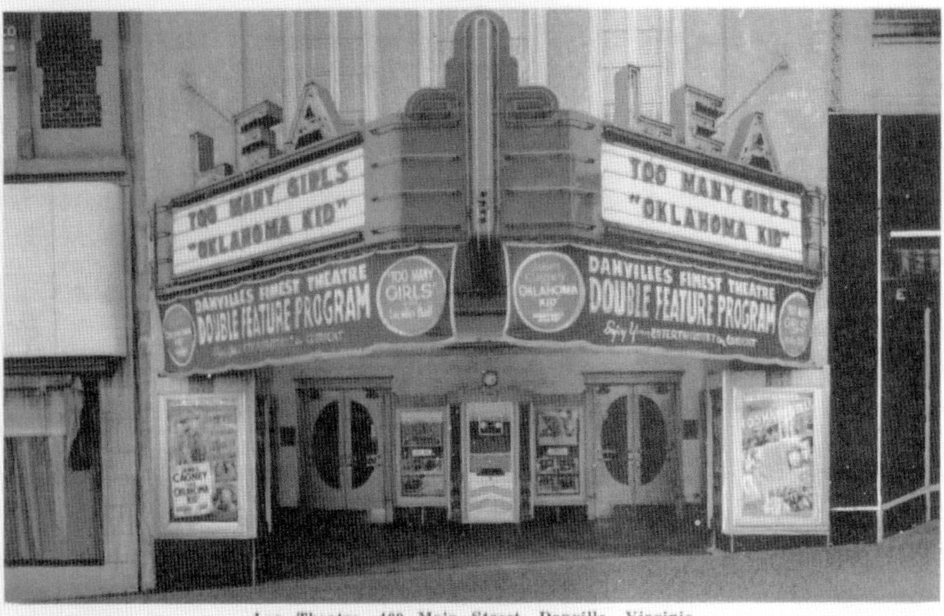

Lea Theatre, 409 Main Street, Danville, Virginia

The Lea Theater at 409 Main Street was originally the Broadway Theater, which burned in the late 1930s. Renovated by Leonard Lea, this popular movie house offered patrons an upstairs lounge and a balcony.

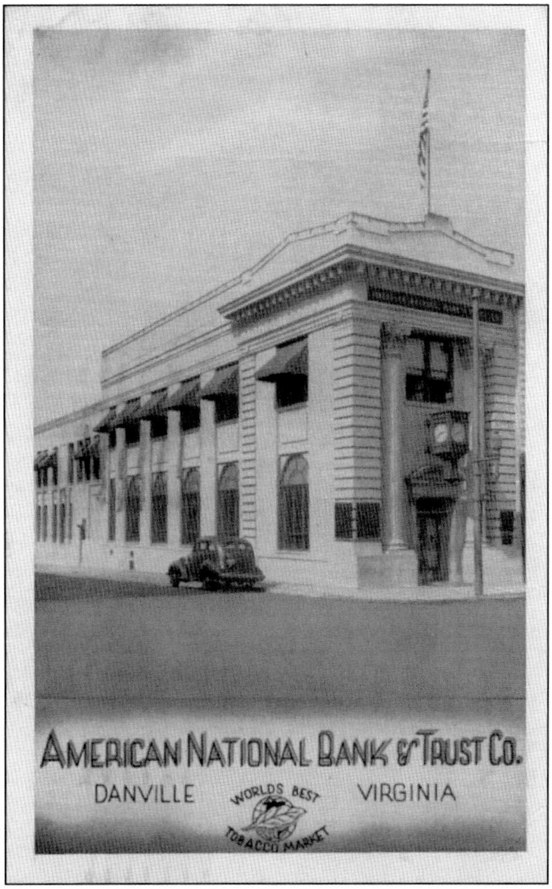

The American National Bank & Trust Company on Main and Market Streets was established in 1909. For many years the bank was known as the "bank with the chime clock." This clock was moved when a new colonial-style brick structure was built at 628 Main Street. The new bank opened in 1973 during the presidency of William H. Jefferson Jr.

American National Bank was the first one in Danville to offer its customers a drive-in branch office. This small structure at Five Forks (the corner of Jefferson Avenue and Loyal Street) opened in 1948, the beginning of a popular trend in banking and ten years before the advent of the ubiquitous credit card.

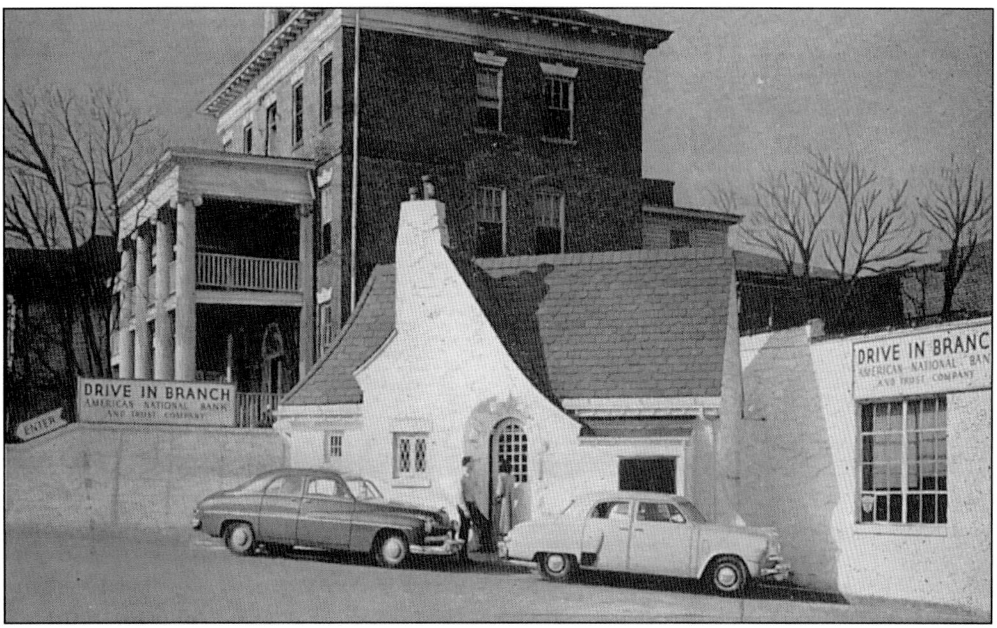

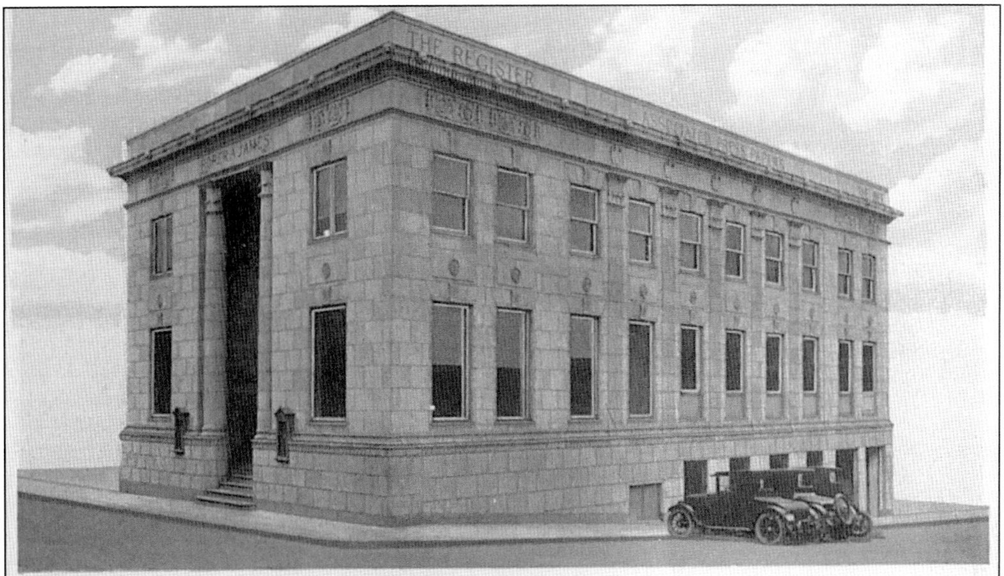

THE REGISTER AND BEE. DANVILLE, VA.
THE FINEST NEWSPAPER PLANT OF ITS SIZE IN AMERICA.

Rorer A. James purchased both the Danville *Register* and *The Bee* at the turn of the twentieth century and in 1922 constructed a new home for his papers at the corner of South Union and Patton Streets. His daughter, Stuart James Grant, at age 17 inherited the businesses and became the youngest woman in the nation to own and manage two successful newspapers. She moved her company to a larger building on Monument Street in 1980.

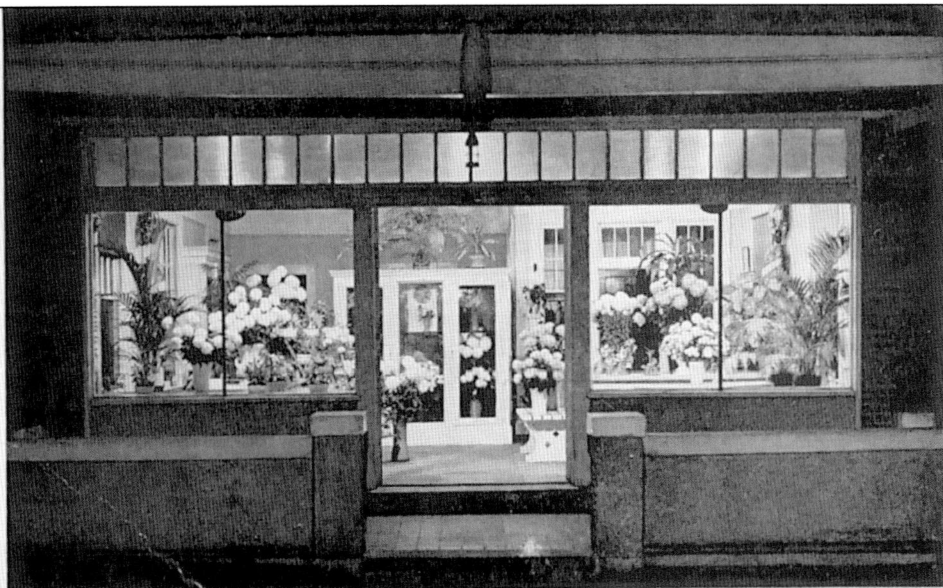

Shop of H. W. Brown, Florist, 431 Chestnut Street, Danville, Virginia

H.W. Brown Florist is the oldest business in town still run by the same family. Opening in October 1883, the shop was once run from the family home at 878 Green Street. The building on Chestnut Street was built in 1925, and the current owners are Tommy Shadrick and his wife, Myrtle.

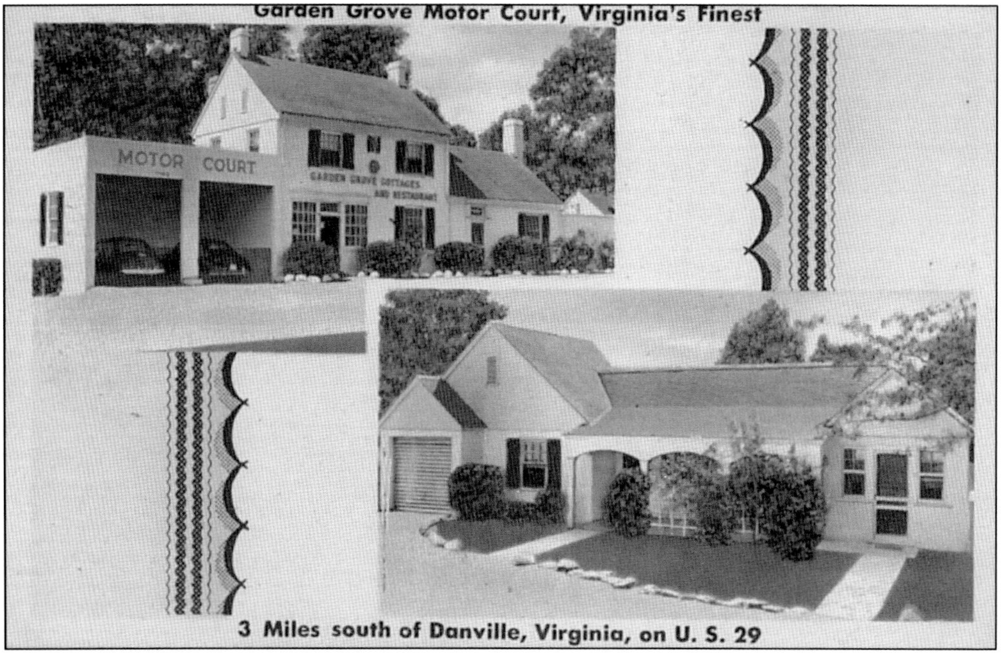

Hotels gave way to motor hotels (motels) by the mid-1950s when the country's economy allowed the average family to own an automobile. The Garden Grove Motor Court was probably the first motel in Danville, built around 1954 on Highway 29 South and advertised to have a private bath and radio in every room.

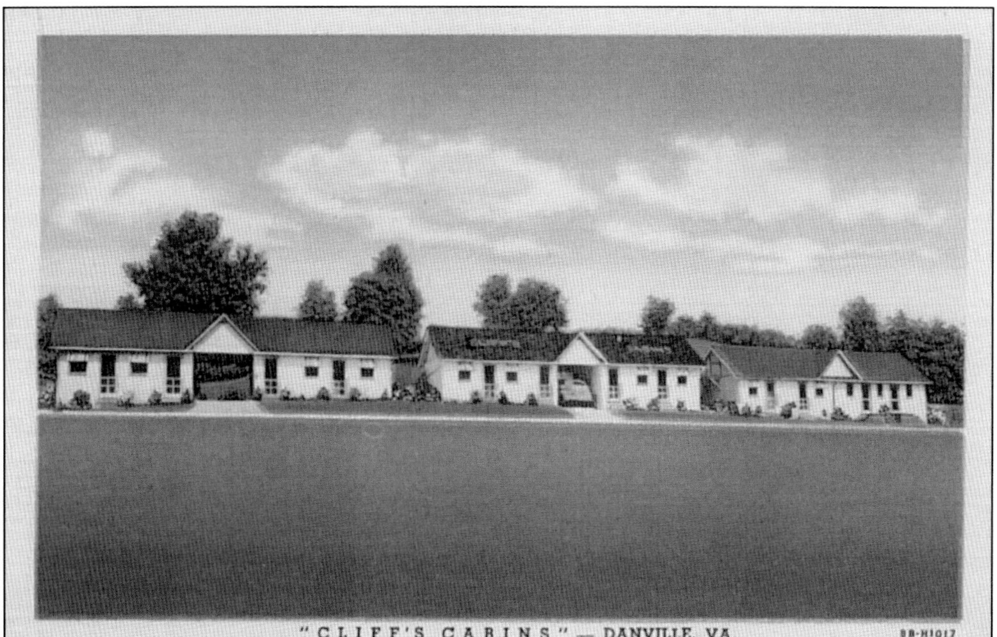

Cliff's Cabins, on Old Riverside Drive, appeared at somewhat the same time. Before the days of single rooms as provided by current motels, patrons wanted a home-like lodging when traveling on vacation. Hence, early motor courts offered individual cabins to visitors.

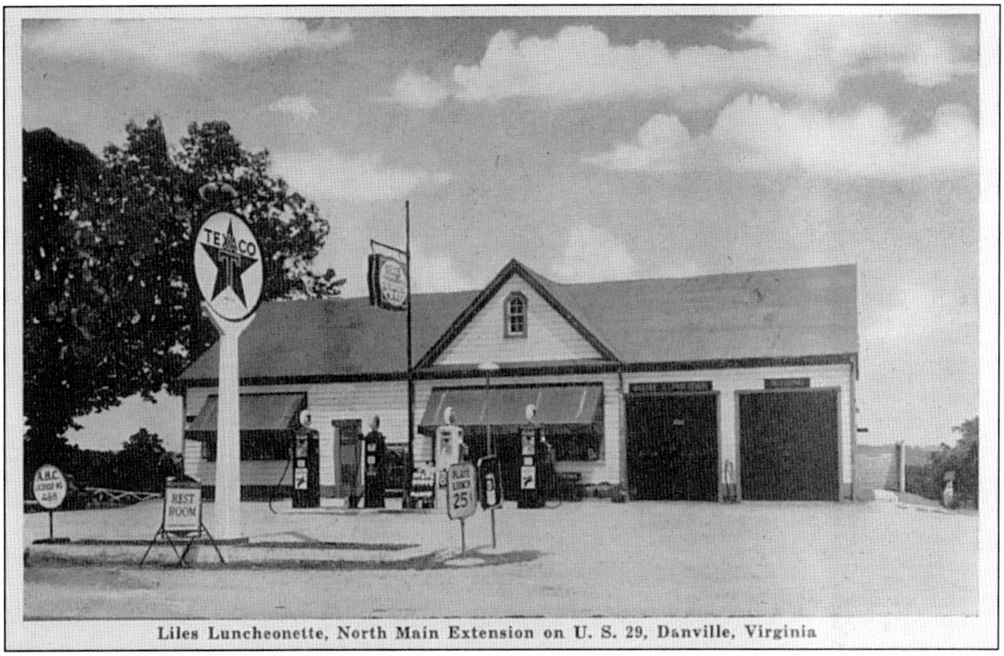

Liles Luncheonette and Texaco station on North Main extension offered plate lunches for 25¢ as well as basic services for cars. In the 1940s and 1950s cars became affordable for the average citizen, enabling families to visit relatives and take vacations more frequently. This growth in privately owned automobiles was matched by a similar growth in gas (or filling) stations along America's highways.

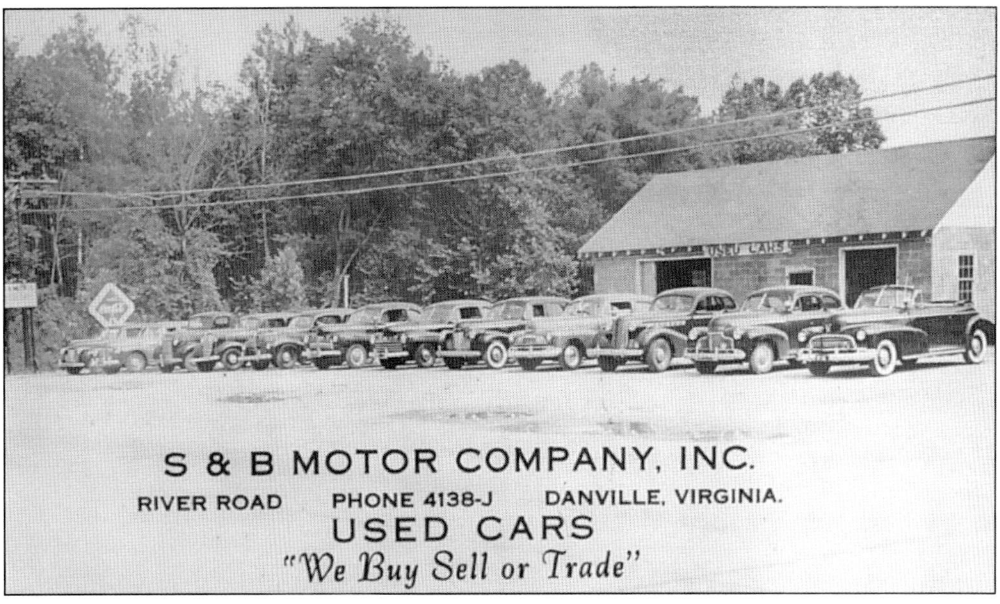

Bruce R. Burton and James M. Simpson started the S & B Motor Company on Loyal Street in 1945. The company moved to River Road (now 2331 Riverside Drive) early in the 1950s, when the shopping strip was first opened. Today a second generation, Sam and Wendell Burton, runs the business.

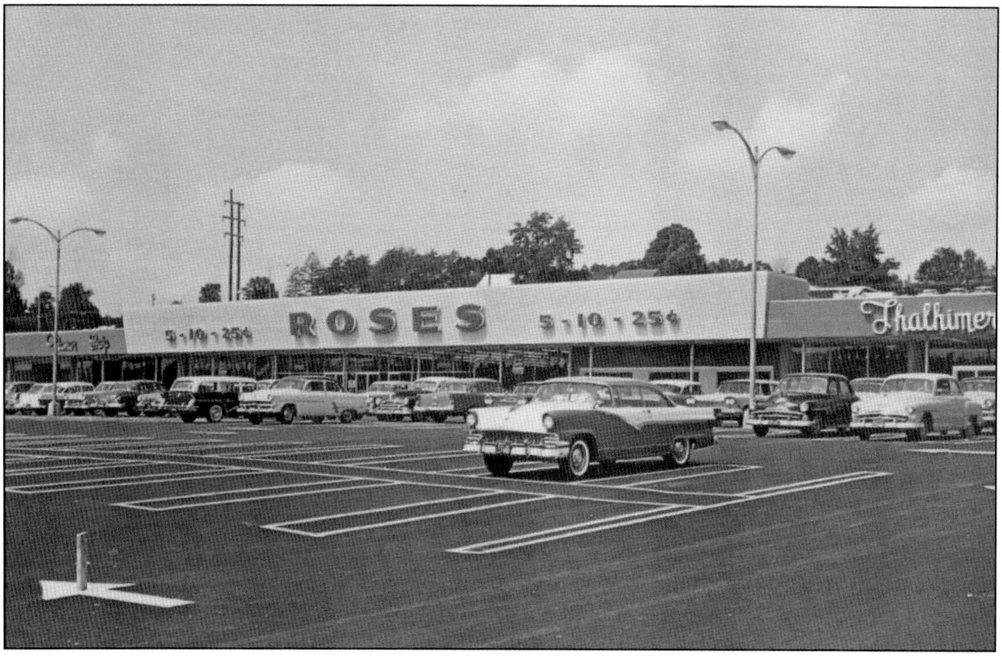

As towns began to swell in size, consumers preferred to shop in their own neighborhoods, causing the innovation of suburban shopping centers. Riverside Shopping Center was built in 1960 by developer John W. Daniel and was followed soon by Nor-Dan and Ballou Park centers in the north and south areas of Danville.

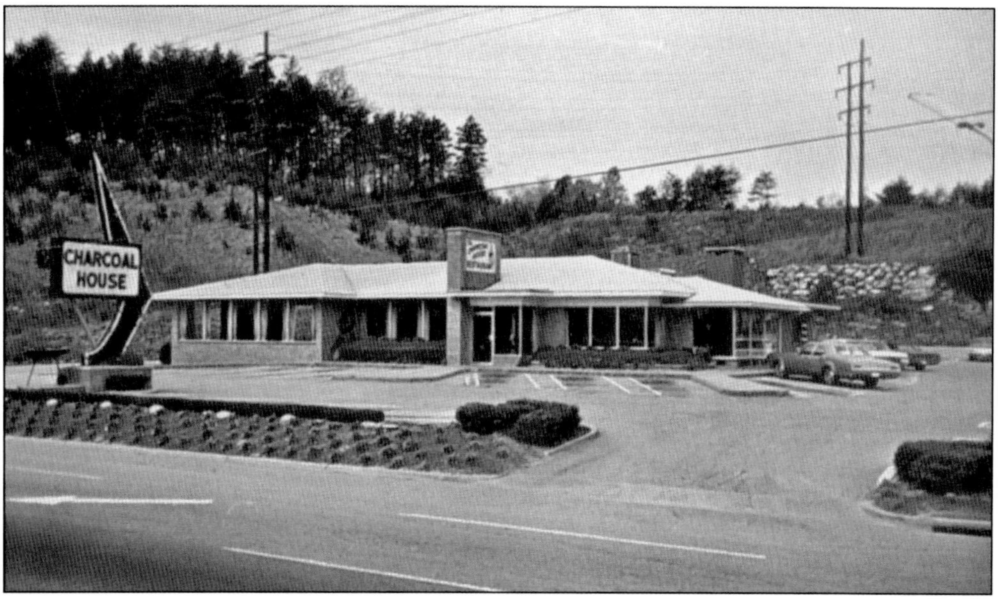

Saïd Shaip owned and managed the Charcoal House at 3426 Riverside Drive from 1958 to 1981. Photographed by Edward G. Jones, this was one of the first restaurants on Riverside Drive. Always the gentleman, "Cy" Shaip offered a combination of foods to his clientele, from steaks cooked on open grills (a method of cooking that became popular in the mid-1950s) to ethnic dishes from his native land, Lebanon, including the ever-popular tabouli.

Five

School Days

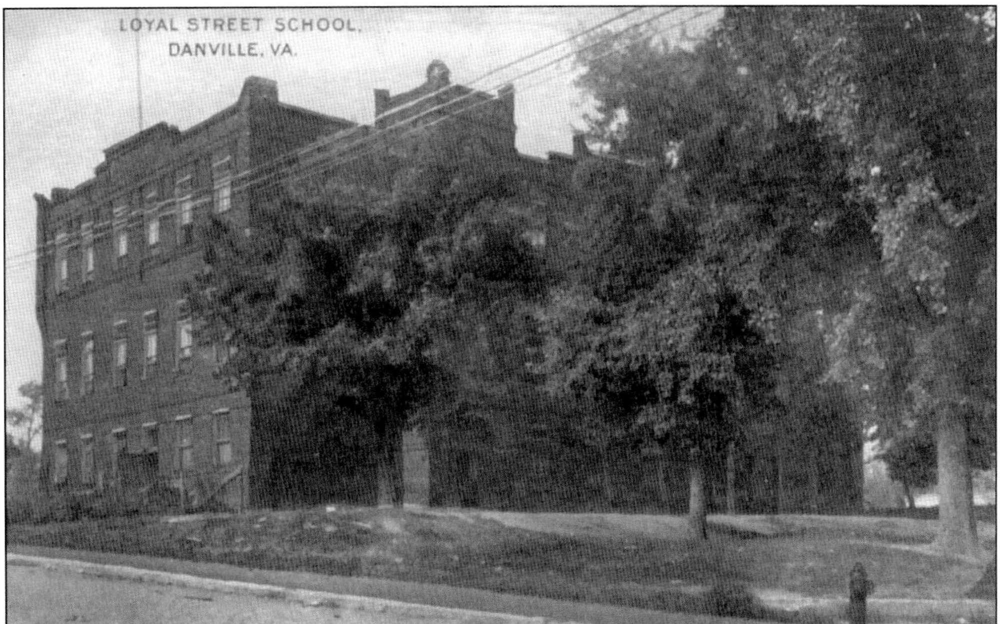

When free public education was proclaimed law in Virginia in 1870, Reverend George W. Dame was named superintendent of the city school system. In 1880 the Loyal Street School was erected at the corner of Loyal Street and Tazewell Alley (now Ridge Street), formerly the site of Stratford College's first campus. For many years the high school department was on the second floor and had a separate principal. At about the same time, the Danville School on Holbrook (later renamed Westmoreland) was built and in 1881 was headed by Reverend William A. Yancey, Danville's first African-American principal.

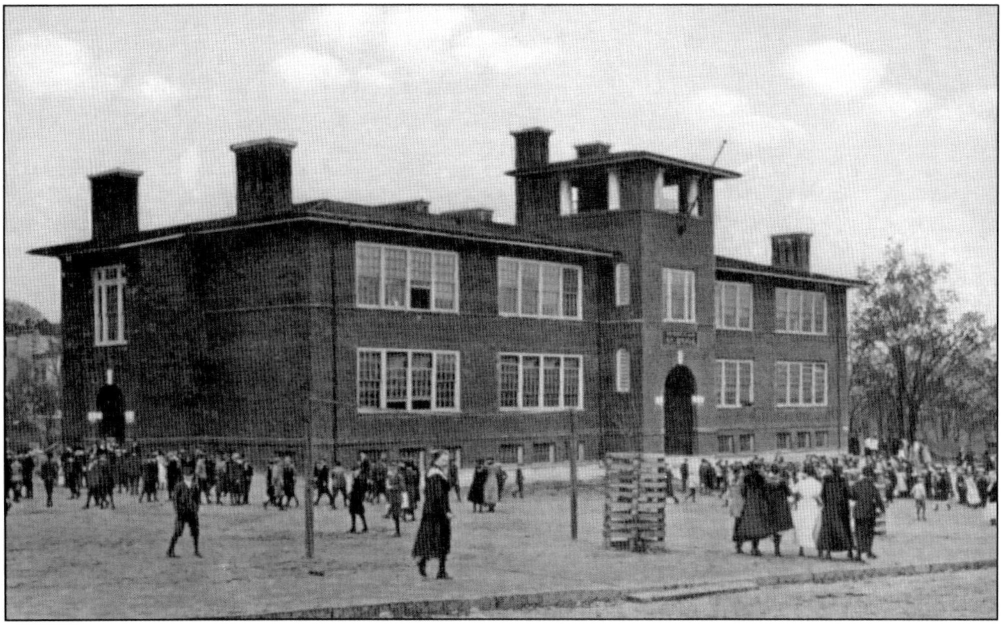

In 1911 the Loyal Street School was leveled and a newer building constructed on the same site. This Robert E. Lee Elementary School, housing grades one to seven, was in use until 1956, when the property was sold to Sears Roebuck and Company.

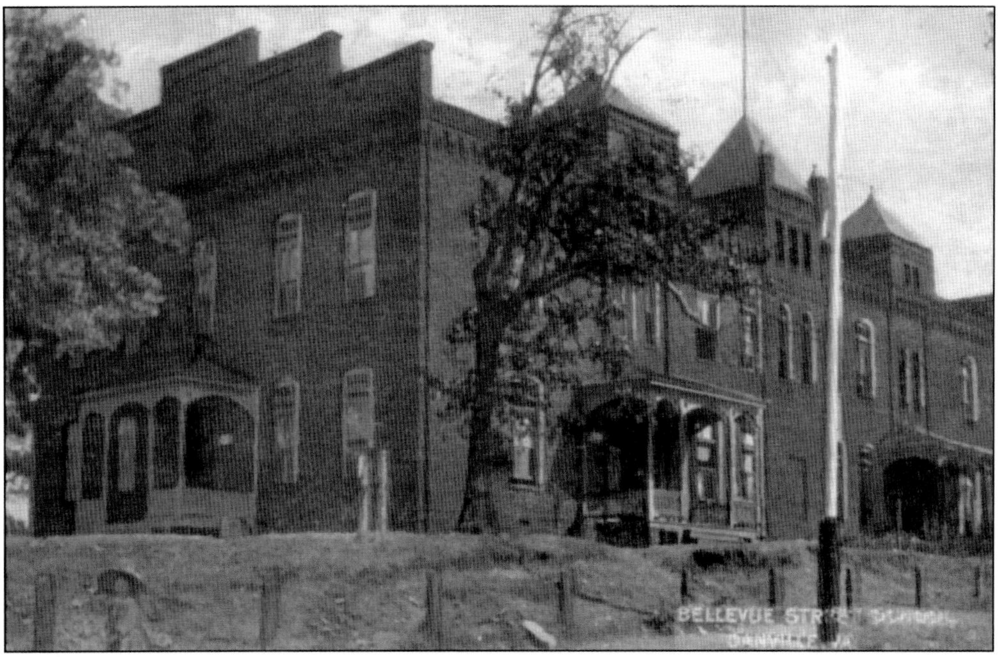

On the north side of town, Bellevue Elementary School was built in 1898 on the hill overlooking the falls in the river. Named for the former home of Leonard Claiborne, an early landowner in North Danville, this school closed in 1981, and most of the building was torn down.

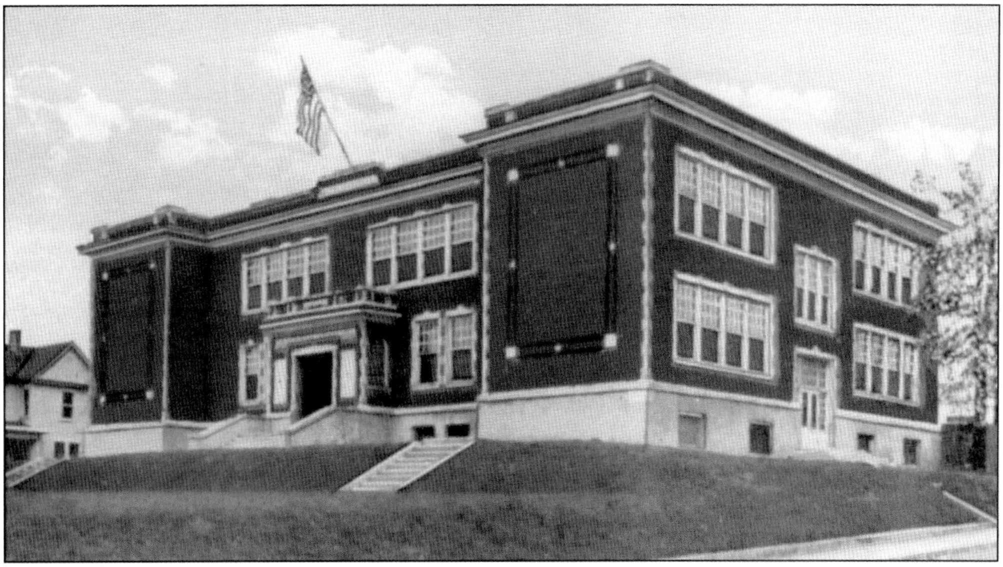

In 1915 the Stonewall Jackson Elementary School was built at 1600 North Main Street. It was at this school that the first Parent-Teacher Association in Danville was formed in 1920. In service for 63 years, the brick building was torn down in 1978. The gymnasium-auditorium building adjacent, built in 1954, was left standing and is now used for a special populations center.

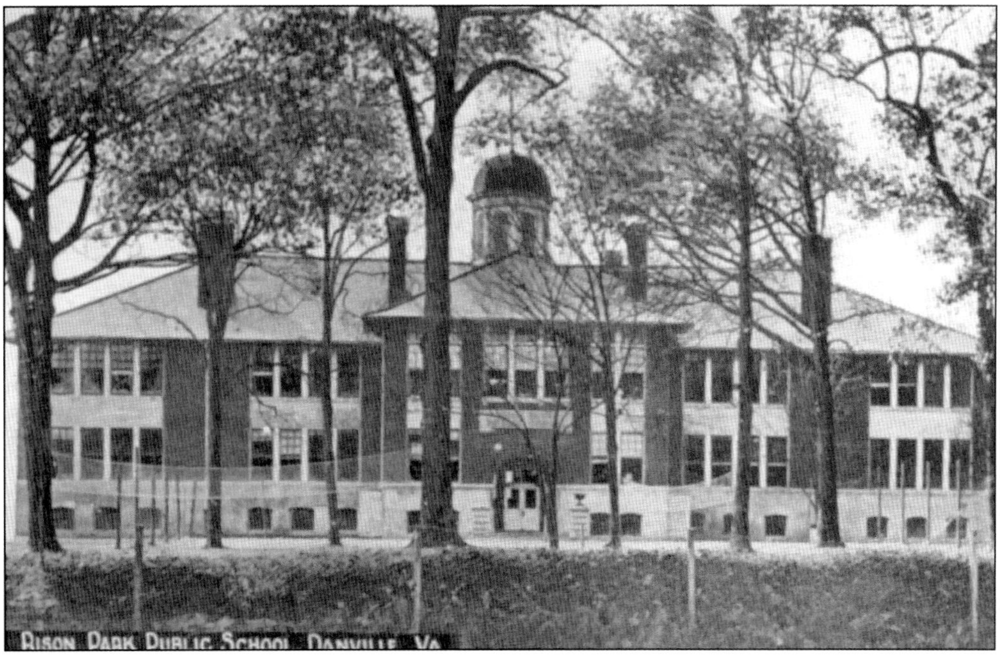

Many Danville students attended school in this building located at 500 Holbrook Avenue. It opened in 1909 as Rison Park Elementary School, built on the oak-shaded estate of Colonel William Rison. Serving as an elementary school until 1926, it was then enlarged and renamed George Washington High School. The former Danville High School on Grove Street (1910–1926) became the John L. Berkeley Elementary School.

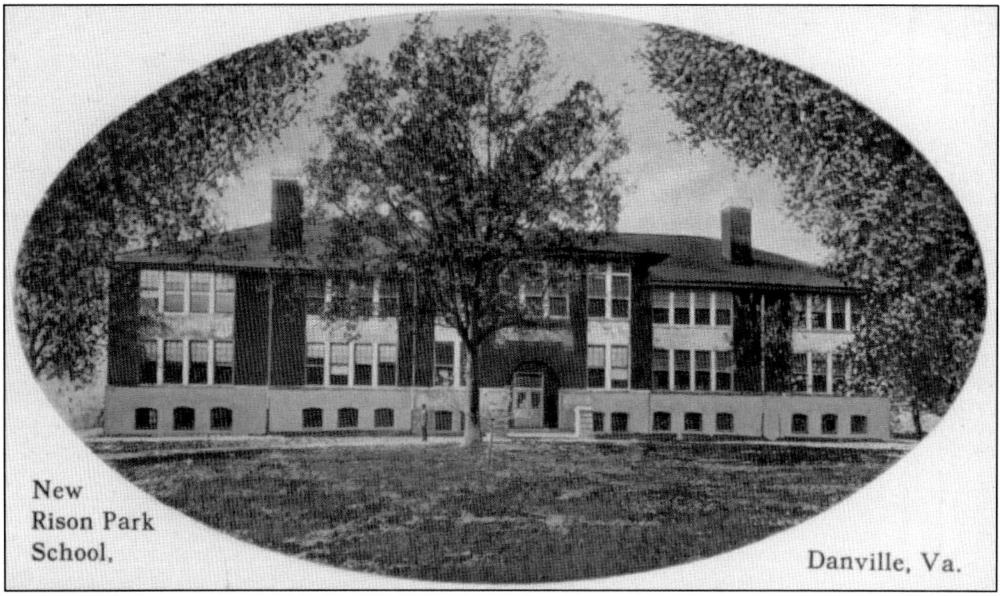

George Washington High School (the old Rison Park School) moved to a new campus on Broad Street in 1957, and this building on Holbrook continued in use as the Robert E. Lee Junior High School for many years. At about the same time, in 1958, the John M. Langston High School on Cleveland Street was built.

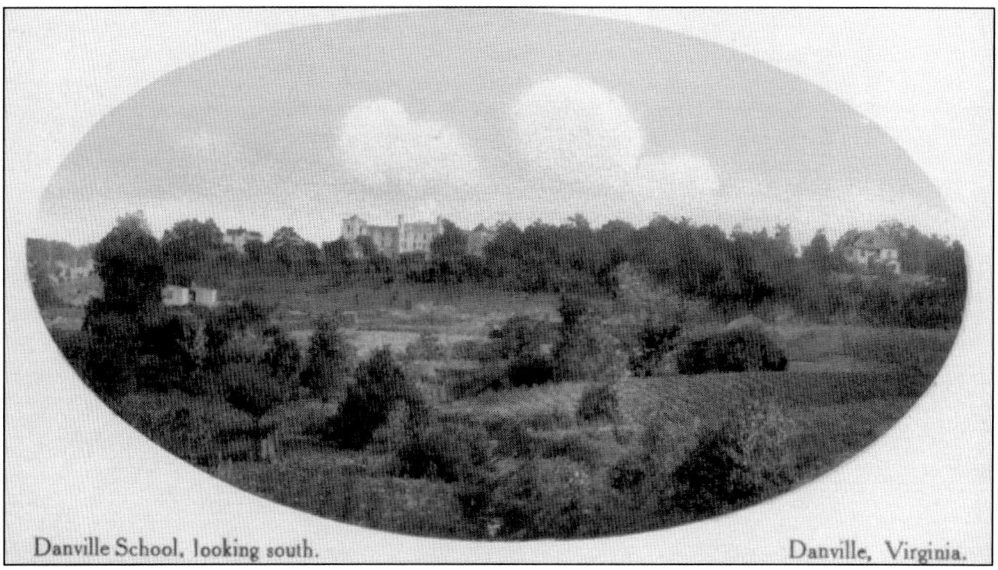

Chartered and built in 1890, the Danville Military Institute (DMI) was an imposing sight for travelers approaching Danville. At the corner of Kemper Road and South Main Streets, the "castle on the hill" served its student body as both a dormitory and classroom building. The school's most famous instructor was General George C. Marshall, who taught there in 1901–1902.

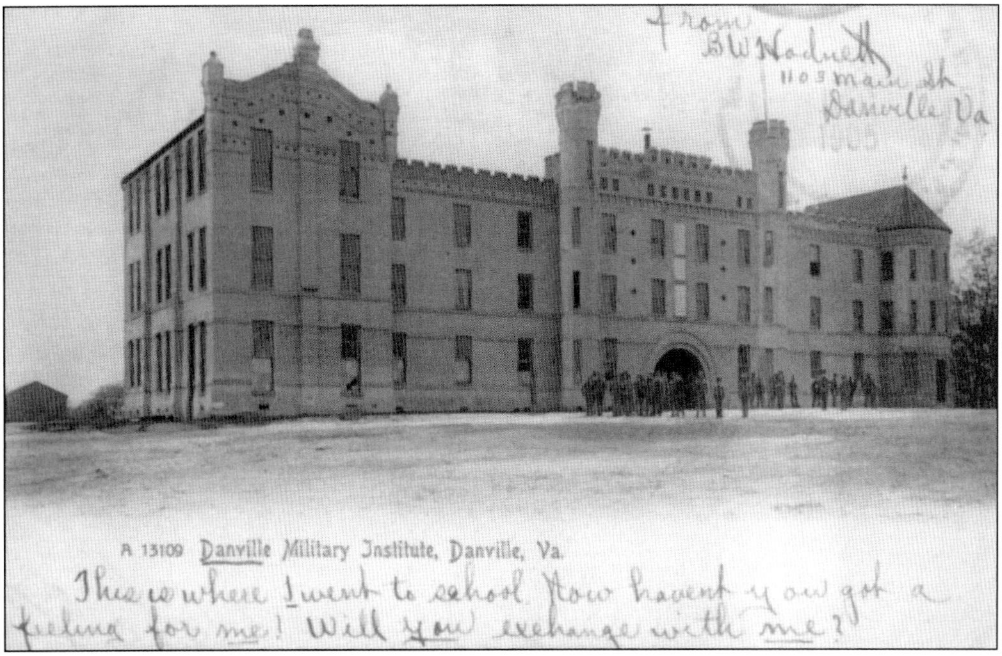

Facing financial difficulties, the military school was sold at auction at the end of World War I. In 1918 the Red Cross used this building as a hospital during the infamous flu epidemic that crippled the nation. During World War II the castle was used to house German prisoners.

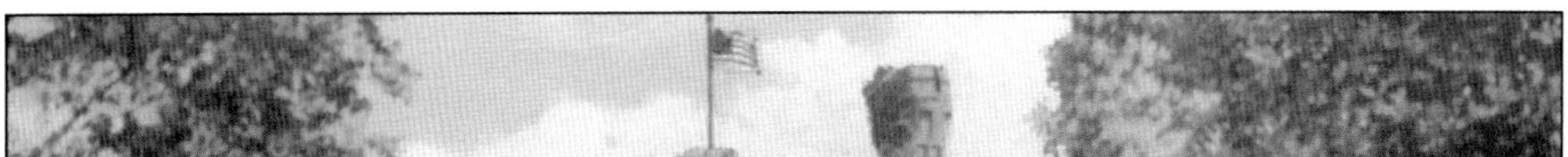

In the 1940s DMI was remodeled and used as a home for the Danville Technical Institute. Virginia Polytechnic Institute-Danville occupied the building for a few years. The building was condemned and torn down in 1974, and the land was used for expansion of the Danville Community College.

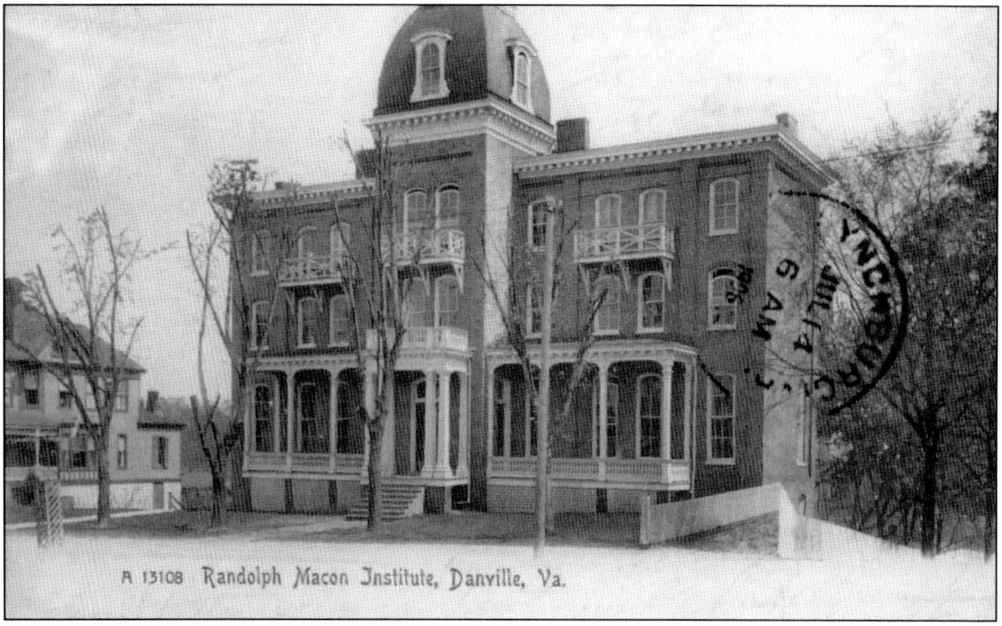

The Danville College for Young Ladies, formerly on Loyal Street, moved to a wooded 30-acre campus on Main Street in 1883. Richmond architect Albert L. West designed Main Hall, which is located in the 1100 block of Main Street. The college had been a part of the Randolph-Macon system of schools from 1897 to 1930, when it cut those ties and changed its name to Stratford College.

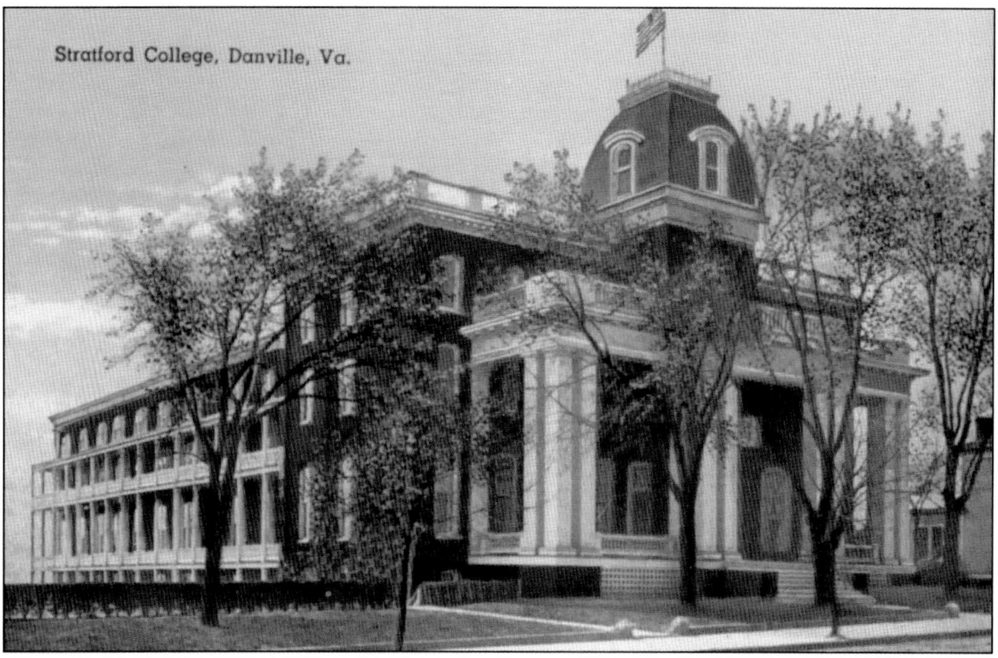

Stratford College began as a two-year girls' school with a four-year high school department called Stratford Hall. The two-story front porch was added around 1910. In later years the college expanded to a four-year college granting liberal and fine arts degrees.

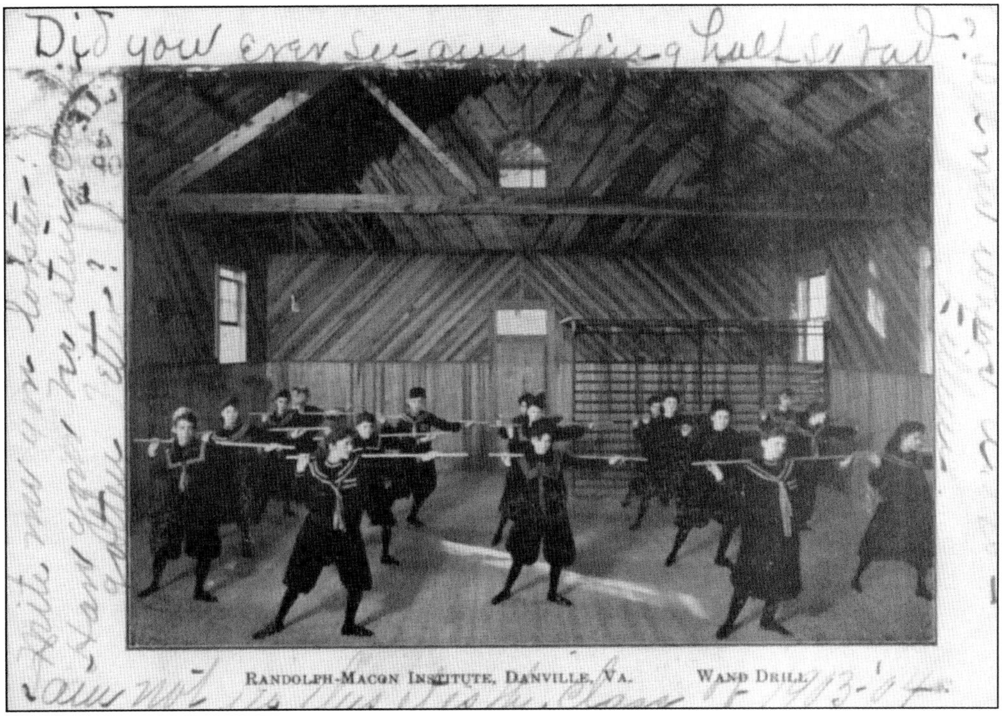

This 1905 postcard reveals the standard gym-suits worn in "calisthenics and physical culture" classes at Stratford. The small gymnasium was later used as an art studio and shop for local artists Jane Appleton and Paul Bond.

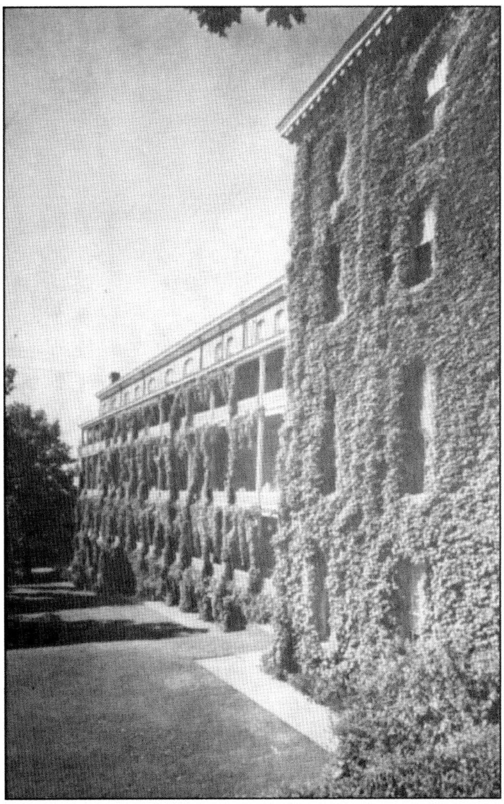

Behind Stratford's Main Hall was a rather long dormitory wing that was covered with ivy, giving the college an atmosphere of permanence. Sadly, in 1974 Stratford College closed its doors forever. The library was sold to Elon College in North Carolina, and the buildings and grounds were purchased by Memorial Hospital.

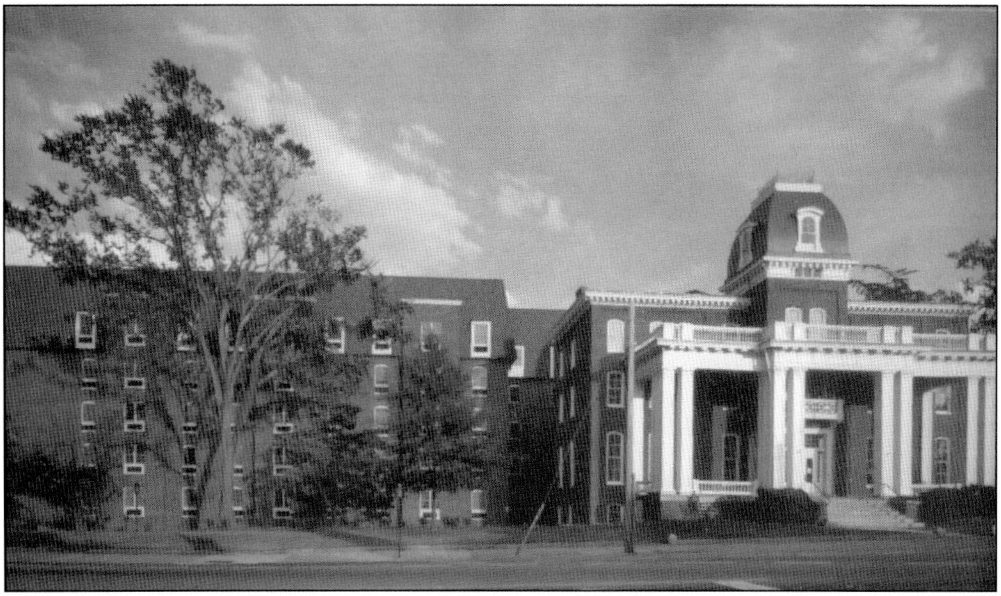

In 1990 the old college campus was renovated and expanded by Memorial Hospital to become the first retirement community in Danville, Stratford House.

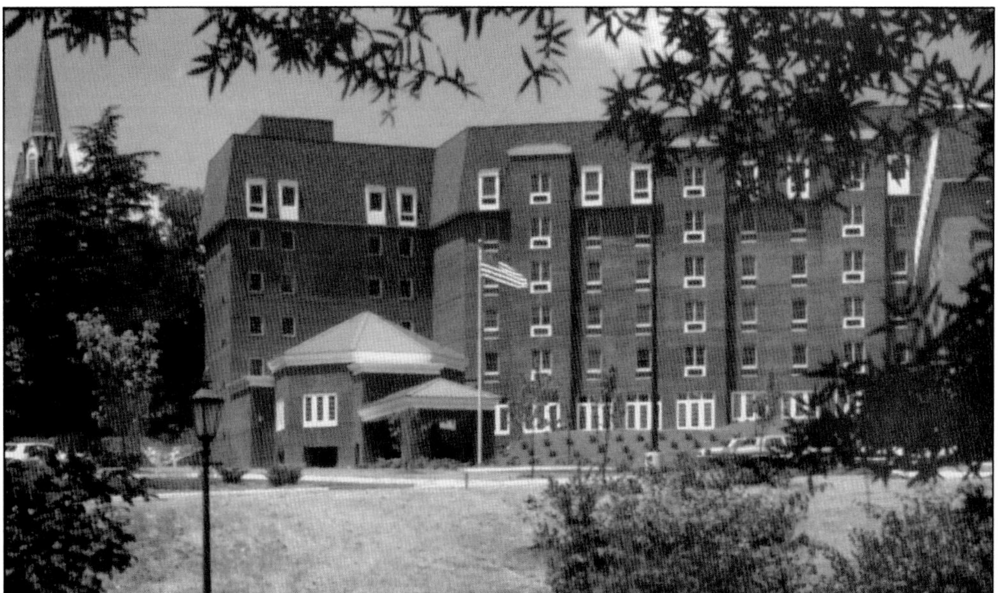

Built to provide a home for older citizens and to accommodate those who need assisted living services, Stratford House offers much to its residents including served dinners, transportation, scheduled outings, and weekly housekeeping.

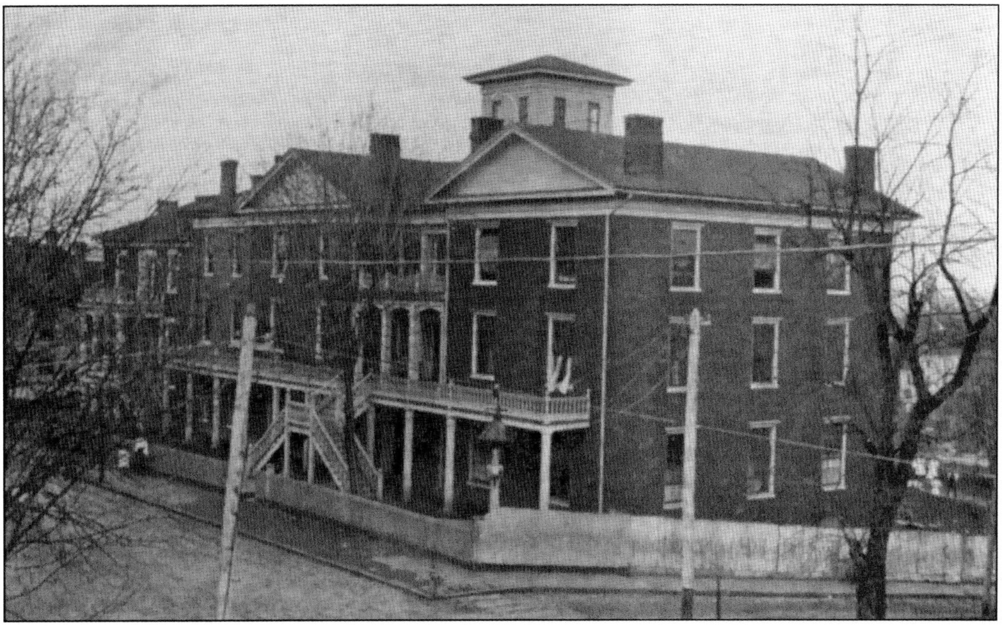

Averett College was chartered in 1859 and sat at the corner of Patton and Ridge Streets. This 1904 view was one of the earliest postcards sold in Danville. Besides a glimpse of the old brick school building, this card shows the type of electric streetlights, suspended in the center of the intersection, in use by the city of Danville.

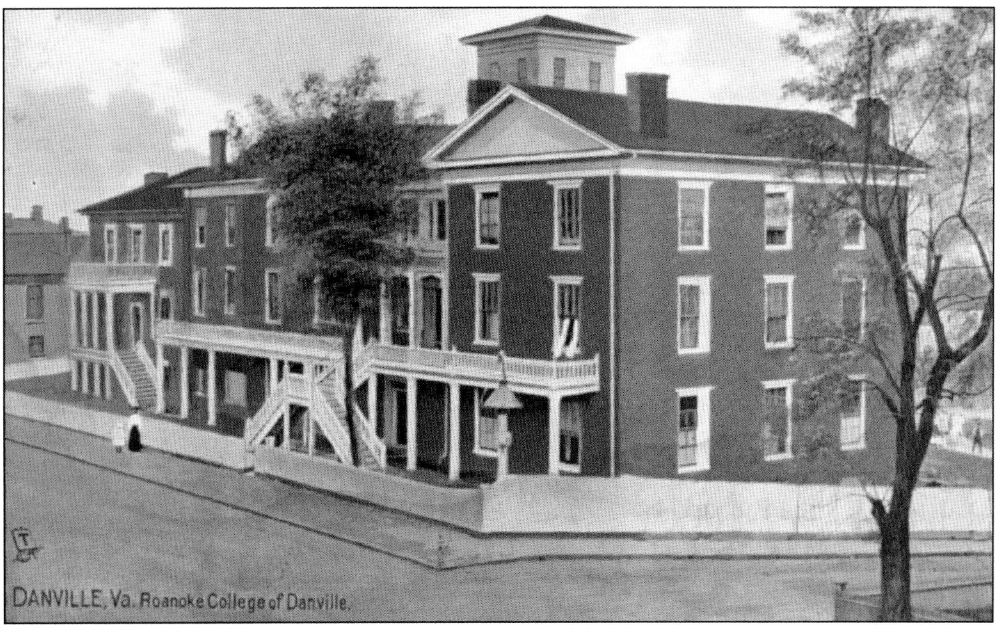

The 1904 view above was published by the Souvenir Post Card Company. When the Raphael Tuck Company wanted to use the same negative (a common practice of the day), the image was air-brushed to clean up the picture by eliminating the light poles and by adding leaves to the trees. Somehow overlooked, the streetlight in the center of the intersection was left hanging from nothing!

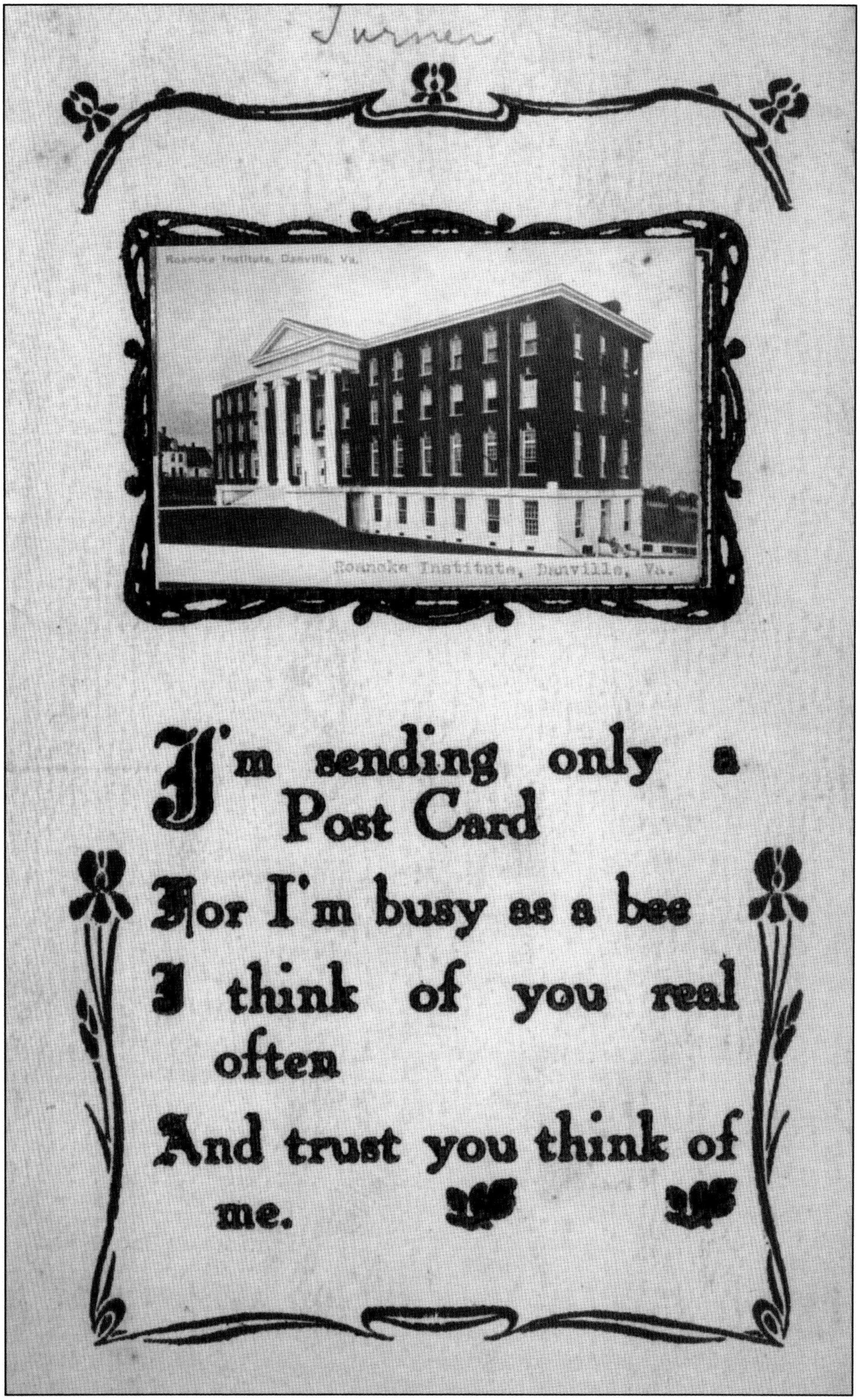

Greeting cards were popular for college girls to send to young men or to family members. An actual photograph of the college was pasted onto this generic card to attract an Averett buyer. Other city buildings have appeared on similar cards by the same publisher.

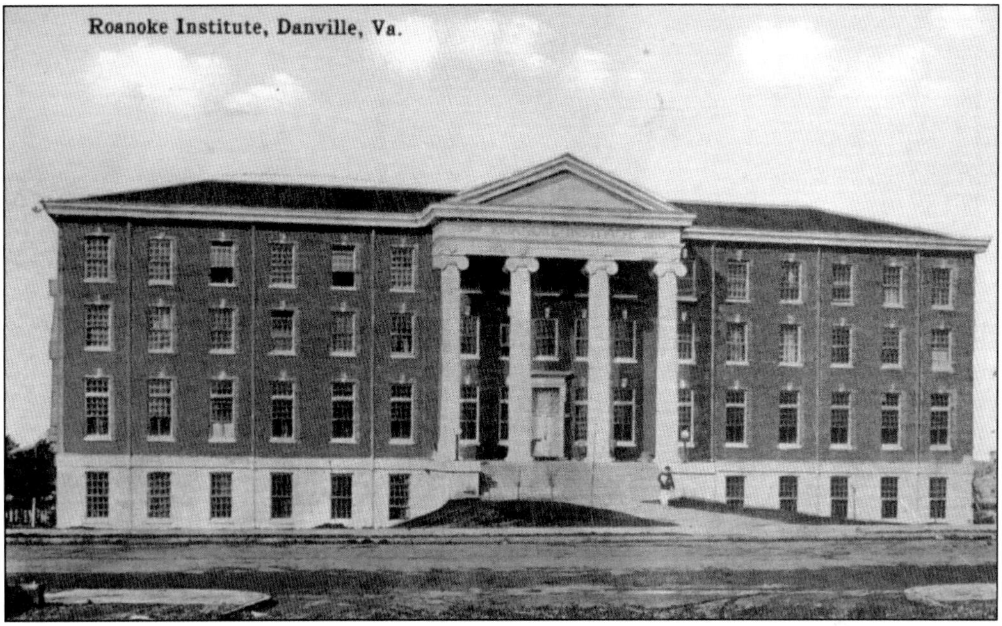

The Roanoke Female College, as Averett was once known, moved from its location on Patton Street in 1911 to a new site at 420 West Main Street before the street was even paved. In 1917 the name of the college was changed to honor a family who had served the college well, and one man in particular, former President John T. Averett.

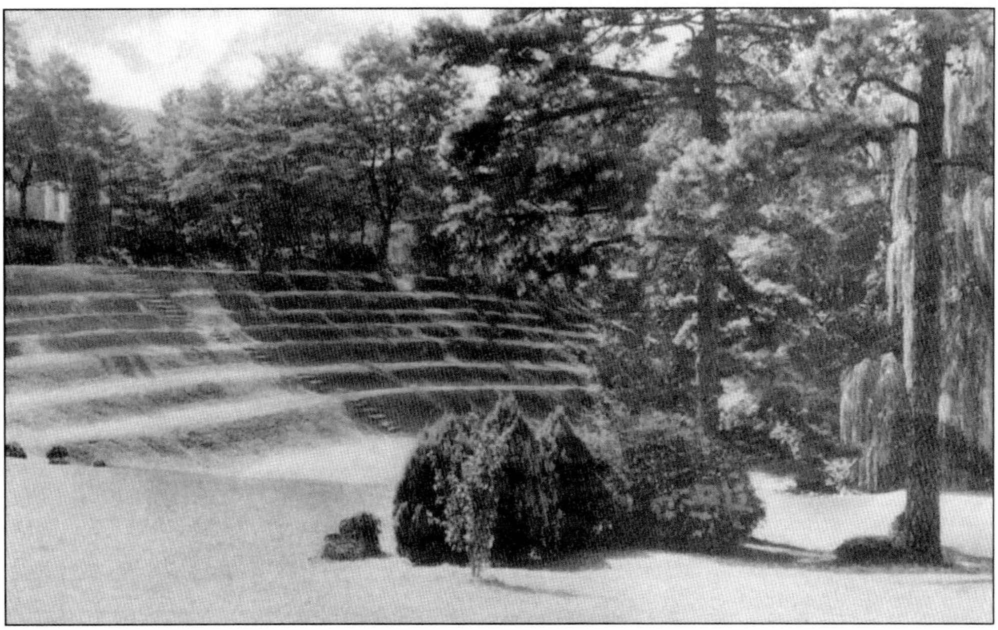

Every spring the public was invited to Averett College to witness the drama and excitement of the May Day festival, which was performed at the foot of the terraced hill behind the college buildings. Usually telling a folk or fairy tale through music and dance, the day's events included the crowning of a May Queen by a noted local citizen.

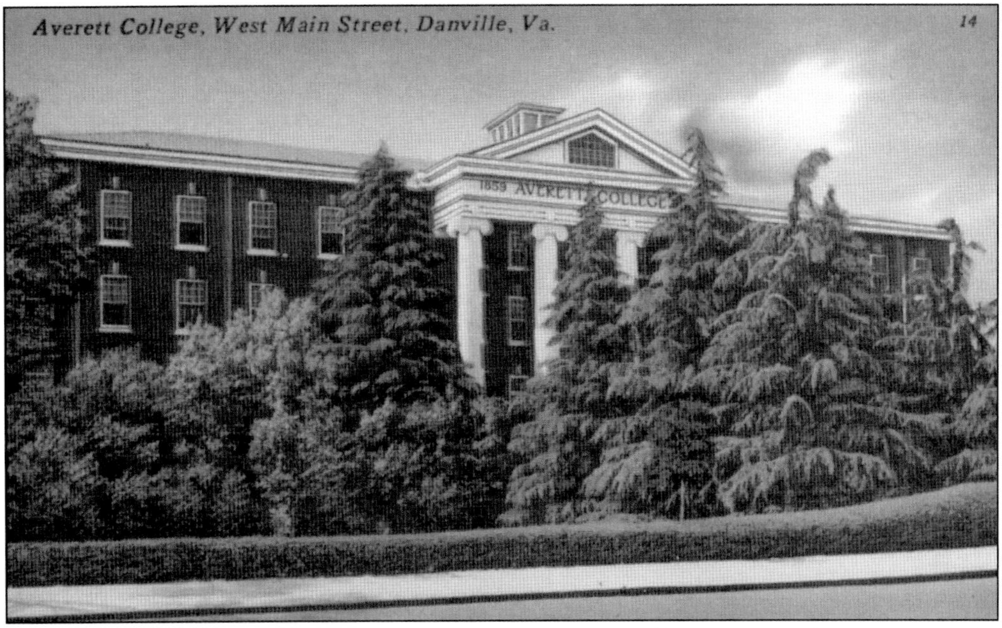

Although an occasional male took classes at Averett, the college remained a two-year girls' school until the early 1970s. In 1974 Averett awarded its first four-year degrees to both males and females. This view taken in the 1930s shows Main Hall almost totally engulfed by trees.

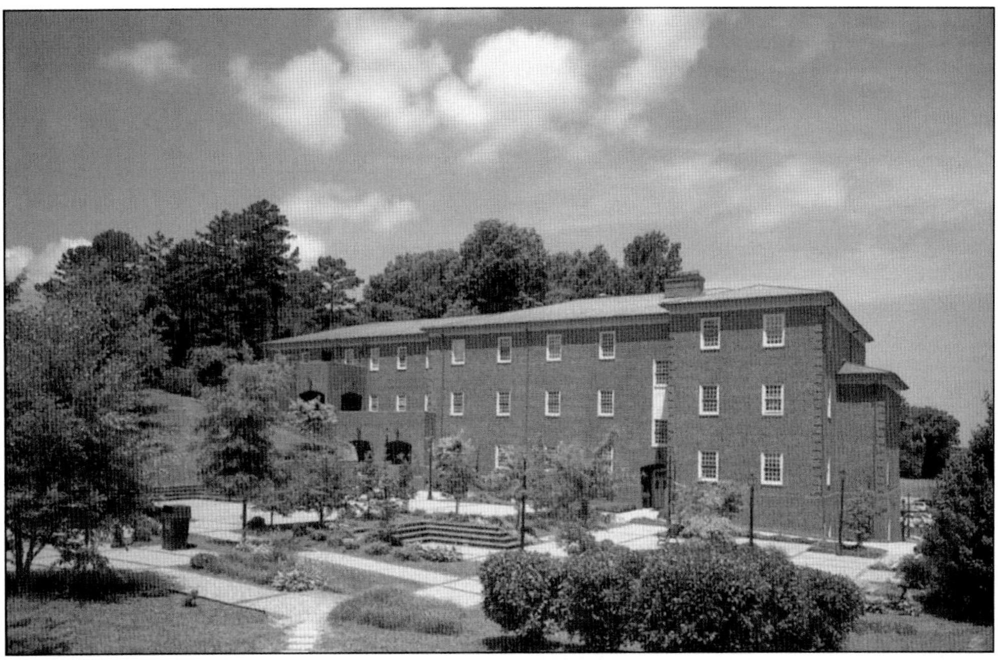

As Averett College continues to provide quality education to its many and diverse students, it has continued to expand its campus to accommodate the numerous programs offered to both undergraduate and graduate classes. Frith Hall, housing science laboratories and general classrooms, was added in 1985.

Six

City of Churches

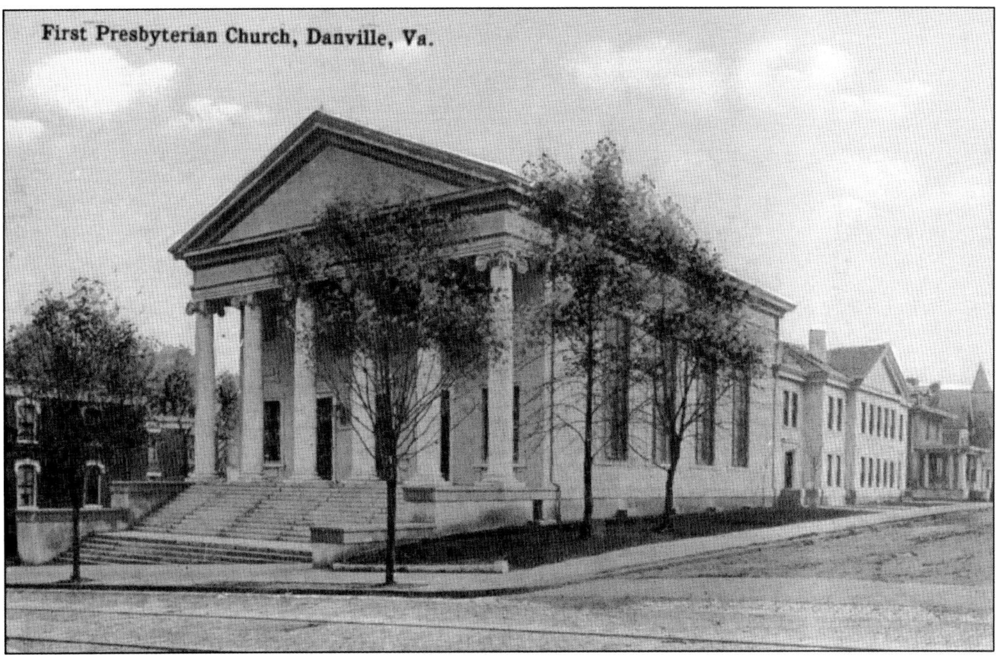

The first religious establishment in Danville was organized as the First Presbyterian Church in 1826. Outgrowing three houses of worship on Jefferson Avenue, the church constructed this fourth edifice in 1912 at the corner of Main and Sutherlin Streets. Behind the Presbyterian Church, one sees the Temple Beth Sholom (House of Peace) at 129 Sutherlin Avenue, which was built in 1900 by the local German Jewish community. Danville architect-builder R.B. Graham designed their Romanesque Revival temple.

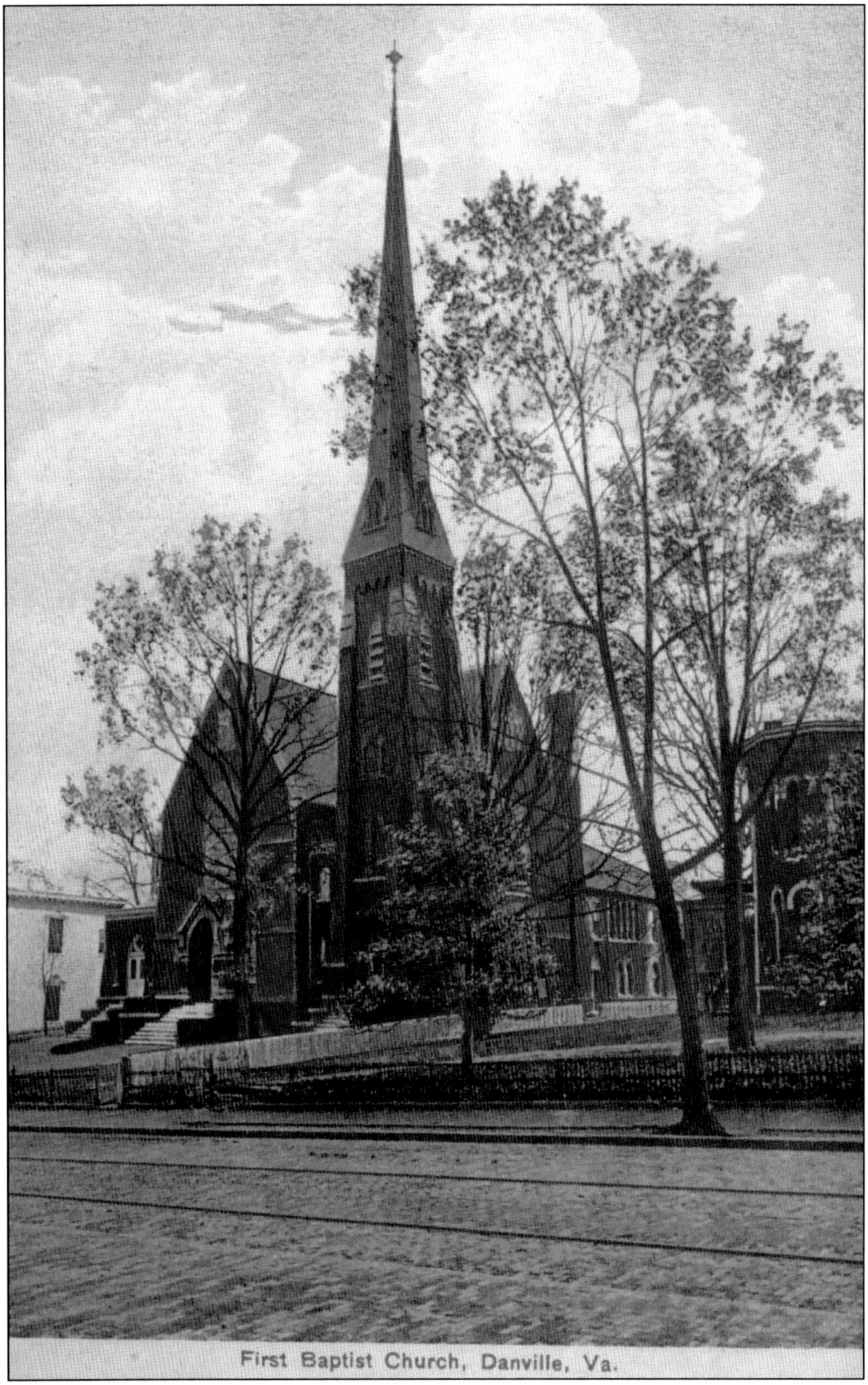

In 1883 the First Baptist Church at 871 Main Street was built when the congregation outgrew their former building on the corner of Ridge and Patton Streets. In 1905 lightning struck this steeple, nearly destroying the church.

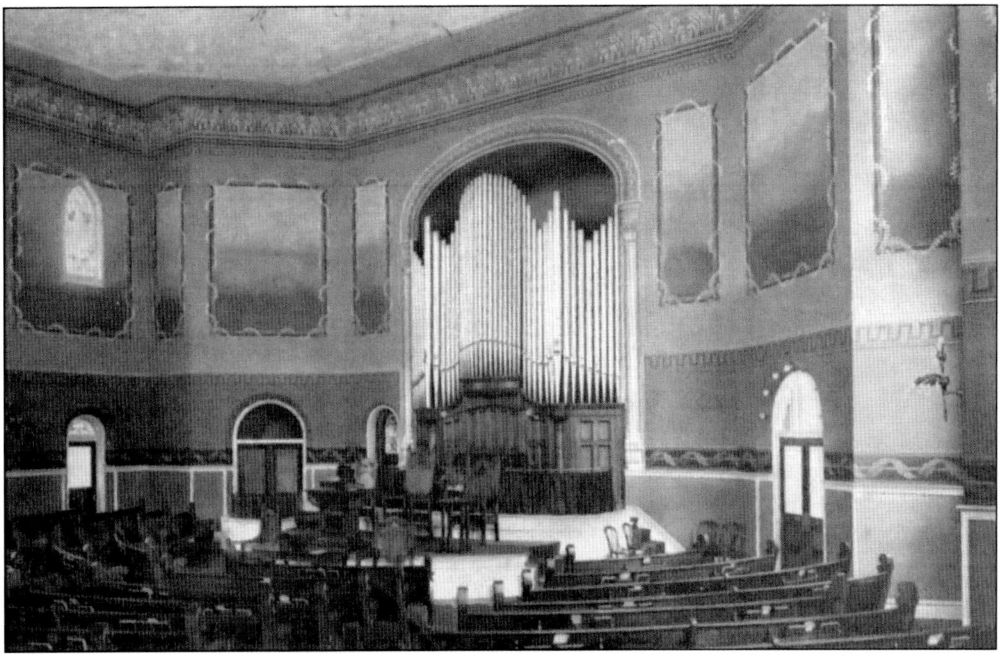

Interior views of buildings were rarely used as subjects for postcards. This 1911 view of the inside of the First Baptist Church on Main Street captures the changes made to the sanctuary after fire caused massive damage.

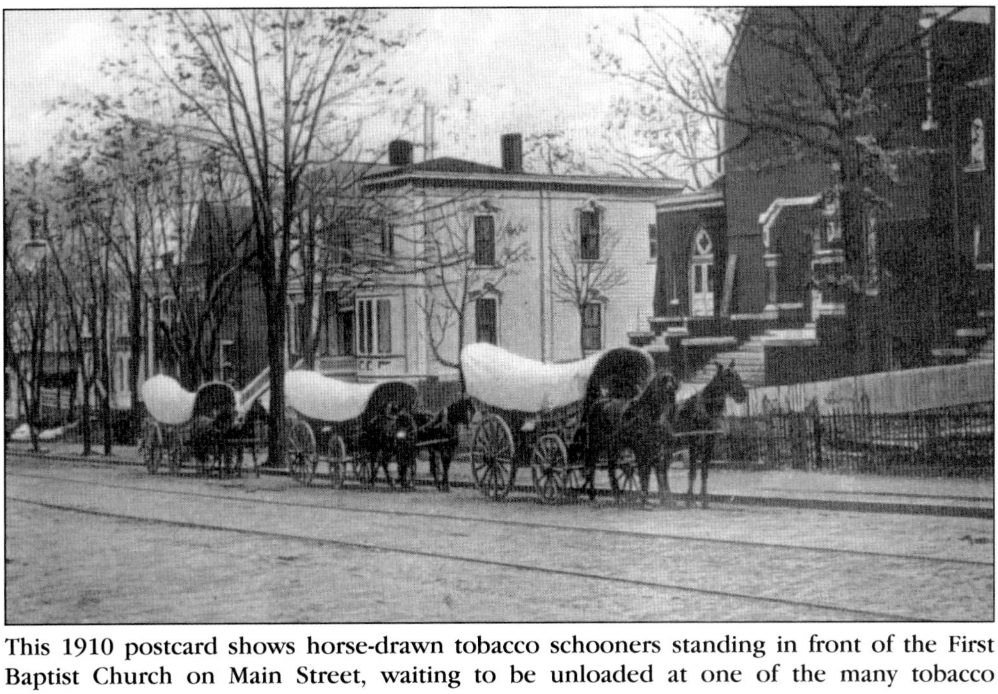

This 1910 postcard shows horse-drawn tobacco schooners standing in front of the First Baptist Church on Main Street, waiting to be unloaded at one of the many tobacco warehouses downtown.

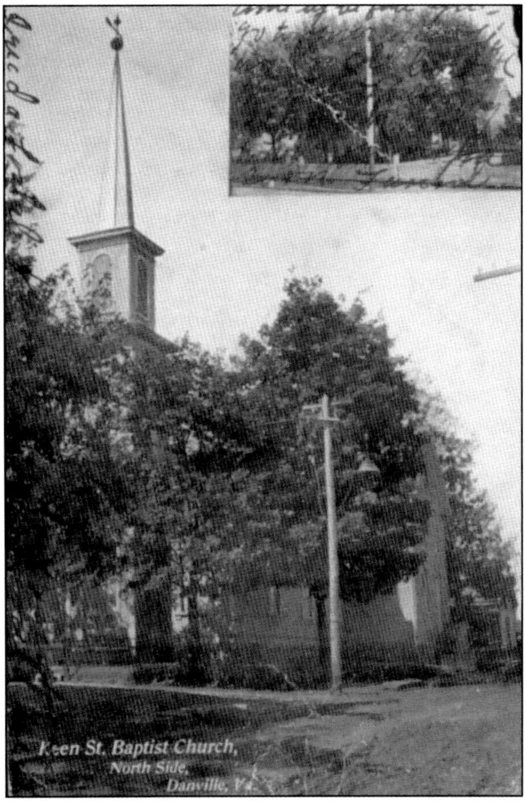

Keen Street Baptist Church on the corner of Keen and Church Streets was originally the home of Calvary Methodist Church and later an Episcopal Chapel. Purchased in 1904 by a group desirous of having a Baptist church in North Danville, Keen Street Baptist grew swiftly and by 1910 needed to enlarge the building. This frame structure was demolished in 1927 for the current brick edifice still in use today.

West Main Baptist Church, located at 450 West Main Street, was established in 1941 to provide a Baptist church near the campus of Averett College. The college was founded by Baptists from this area and still remains affiliated with the Baptist General Association of Virginia. The sanctuary of this brick building was completed in 1949.

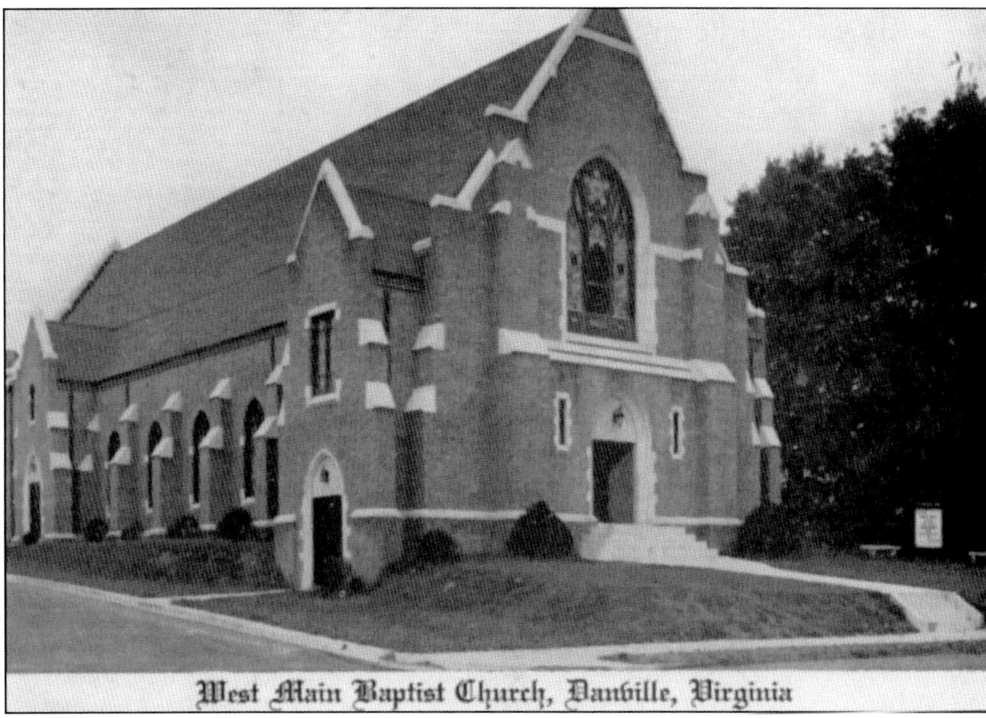

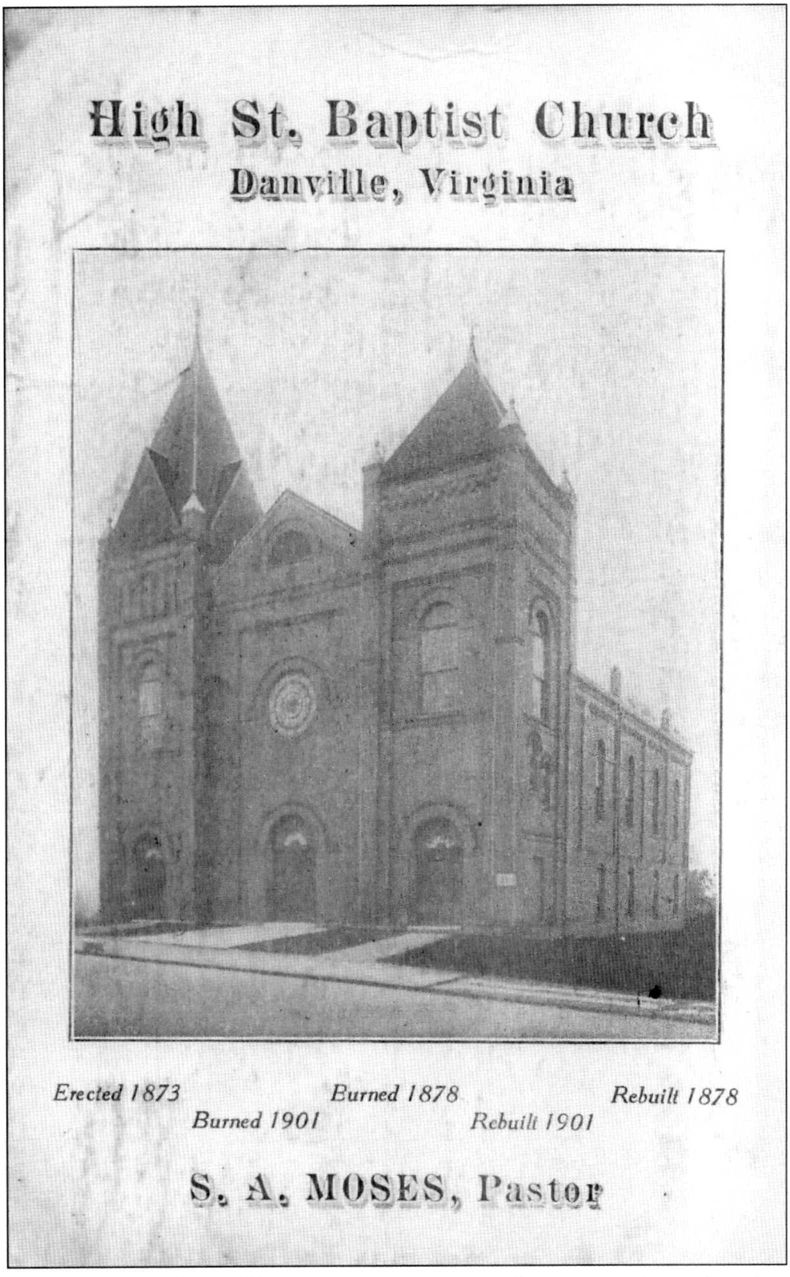

High Street Baptist Church at 630 High Street, the first African-American church in Danville, was organized in 1865. Two local groups grew from this original church, Loyal Baptist Church in 1866 and Calvary Baptist in 1892. The first ordained minister of High Street was the Reverend Harrison Scott, who served for eight years. The present edifice is the third one on this site since two previous ones burned down in 1878 and 1901. Dr. Martin Luther King Jr. was a speaker in this church during the 1960s. In June 1995 a severe windstorm ripped off the roof and this church again sustained much damage, but in 1996 renovations were completed and the church received an award from the Danville Historical Society for its quality restoration.

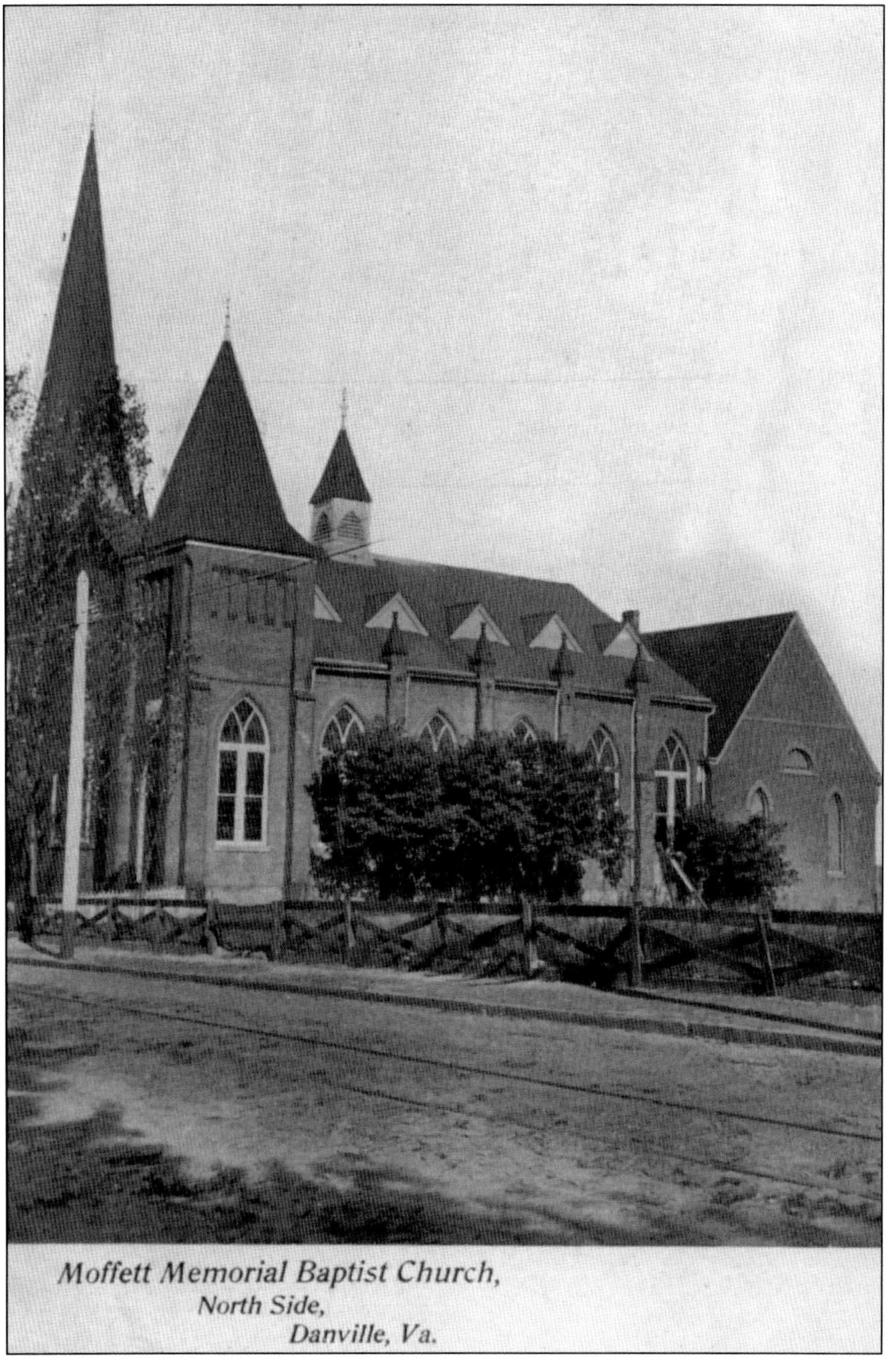

Moffett Memorial Baptist Church at 1026 North Main Street began its days in the 1880s as the North Danville Baptist Church. The first pastor, John R. Moffett, arrived in 1887 and by 1889 dedicated this new sanctuary. A staunch advocate for temperance, Reverend Moffett was murdered, shot at close range by J.T. Clarke. Four days after Moffett's death, the church was renamed in his memory. Struck by lightning and totally destroyed in 1971, Moffett Memorial was rebuilt in 1973 .

A fine example of Romanesque Revival architecture, the Main Street Methodist Church at 767 Main Street was completed in 1873. Later damaged by wind, this handsome structure was redesigned in 1891 by architect William M. Poindexter. The brick parsonage next door was used until the 1920s, when an educational building replaced it. The 11 bells of the carillon were given in 1909 in memory of James G. Penn, a tobacconist.

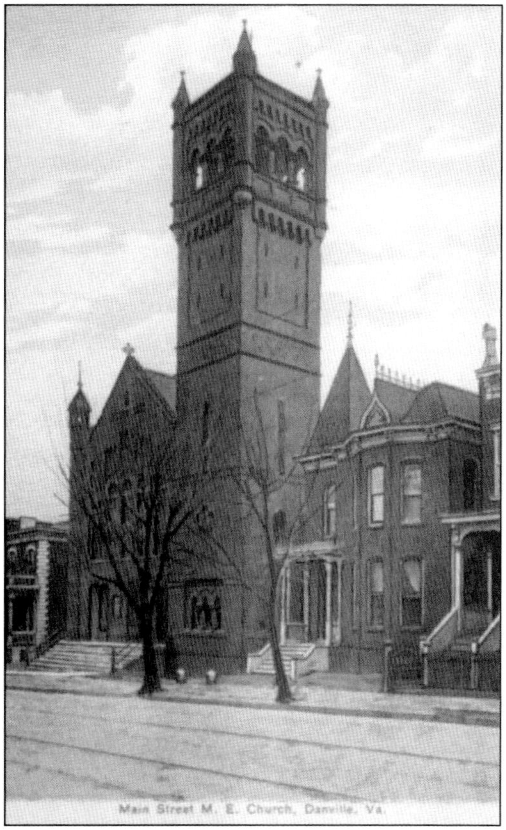

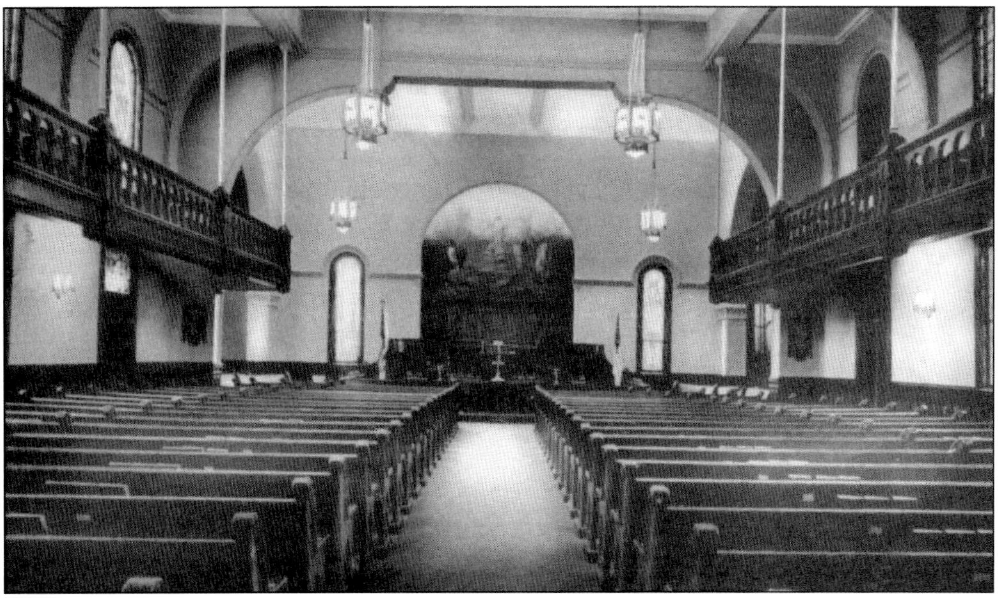

This interior view of Main Street Methodist Church reveals the pride of the congregation, a mural of the Transfiguration painted by G. Lecchi in 1908. By the turn of the twentieth century, Danville had gained another epithet: the "City of Churches."

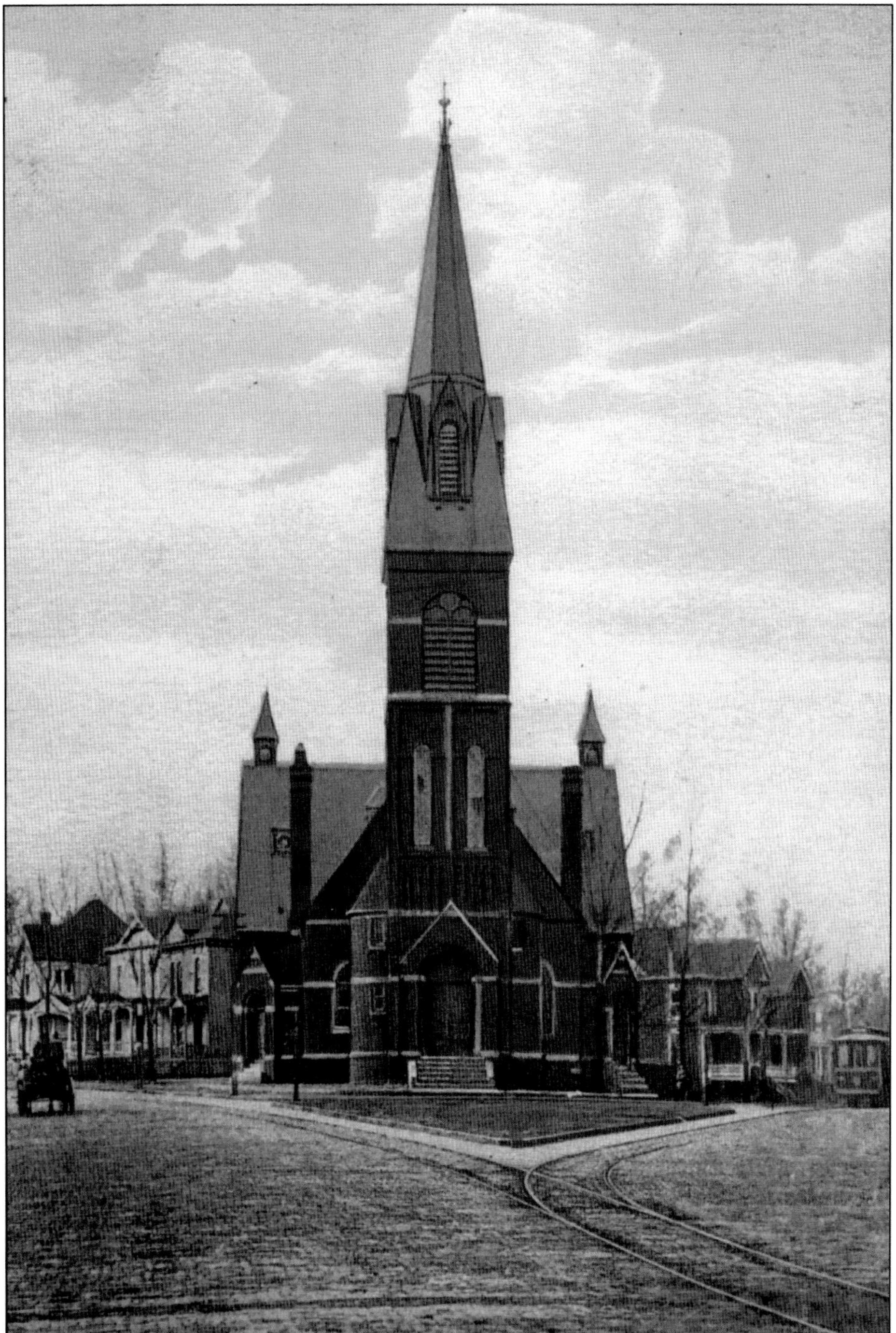

Mount Vernon Methodist Church, a High Victorian Gothic edifice sitting in the crossroads of South and West Main Streets, was designed by Baltimore architect Charles L. Carson and completed in 1885. At that time the only building nearby was the "Methodist" college, later known as Stratford College.

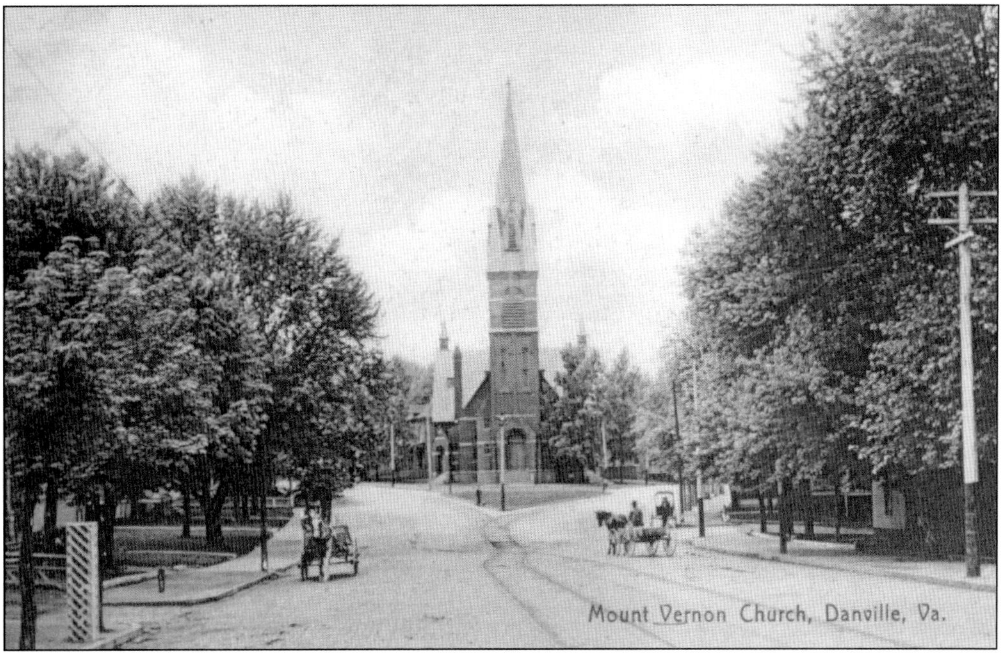

Brick-paved streets and tree-lined yards created beautiful scenes for many streets in Danville during the days before World War I. The road to the right of Mount Vernon Church that headed on to Greensboro, North Carolina, was once known as the Salisbury Road.

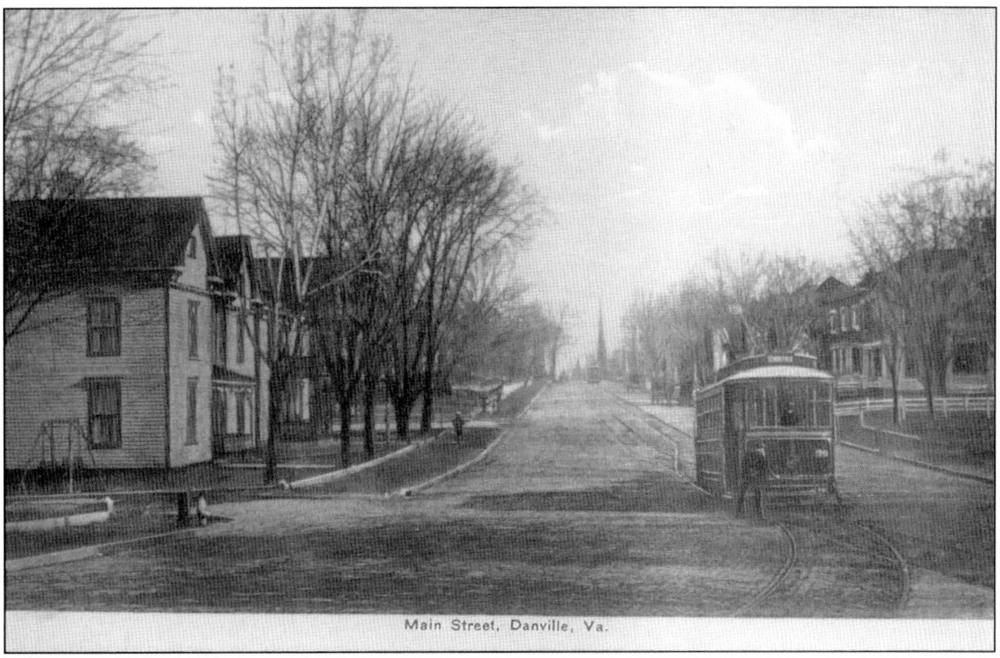

Electric streetcars began to run in Danville in the fall of 1888. They were always green and cream, the colors of the Danville Traction & Power Company. Looking away from Mount Vernon Church, the trolley tracks split between South and West Main Streets.

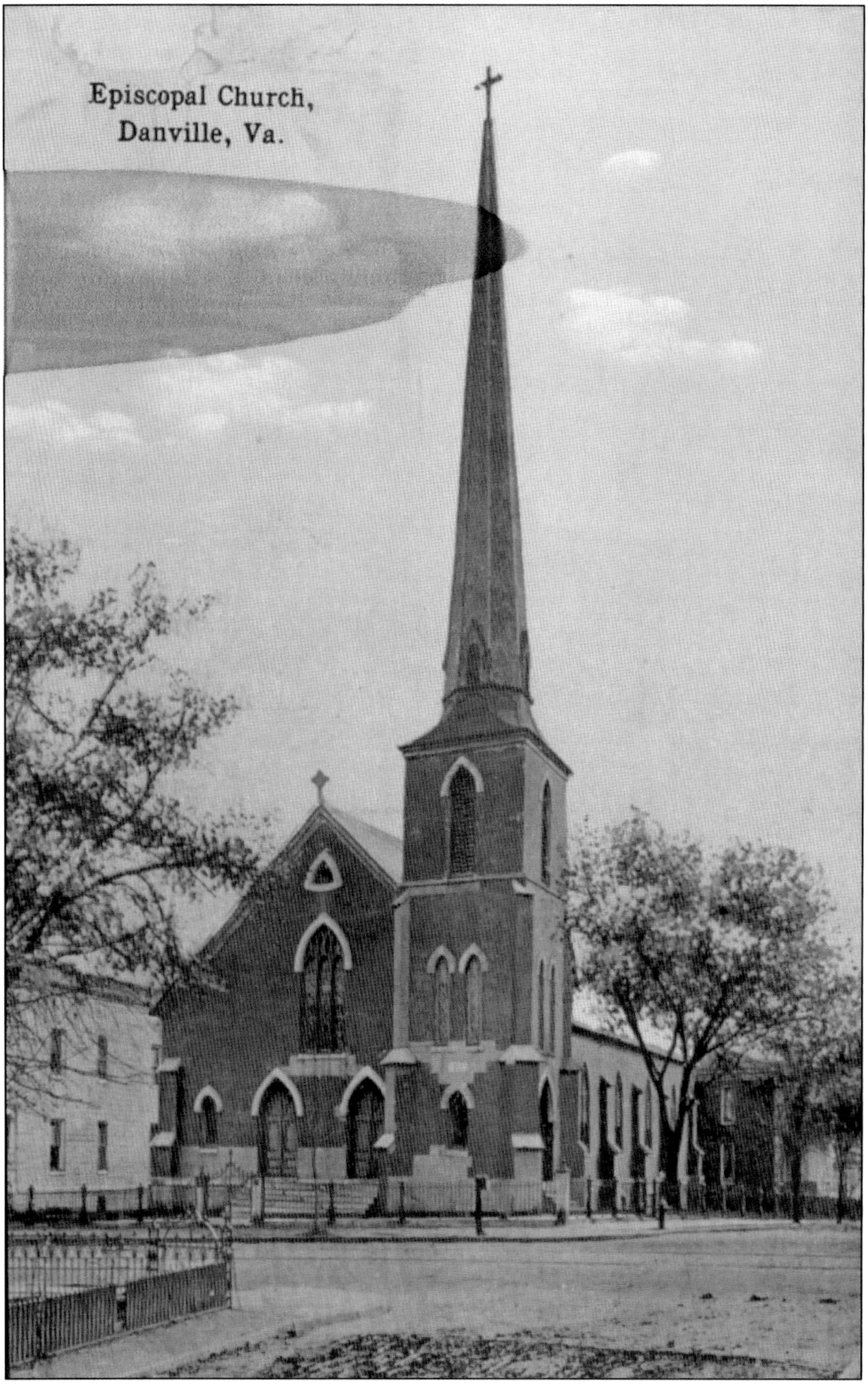

The Episcopal Church of the Epiphany was built in 1879 at the corner of Main and Jefferson on the site of an earlier frame structure. This church was founded in 1840 by Reverend George Washington Dame, who also served as an educator in the area.

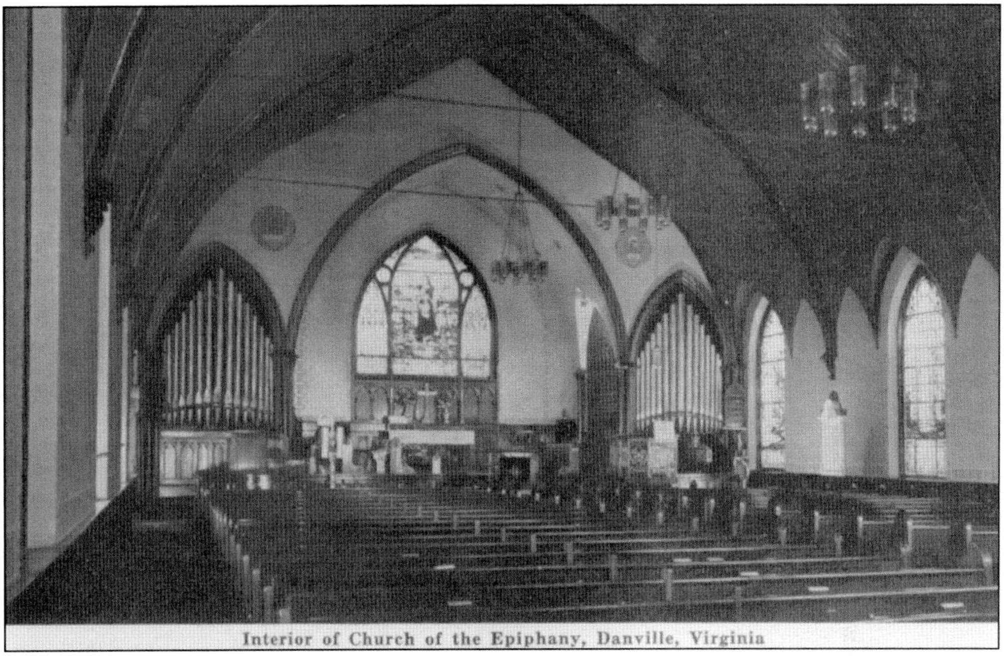

This 1940s view of the interior of the church shows the magnificent stained-glass window placed there as a memorial to Reverend George W. Dame.

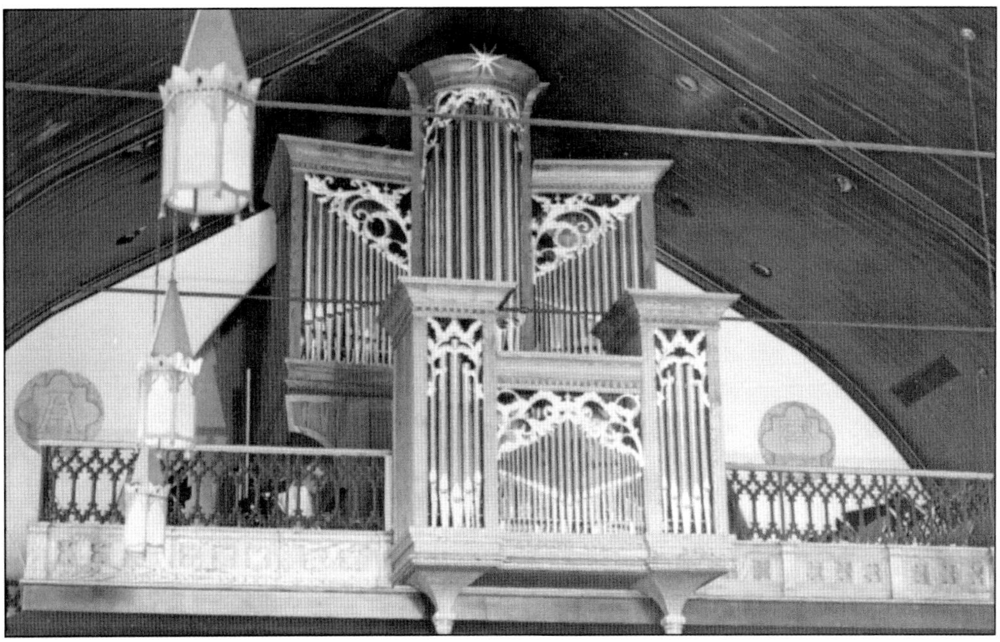

In 1979 the Episcopal Church of the Epiphany installed a new American-built mechanical organ, the largest of its kind in Virginia, produced by the Andover Organ Company of Methuen, Massachusetts. This photograph by Beth Riley shows the organ in all its splendor. The dedication concert featured Earl L. Miller, the church organist.

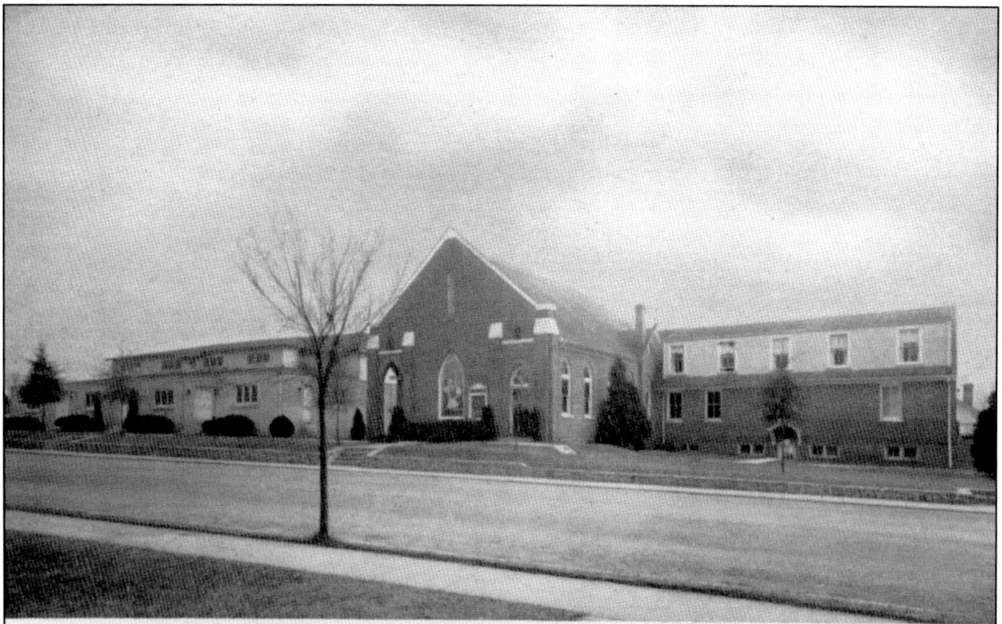

Third Avenue Christian Church and Tabernacle, Danville, Virginia

The Third Avenue Congregational Christian Church at 215 Third Avenue was founded in 1916 as a mission-oriented organization. The Reverend Matthew Thomas Sorrell, who served the church from 1926 to 1954, held the longest pastorate. With the aid of his church members and his assistant, Percy Ricketts, Reverend Sorrell was the founder of the Faith Home, a home and school for both boys and girls who were orphaned or who came from broken homes.

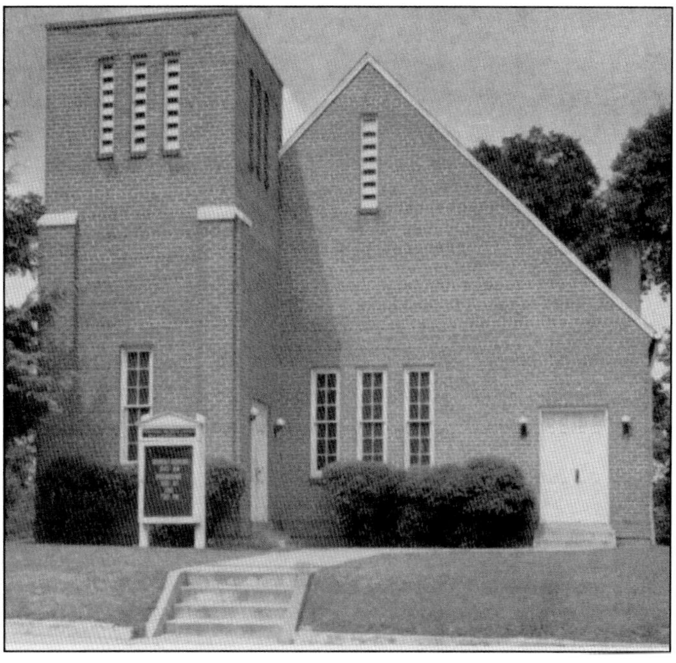

Larger now with the addition of a new sanctuary built in the mid-1950s, the First Pentecostal Holiness Church at 1810 North Main Street was originally built in 1931. The first pastor was Reverend Francis A. Dail, who served this congregation for 18 years.

The first religious group organized in North Danville was Methodist. Thomas B. Fitzgerald, architect, builder, and owner of a brickyard on Clay Street, built Calvary Methodist Church in 1886 at 924 North Main Street. In 1912 lightning heavily damaged Calvary's steeple and a square tower was built to replace it. The congregation merged with two others in 1988 to form St. Luke's Methodist Church at 3090 North Main Street.

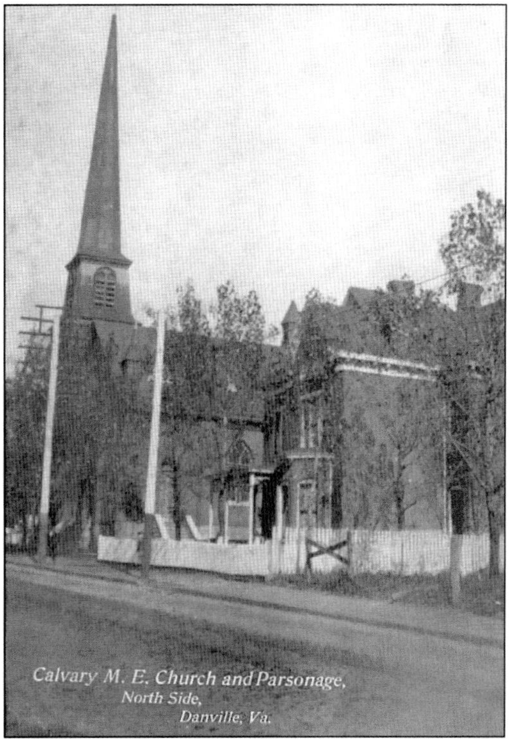

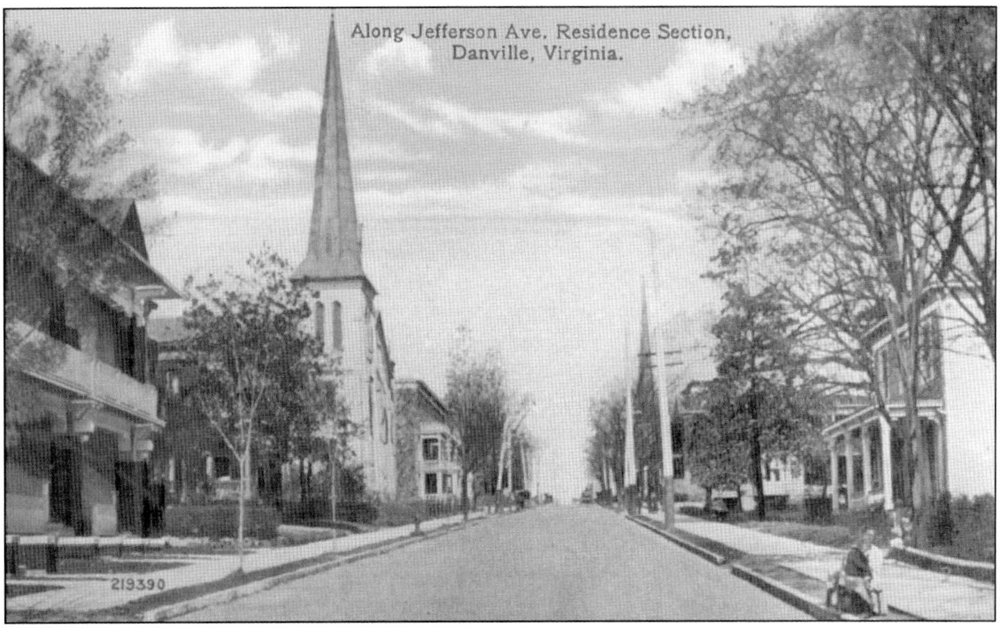

The First Christian Church dates back to 1884, but the congregation moved into this edifice on Jefferson Street in 1912, when the First Presbyterians moved to a new church on Main Street at Sutherlin Avenue. The sanctuary features the original Moller organ installed in 1900 by the Presbyterians. This 1912 postcard view of the homes on Jefferson Avenue was taken before lightning destroyed the church's steeple.

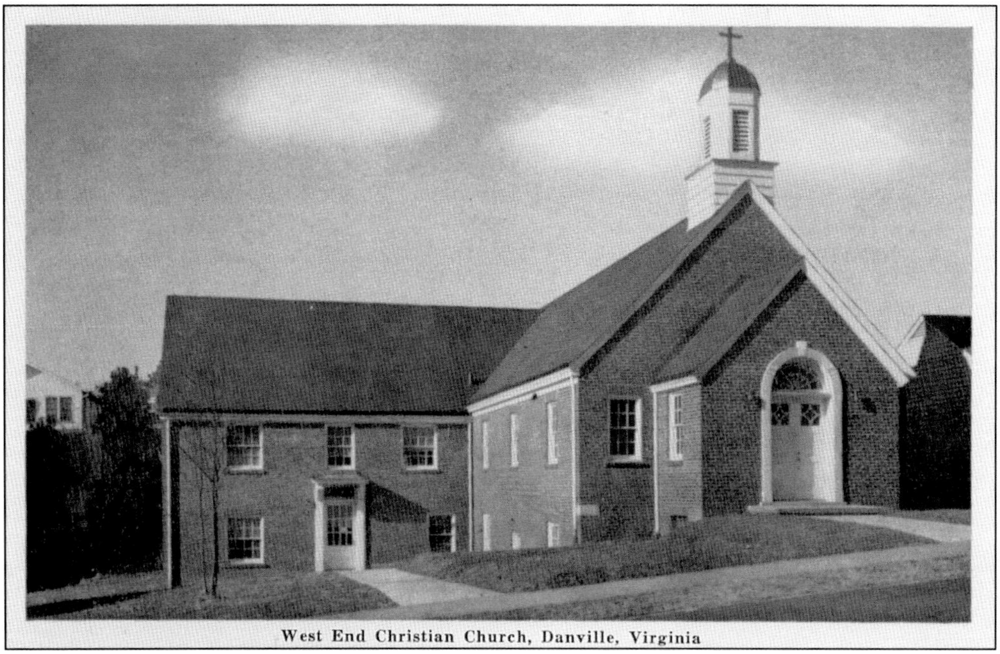

The West End Christian Church (Disciples of Christ) at 130 Montague Street was founded in 1929. Members held meetings in a small cottage on Marshall Terrace until they purchased two lots on Montague and erected the current building in 1939.

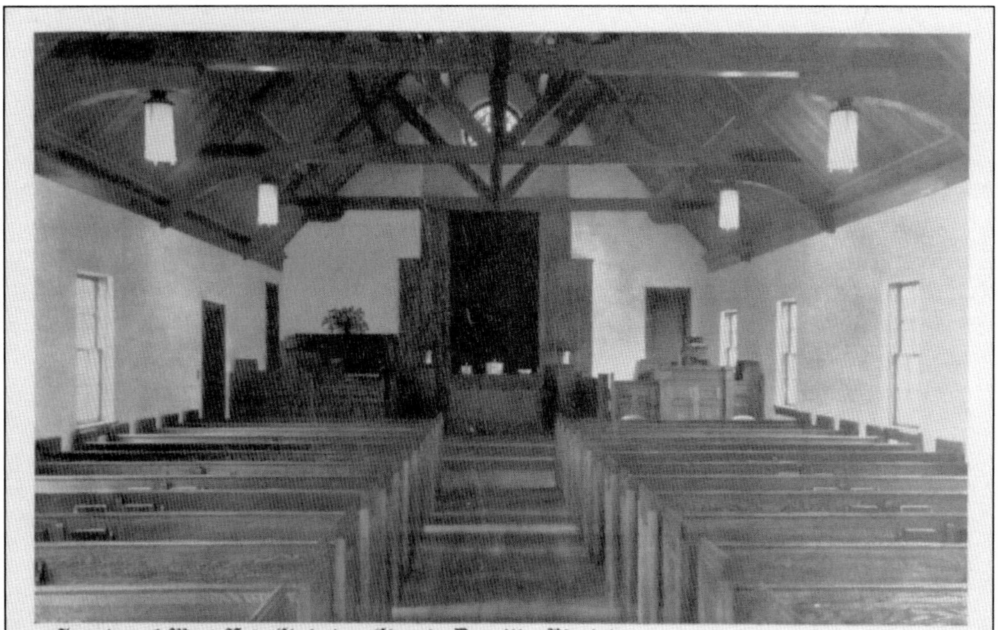

This interior view shows the sanctuary of West End Christian Church as it appeared in the 1940s soon after its completion.

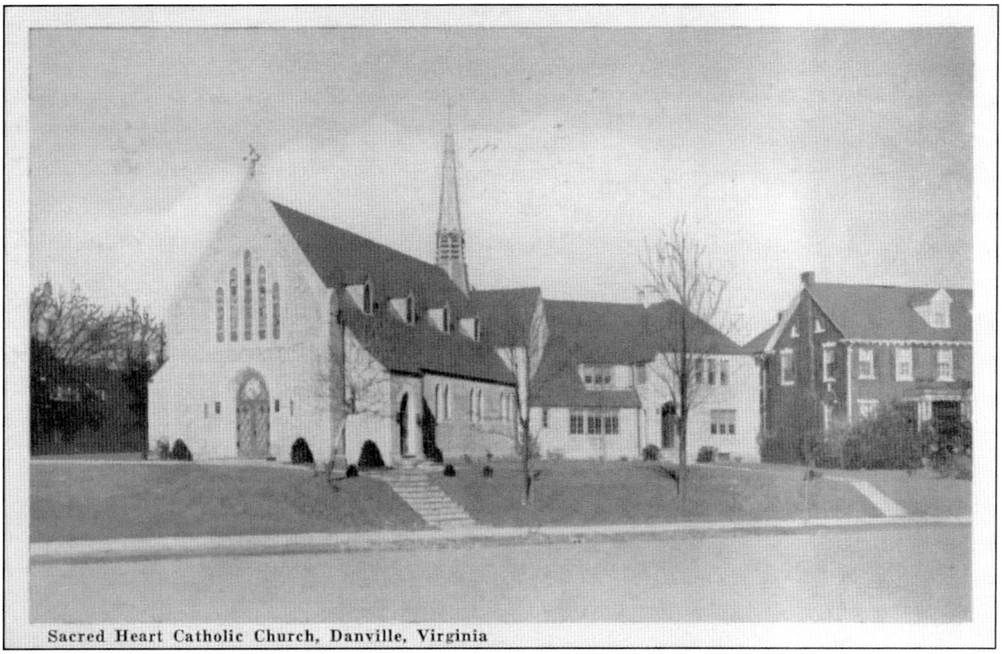

Sacred Heart Catholic Church at 288 West Main Street was completed in 1939 to serve the growing numbers of Roman Catholics in Danville, a group that was organized in 1875. This Gothic-inspired building sits in the intersection of West Main and Randolph Streets on part of the old H.C. Ficklen farm.

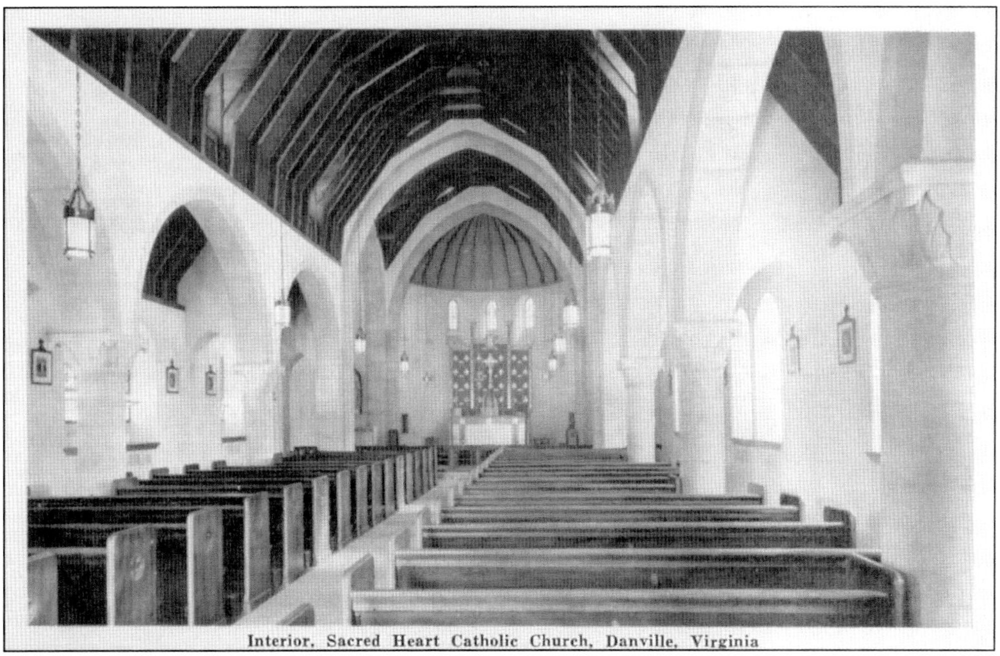

This 1940s interior view shows the original sanctuary of Sacred Heart Church. Until the mid-1960s Roman Catholic services were conducted in Latin. Masses were first offered in Spanish as well as English during the pastorate of Father Michael M. Duffy.

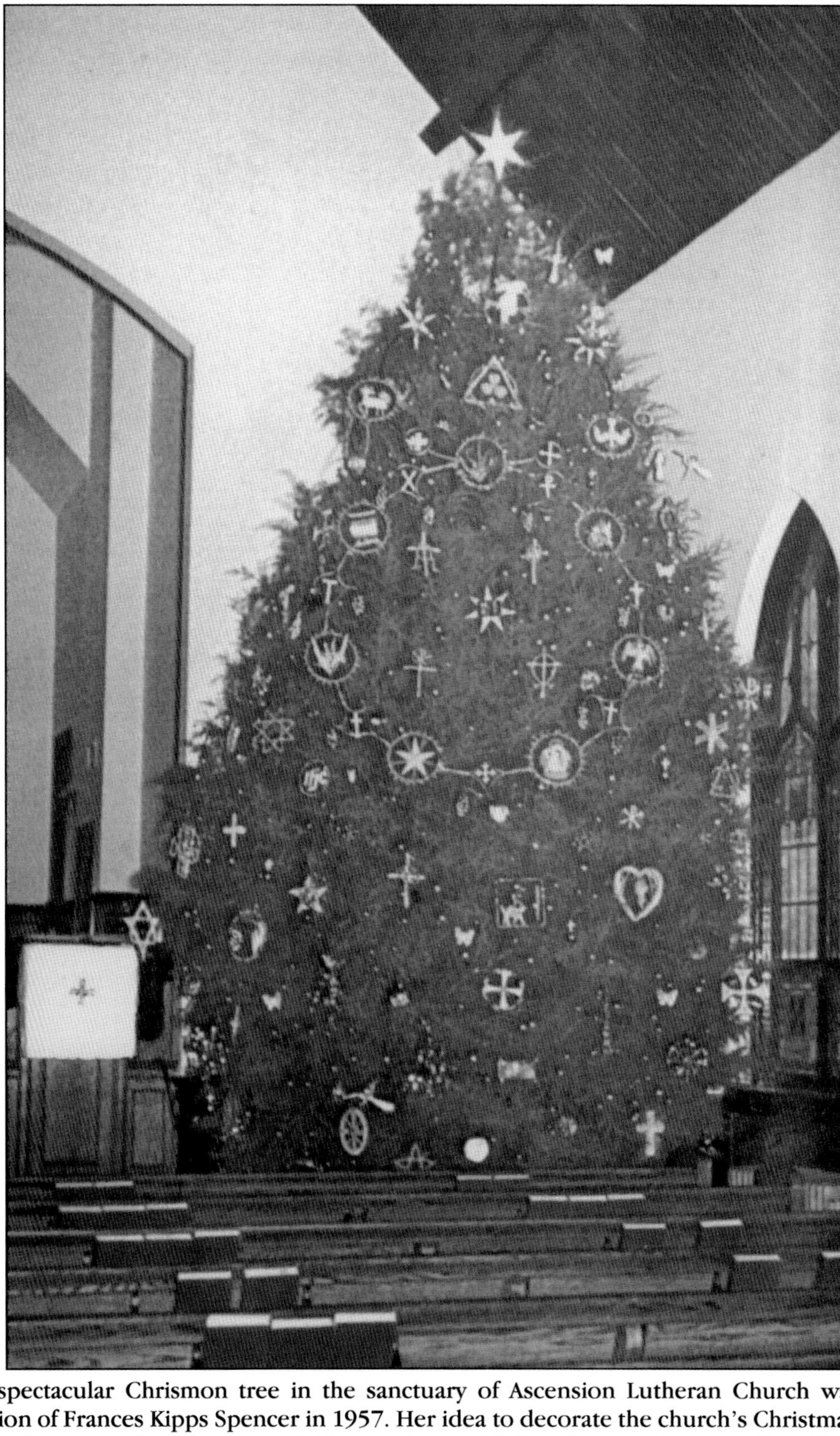

The spectacular Chrismon tree in the sanctuary of Ascension Lutheran Church was the creation of Frances Kipps Spencer in 1957. Her idea to decorate the church's Christmas tree with religious symbols has spread all over the world. Tourists are drawn to Danville every year to see her original gold-and-white ornaments.

Seven

RESIDENCES

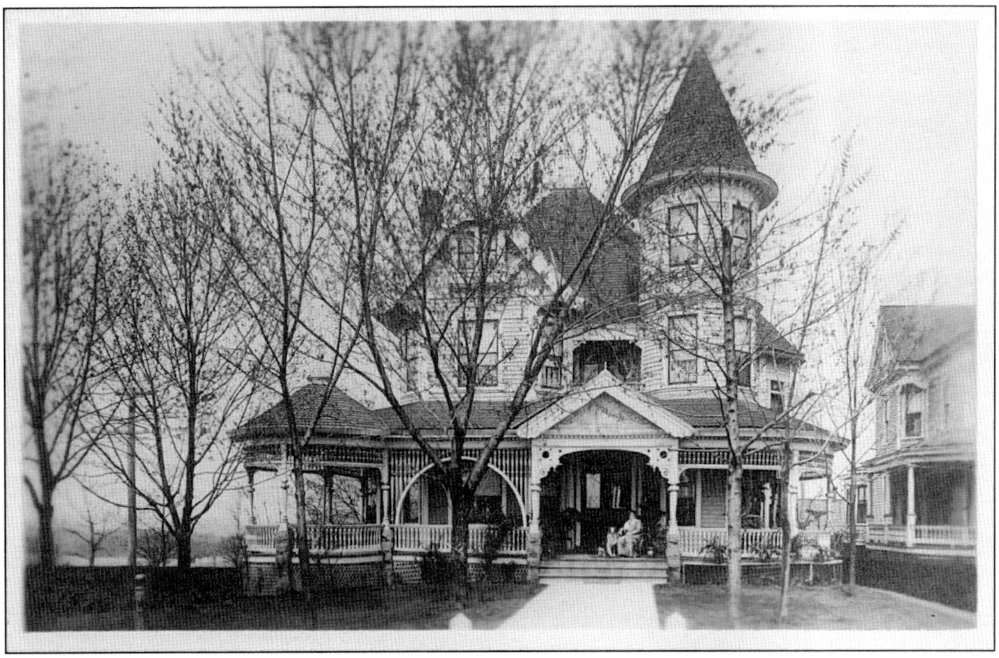

The Peter Collins Penn house at 322 West Main Street was designed from mail-order plans by Tennessee architect G.F. Barber. Completed in the late 1890s, this Queen Anne dwelling, currently owned by Margaret and Wesley Dove, was the first Victorian house in Danville to be included in a collection of handmade historic miniatures by Shelia Thompson of Charleston, South Carolina.

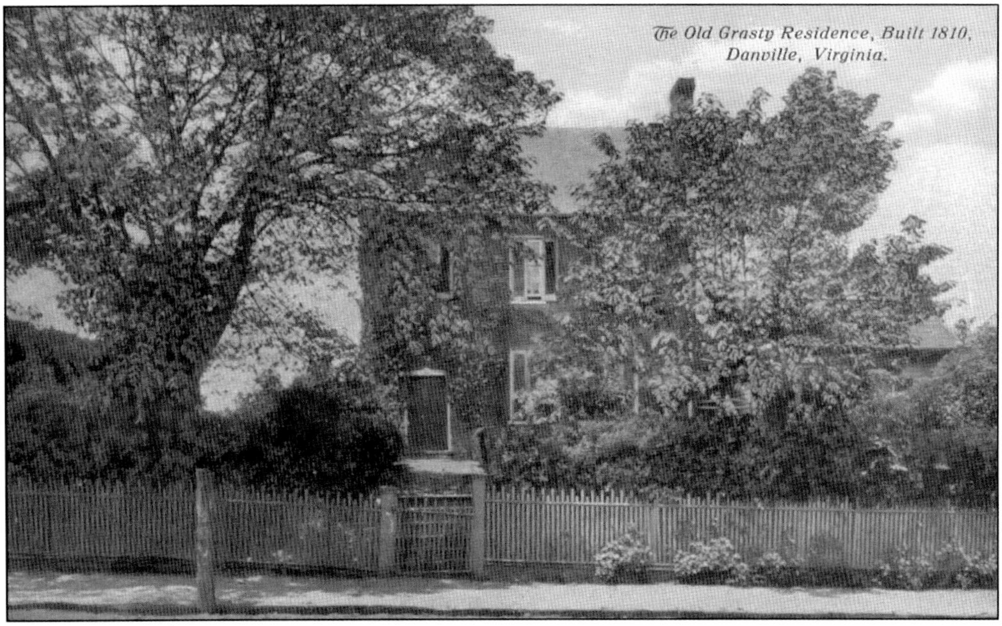

Many fashionable homes were located on Wilson Street in the earliest days of Danville. Colonel William C. Grasty built this brick residence at 722 Wilson Street in the early 1800s. William H. Wooding, father of Mayor Harry Wooding, once owned this beautiful old house with its fine trees and boxwood-lined walkways. The residence, later razed in 1939, was a center for entertaining the Confederate President and his officers during their brief stay in 1865.

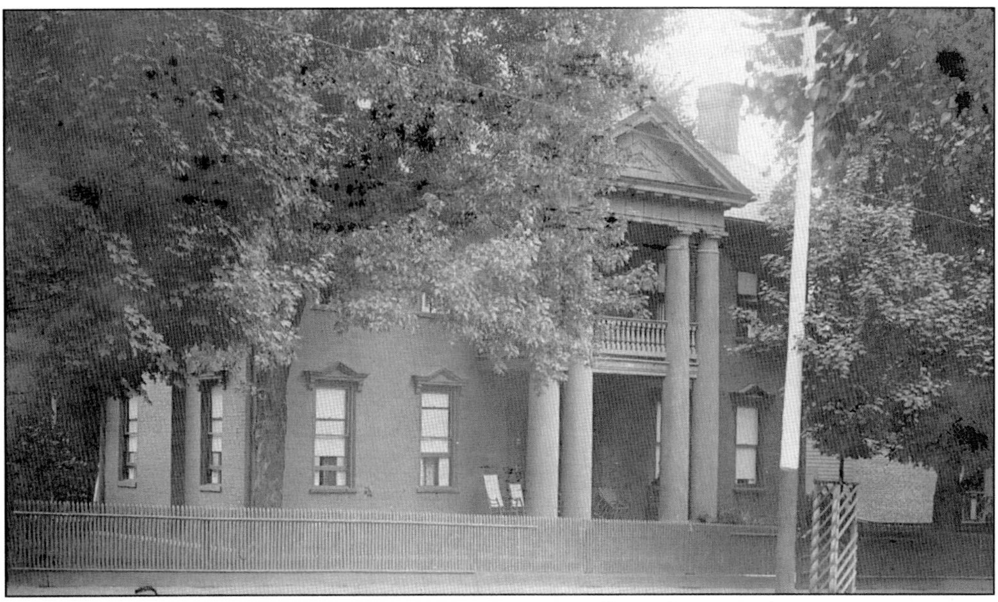

The nearby house at 770 Main Street, currently the office of Garrett & Garrett, attorneys, is the oldest documented residence in the city. Built in 1830 by Danville's first mayor, Captain James Lanier, it is remembered by many as the office of Dr. Samuel Newman, the city's first pediatrician.

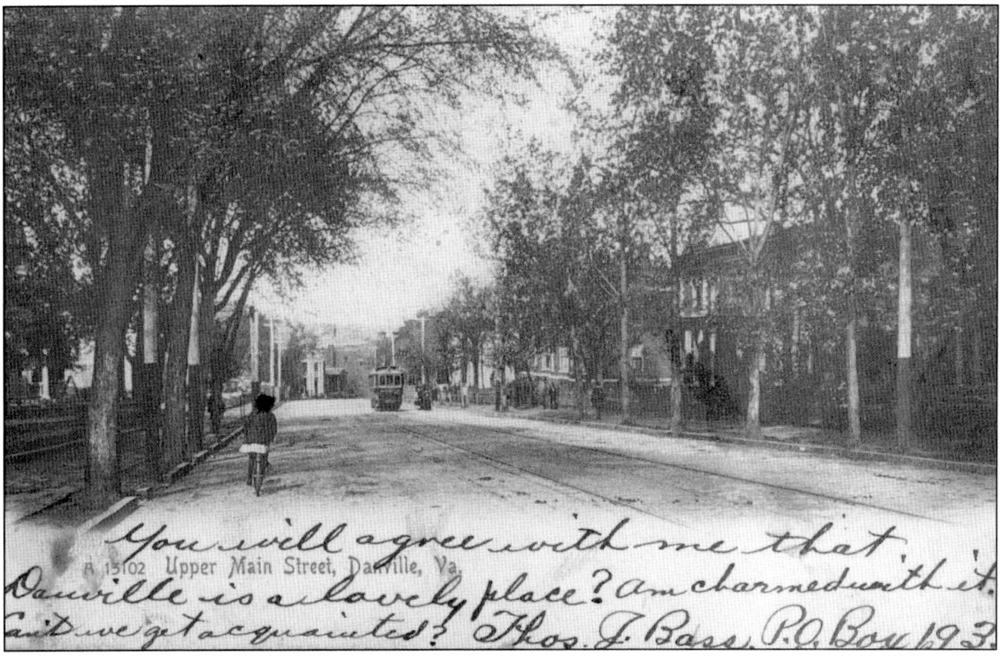

This 1905 postcard view of the 700 block of Main Street shows how charming the city looked with trees adorning the yards of the elegant mansions on each side of the street.

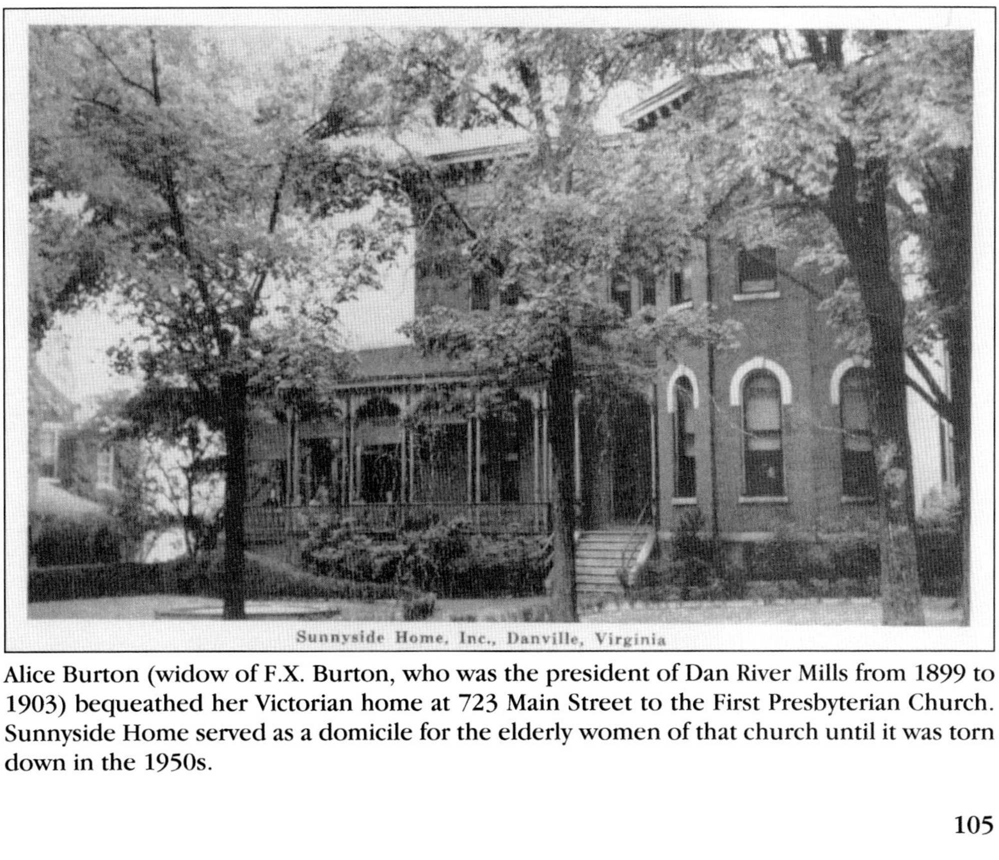

Alice Burton (widow of F.X. Burton, who was the president of Dan River Mills from 1899 to 1903) bequeathed her Victorian home at 723 Main Street to the First Presbyterian Church. Sunnyside Home served as a domicile for the elderly women of that church until it was torn down in the 1950s.

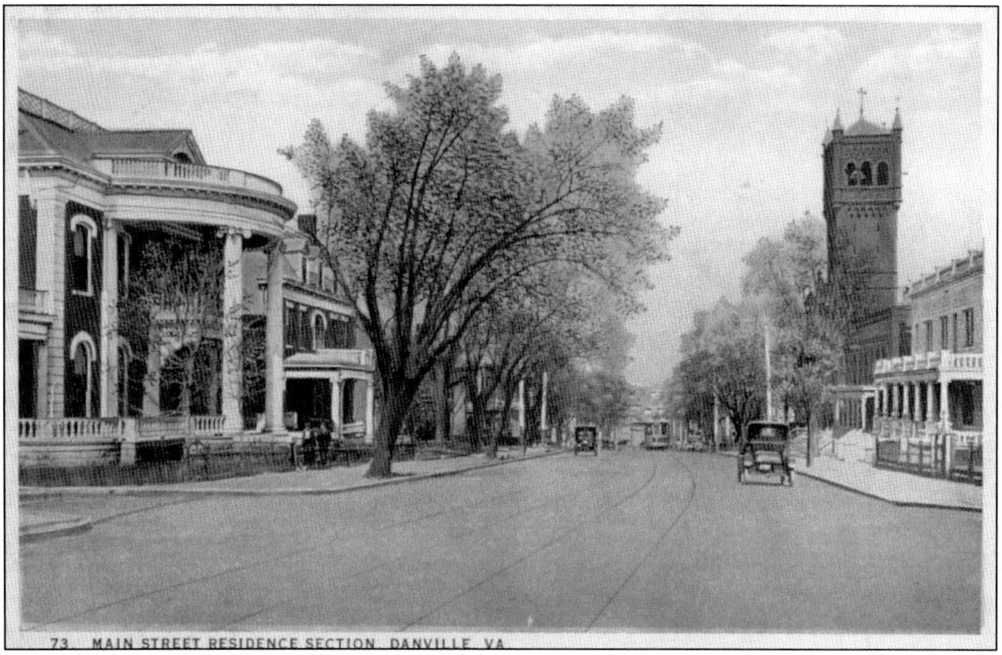

At the far end of the same block as late as 1972, the Lawson/Overbey house was saved from being replaced with a service station. This house at 782 Main Street, built in 1881, was one of many elegant houses constructed by Thomas B. Fitzgerald.

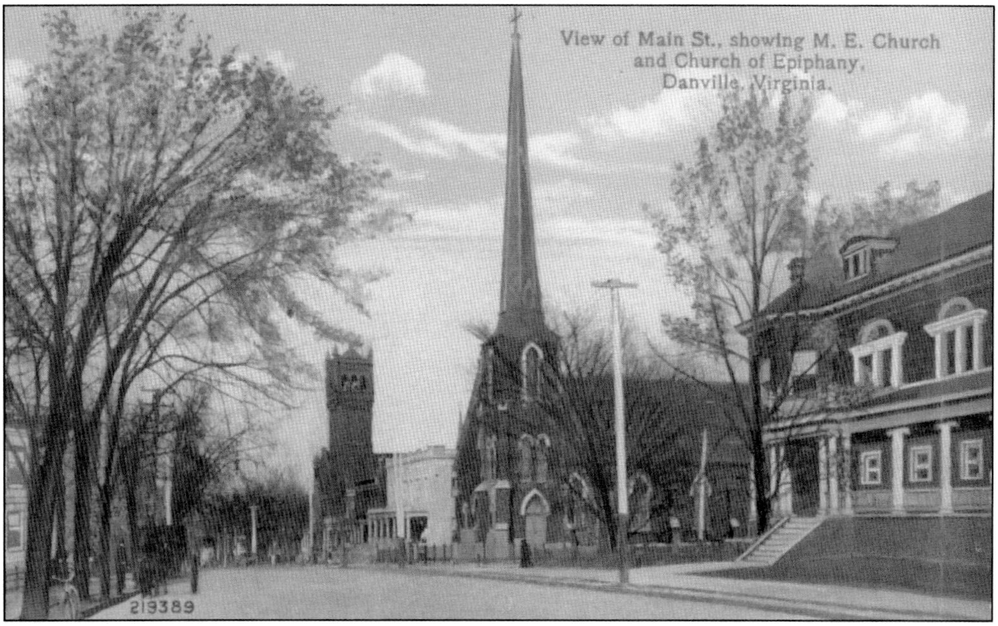

Dr. Bruce James built the brick house at 803 Main Street in 1899, which served as his home and office. This residence was to serve several later doctors as well, including Dr. Henry Langston. This postcard exemplifies a publisher's tendency to "stretch" a building to improve the appearance, as the actual house has one Palladian window upstairs (not two) and is narrower than the photograph indicates.

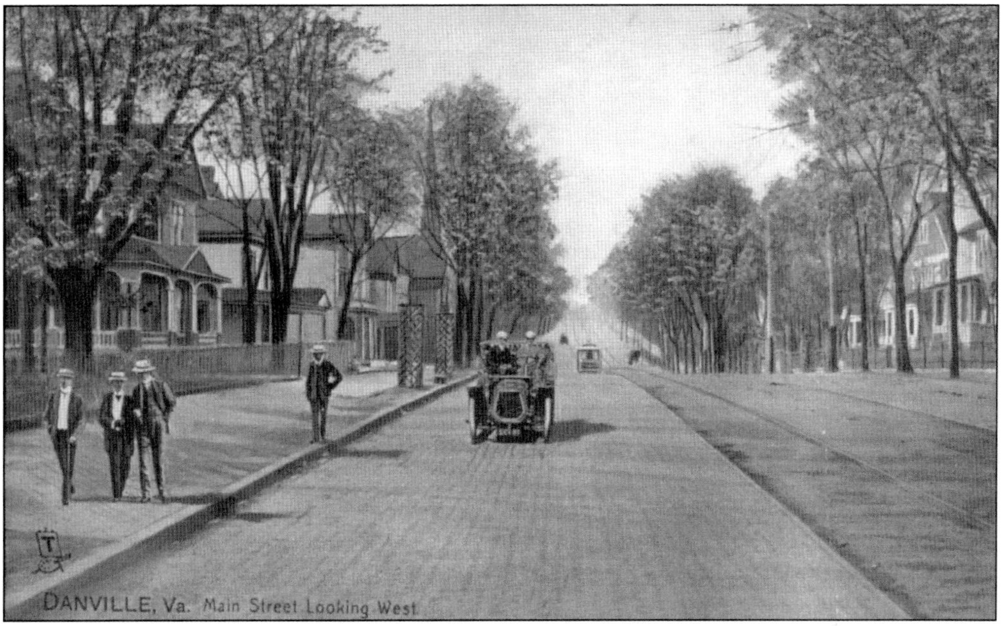

Looking away from downtown one sees samples of the finest Victorian and Edwardian homes built in Danville during the years from 1880 to the turn of the century. This 1-mile stretch of houses built by wealthy tobacconists on Main Street has been called "Millionaires Row."

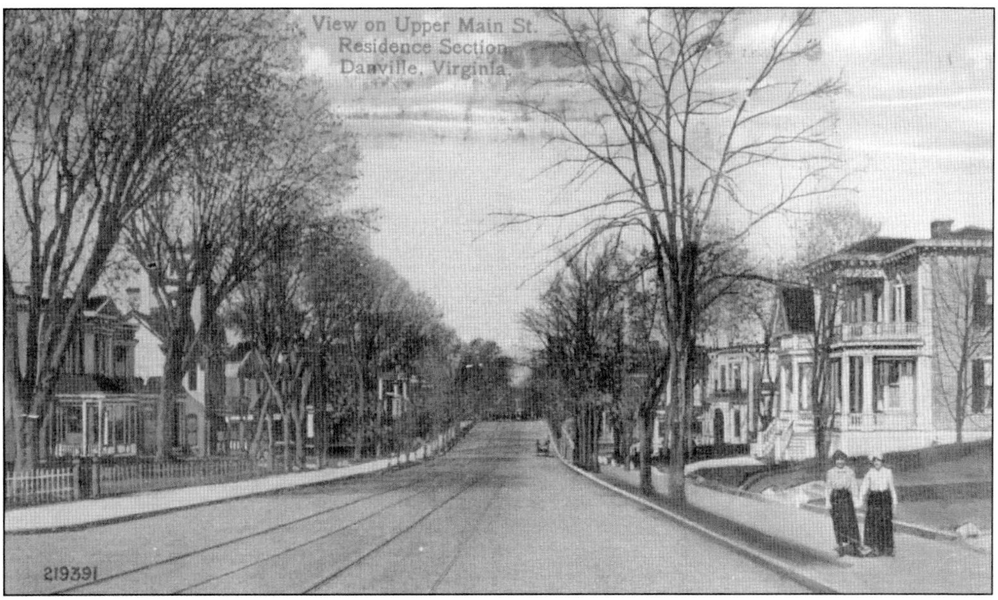

Many houses on this 800 block of Main Street have been removed over the years. This view, taken from the front of First Baptist Church and looking in the direction of town, reveals what Danville looked like around 1910. This stretch of Main Street with its dip in the road was called "Penn's Bottom" because several of the wealthy Penn families built close together in this area.

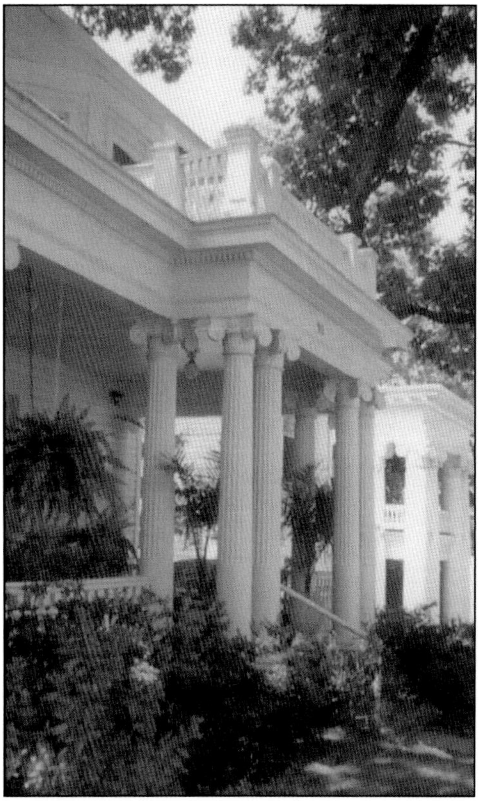

Thanks to the efforts of the Danville Historical Society, the City Council in 1972 enacted a Historic Zoning ordinance to promote and rehabilitate the architecturally significant structures on Main Street and adjoining neighborhoods. This commemorative card #5, photographed by Dan Vaden, shows the H.L. Boatwright house at 904 Main Street, which was built around 1860, and the French H. Conway house at 912 Main, which was built in 1898.

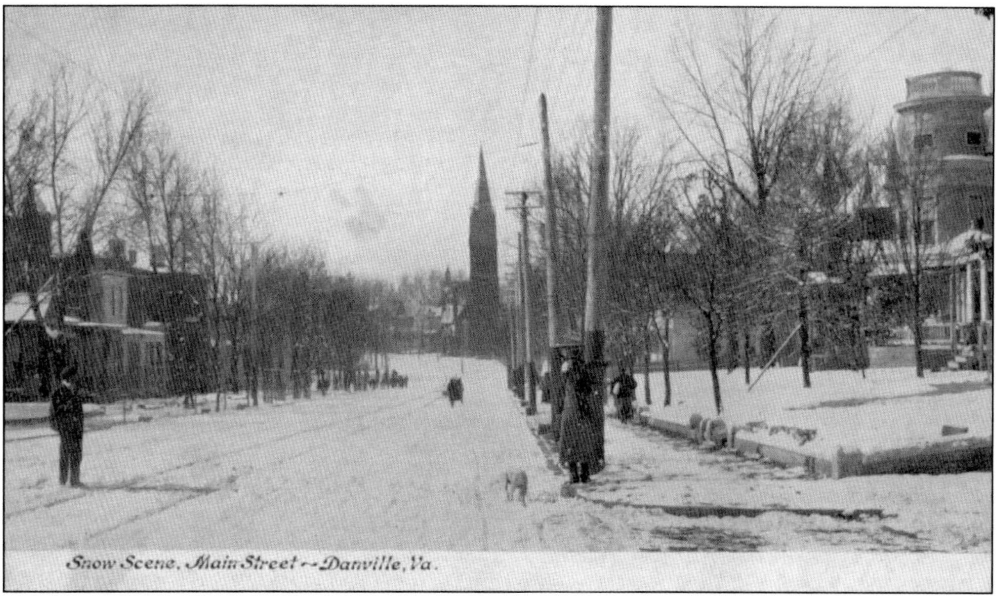

On the far right of this rare snow scene is the Barnes Penn house at 1012 Main Street. It has often been called the "wedding cake" house because of its intricate ornamentation. This house, sporting a balustrade at the top of the round tower, was the second Queen Anne house from Danville to be included in the collection of Shelia's historic miniatures.

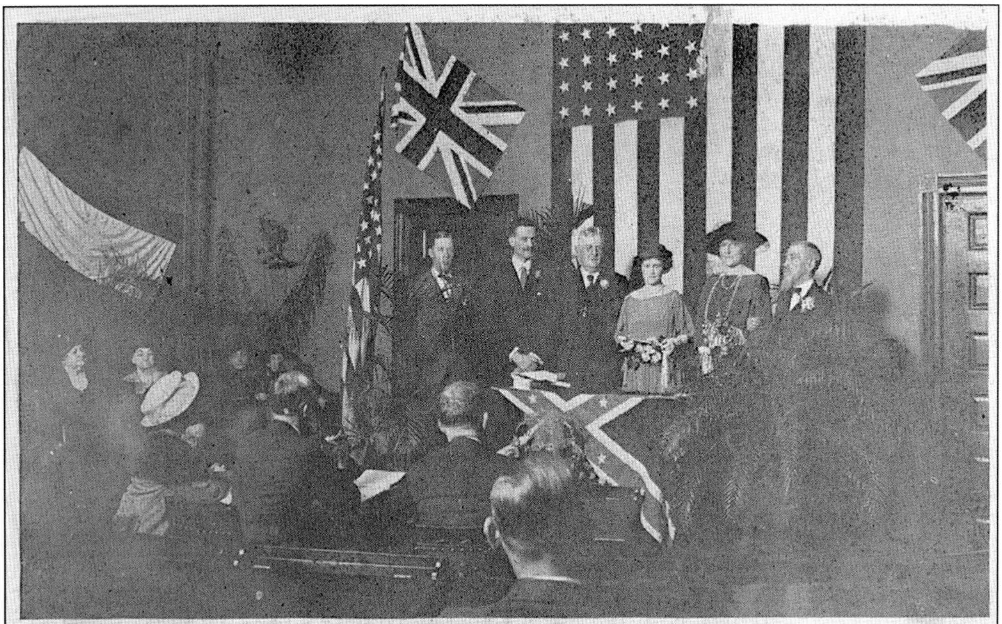

Lady Astor Receiving the Key to Danville, Va.

In 1922 Lady Nancy Astor returned to the city of her birth to receive a key to the city from the mayor. Standing with her on the platform (from left to right) are as follows: unidentified man; her husband, Lord Waldorf Astor; Colonel A.B. Carrington; Nancy Astor; Irene Gibson (her sister who married Charles Dana Gibson, artist and creator of the Gibson Girl of the 1890s); and Mayor Harry Wooding.

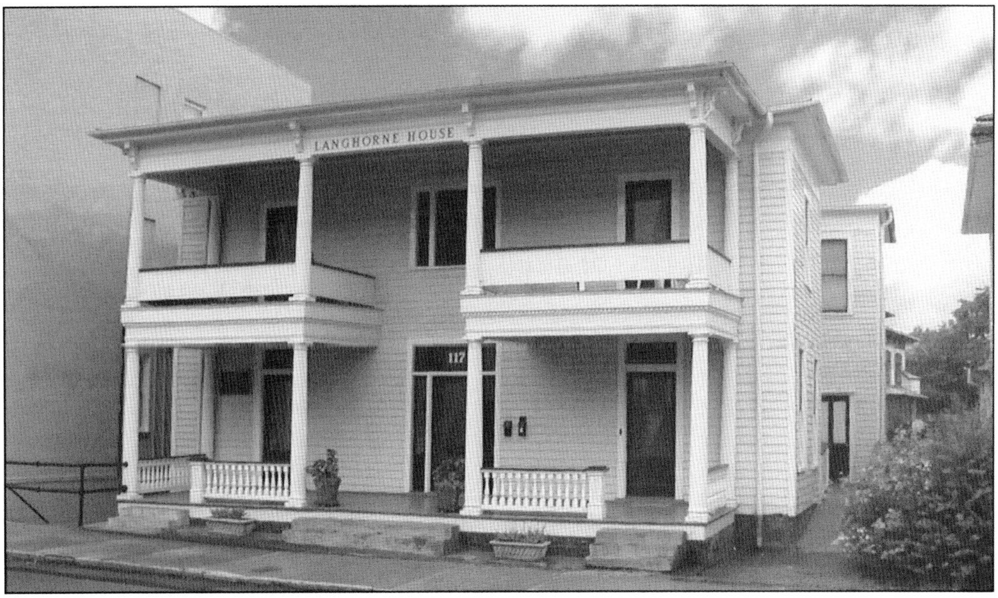

Saved from demolition in 1988 largely through the efforts of Stuart James Grant, the Langhorne house at 117 Broad Street is being restored as a permanent museum to the Langhorne family and especially the famous daughters, Nancy Langhorne Astor and Irene Langhorne Gibson.

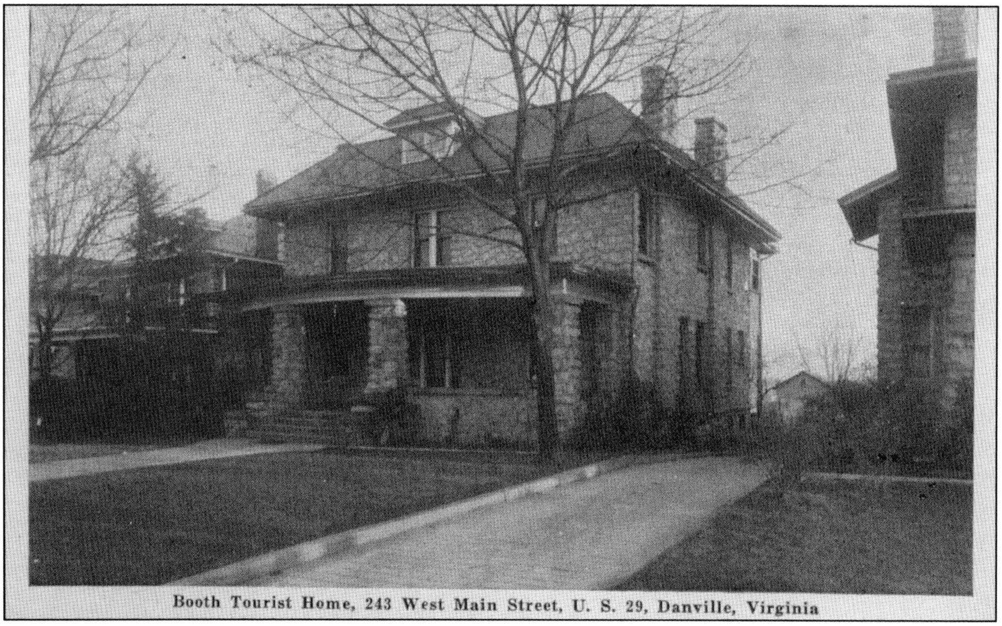

In 1937 Charles L. Booth survived the closing of the Commercial Bank, where he had worked for 40 years by opening the Booth Tourist Home at 243 West Main Street. Booth's bird dog, Mary, used to hitch a ride on the streetcar to go downtown to find her master. Later, Mary caught a return trolley and got off in front of the Booth house. Mr. Booth settled with the company at the end of each year. Danville Traction Company finally gave in and awarded the dog an annual pass to ride free of charge. Mary never took a wrong car.

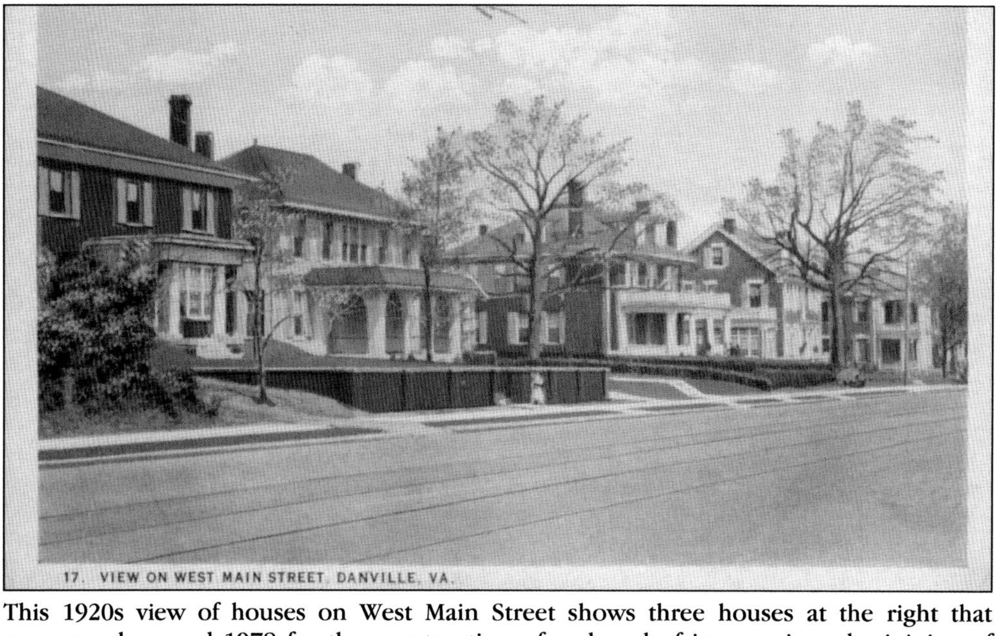

This 1920s view of houses on West Main Street shows three houses at the right that were razed around 1978 for the construction of a cloverleaf intersection, the joining of Highway 29 with Highway 86. The two houses visible at the left (244 and 240 West Main Street) survived the demolition.

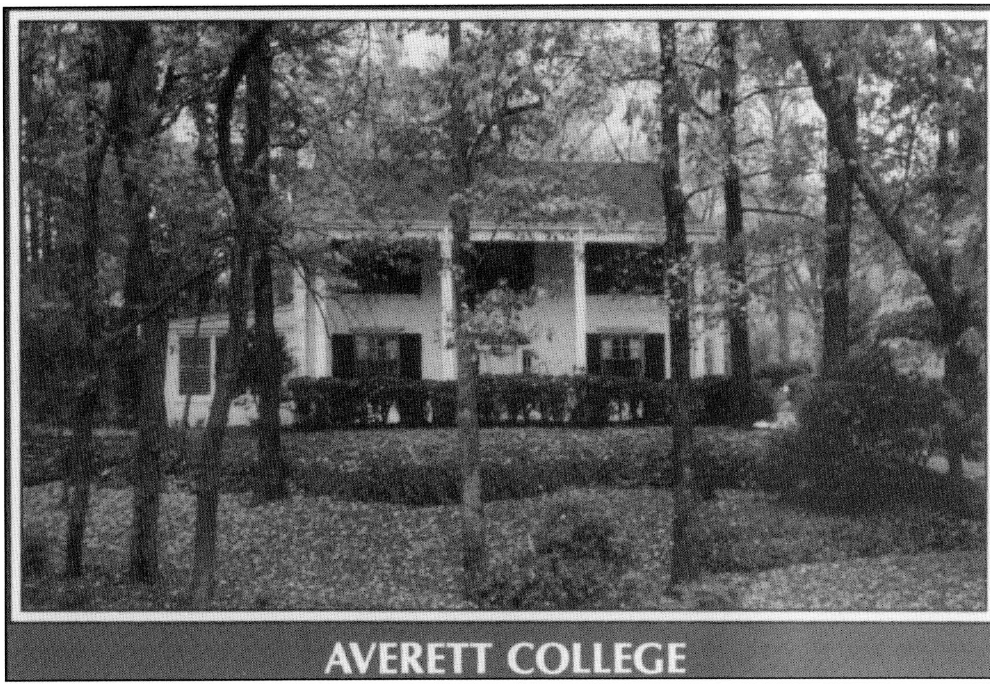

In 1984 the house and grounds at 500 Hawthorne Drive in Forest Hills were donated to Averett College by Mrs. A.B. Carrington Jr. for use as the home of the college president and his/her family. Dr. Frank Campbell and his wife, Janet, are the current residents.

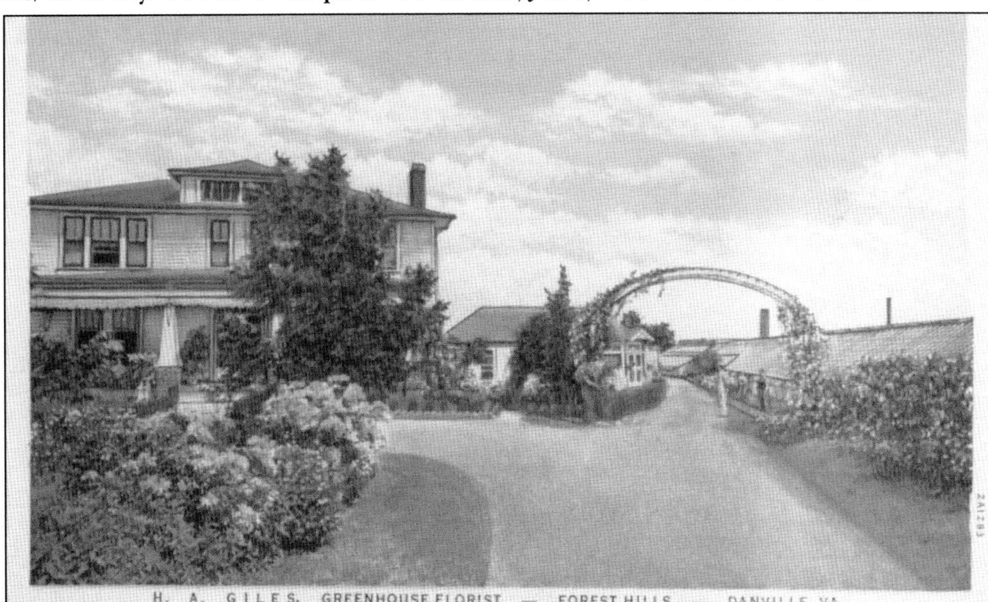

For many years the social life of Danville citizens was enriched through the skill and guidance of Earline and Charlie L. Giles from their Flower Shop on South Main Street. This couple directed many wedding and funeral services. They raised their own flowers in greenhouses located beside the family home at the far end of the cul-de-sac that once ended Mt. View Road.

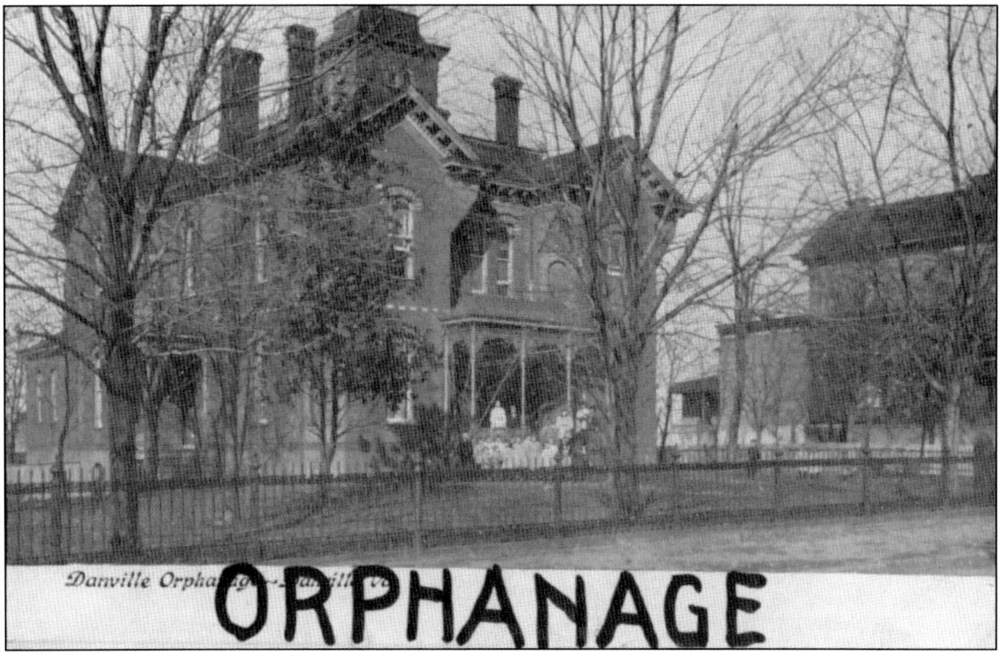

Thomas Benton Fitzgerald built his own home at 1015 North Main Street, an ornate brick structure that he later gave to Calvary Church to be used as an orphanage. His house was demolished when the City built Woodrow Wilson School on the same site in 1926.

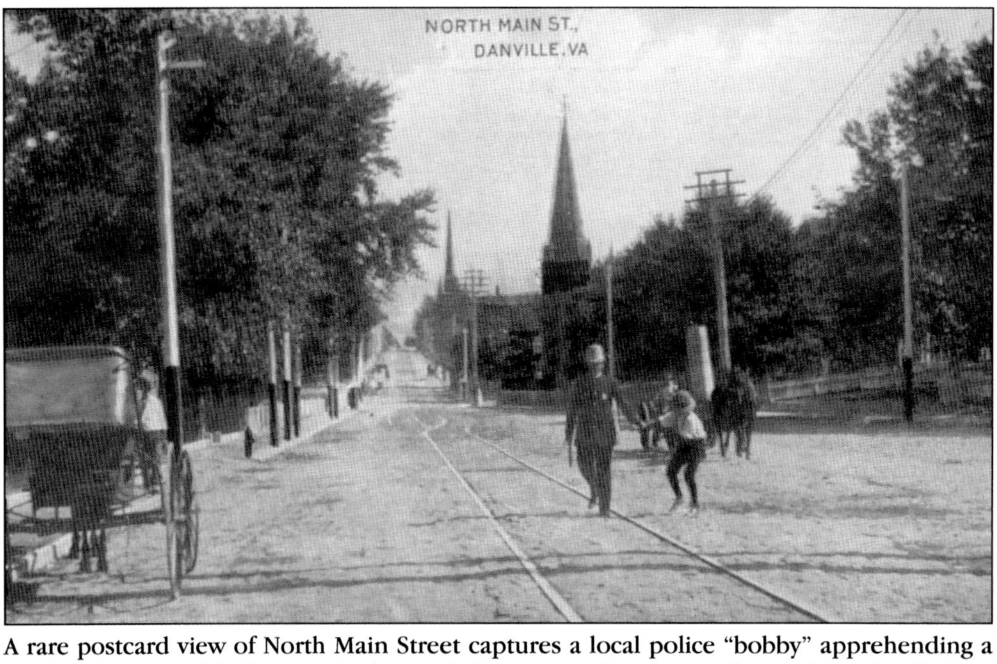

A rare postcard view of North Main Street captures a local police "bobby" apprehending a law-breaker. Dated before 1912, this card shows two church steeples at the right, Shelton Memorial Presbyterian and behind it, Calvary Methodist Church before the steeple was replaced with a square tower.

Eight

POSTSCRIPTS

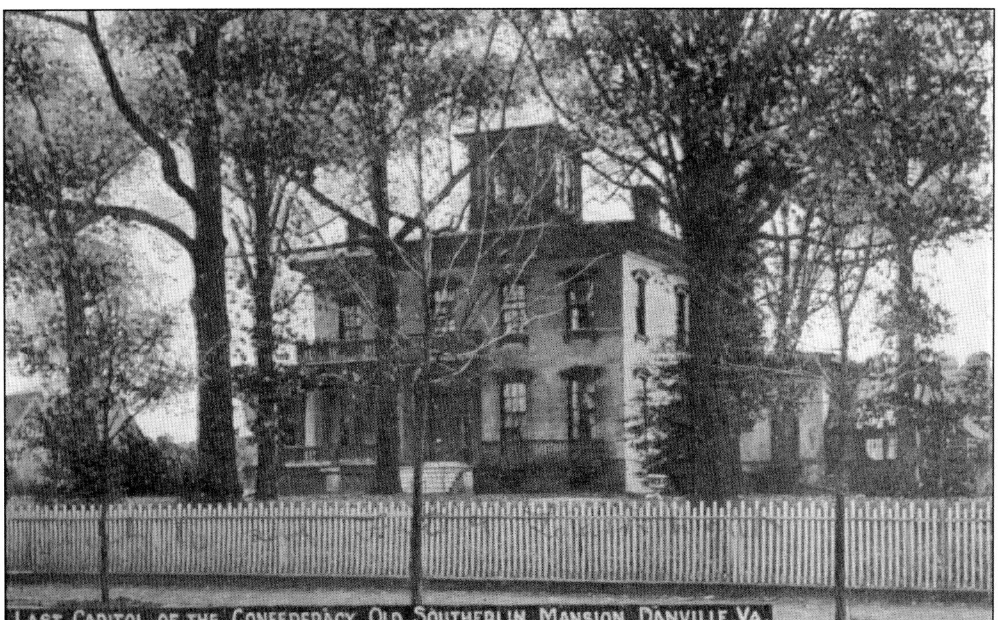

Built in 1857, this Italian-villa styled mansion was home to one of Danville's most prominent citizens, Major William T. Sutherlin. It is obvious that the card was printed in Germany or England, as the publisher misinterpreted the spelling of Sutherlin's last name.

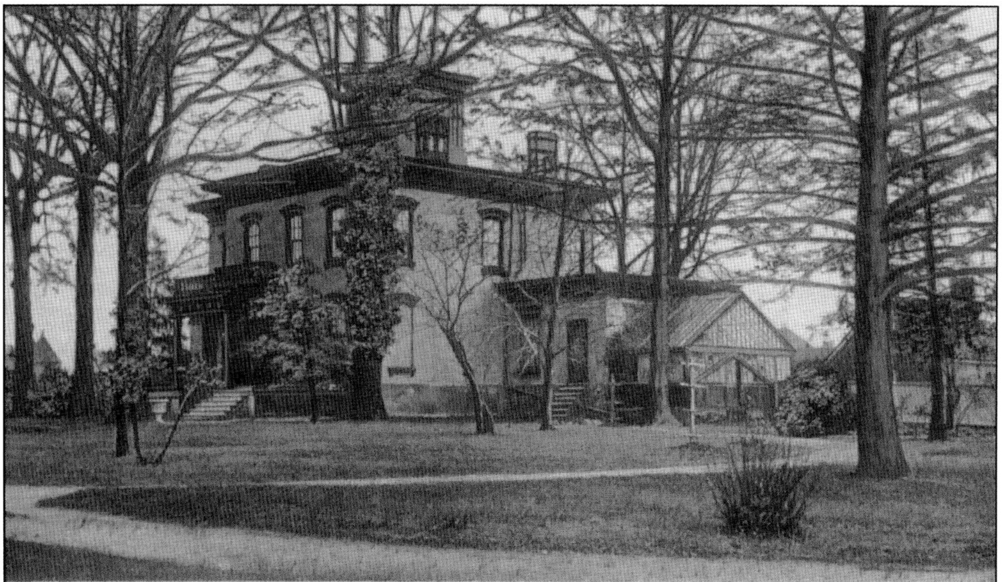

Major Sutherlin's Residence, the Last Capitol of the Confederacy, Danville, Va.

From April 3–10, 1865, when Jefferson Davis, President of the Confederacy, was forced to flee Richmond with his government officials, he traveled to Danville and stayed as a guest in the home of Major Sutherlin.

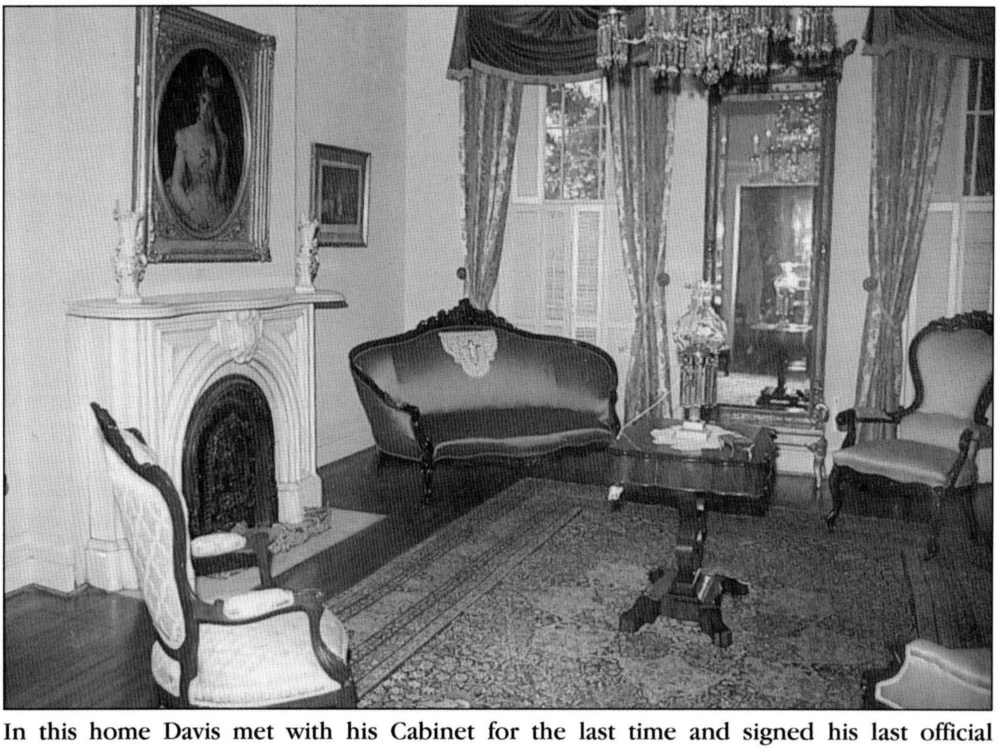

In this home Davis met with his Cabinet for the last time and signed his last official proclamation as President of the Confederacy. Hence, Danville gained the epithet, the "Last Capital of the Confederacy."

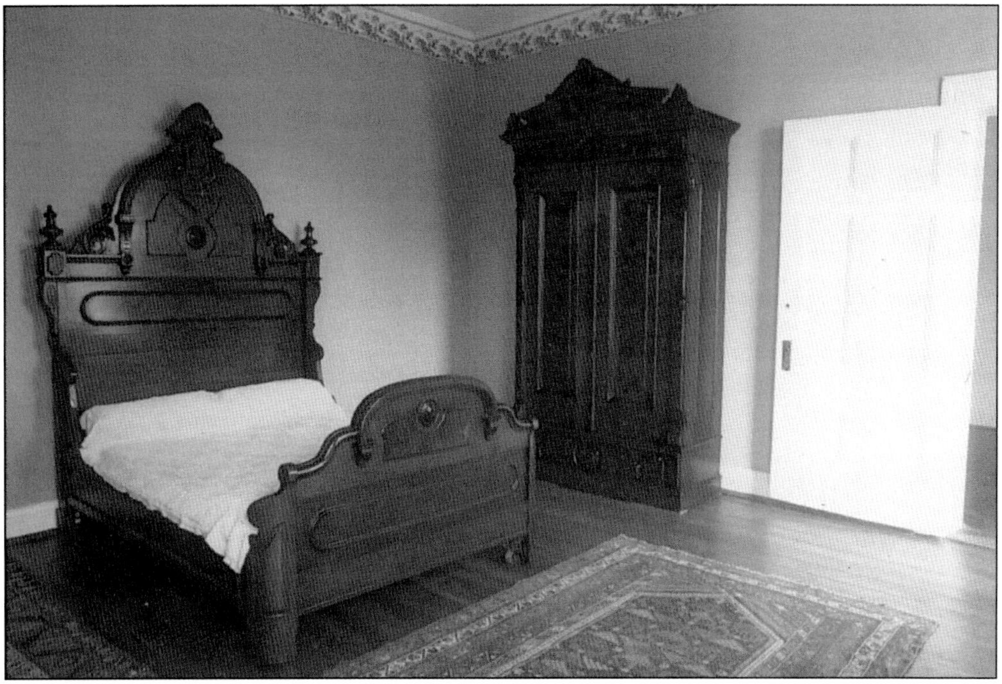

An upstairs bedroom in the Sutherlin mansion features a suite of walnut furniture that was original to the house, sold at auction before World War I, yet returned to the house in 1979, when purchased by the board of the Danville Museum of Fine Arts and History. The elegantly carved bed, a clothes closet, bureau, and washstand may have accommodated the Confederate president during his stay in 1865.

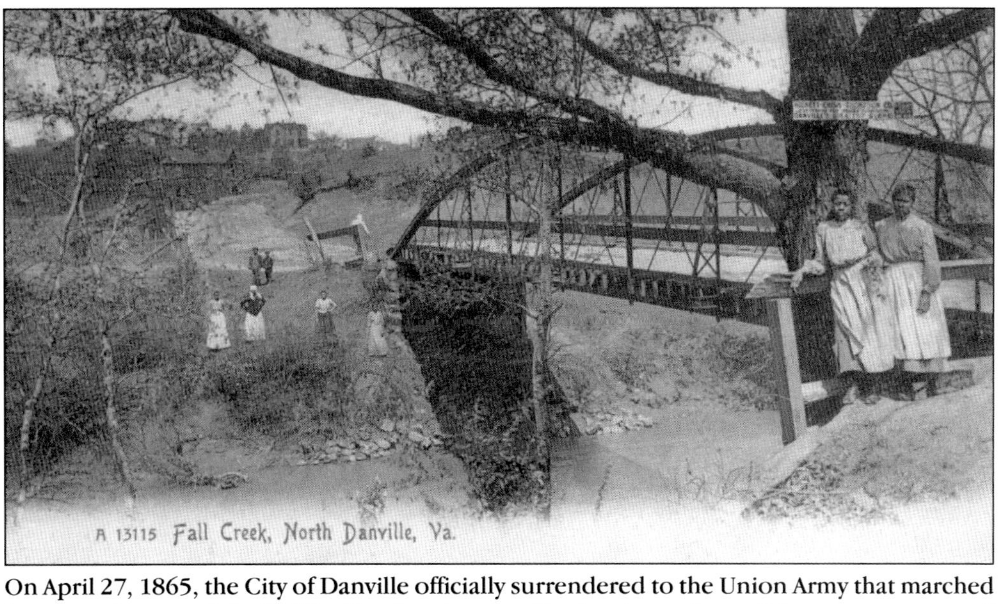

On April 27, 1865, the City of Danville officially surrendered to the Union Army that marched into town by way of the Halifax Road to the east. The local members of the common council met the Federal commander on the main road between the railroad track and the bridge that crossed Fall Creek.

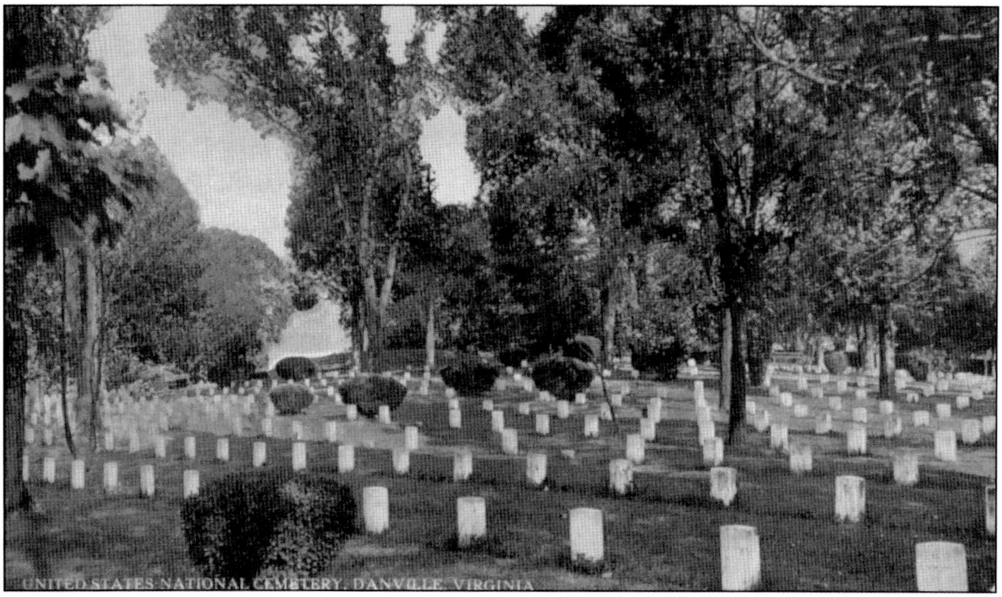

The National Cemetery on Lee Street sits in the northeast corner of Green Hill Cemetery, thought to be named for Nathaniel T. Green, who sold this land to the City when the Grove Street Cemetery was nearly at capacity. Created in 1867 for the burial of Federal prisoners-of-war who died in Danville prisons, the cemetery is enclosed by a stone wall that separates it from the city graveyard.

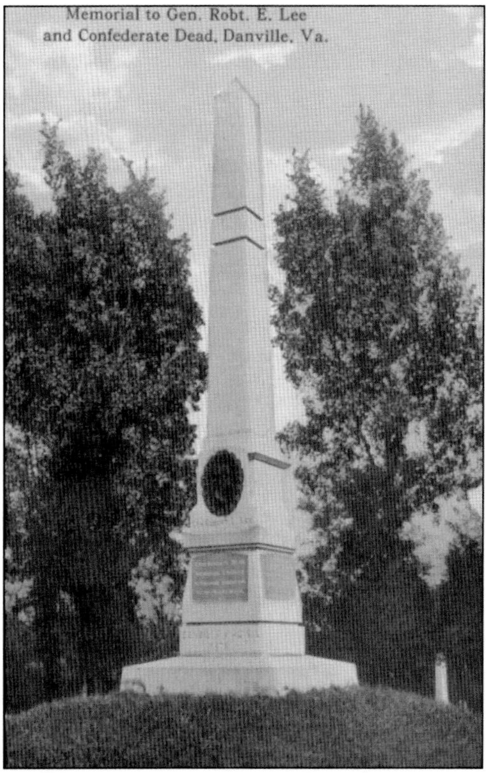

A monument to the Danville soldiers who died in the Civil War was placed in Green Hill Cemetery in 1878 by the Ladies Memorial Society, which was later known as the Anne Eliza Johns Chapter of the United Daughters of the Confederacy.

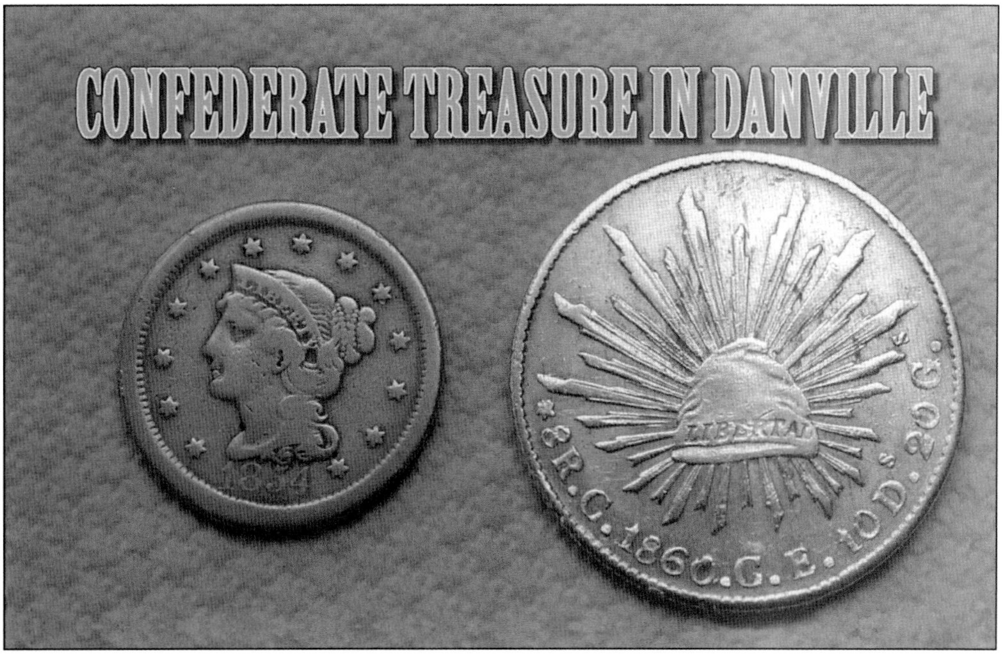

This contemporary postcard displays one 1860 Mexican silver dollar (8 Real or "piece of eight") and one 1854 copper cent found together in the vicinity of Danville in July 1998. Local author J. Frank Carroll's *Confederate Treasure in Danville* states that the bulk of similar coins (stored in kegs) has yet to be found.

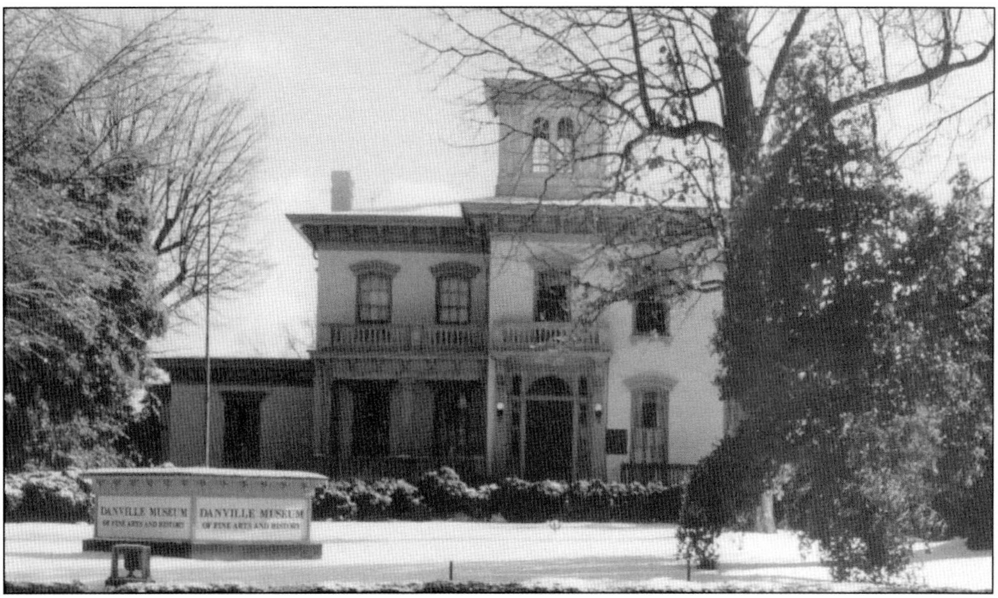

Since Danville receives little snow in the wintertime, any postcard scene with snow on the ground is unusual. This recent photograph by Bruce Spangler gives a quiet presence to the Museum of Fine Arts and History at 975 Main Street. The city's only art museum, which opened in 1974, is affiliated with the Virginia Museum of Fine Arts in Richmond and offers the public a variety of exhibits and programs.

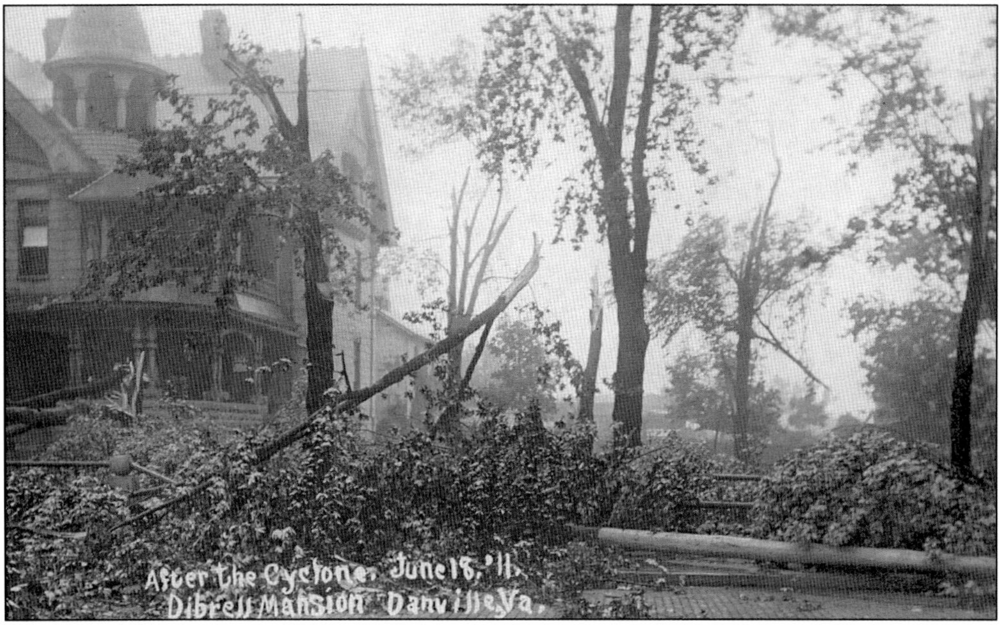

A ferocious tornado (or cyclone as it was called on June 18, 1911) swept through Danville on a Sunday afternoon causing severe damage to a large section of the city. O.W. Cole, photographer, captured the aftermath of this weather phenomenon with his camera and produced at least 14 if not more postcard views of its destruction. Here one sees the R.L. Dibrell mansion on Main Street just across from the Sutherlin home.

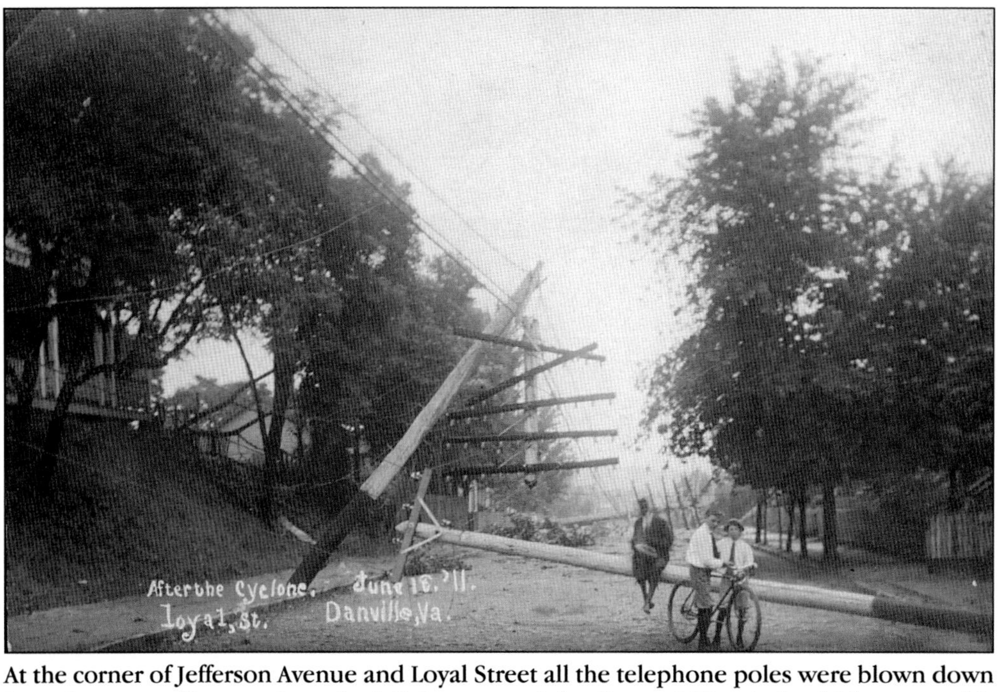

At the corner of Jefferson Avenue and Loyal Street all the telephone poles were blown down into the street. The porch at the left is a part of the General Hospital, which sat on this corner. The people in this scene are unidentified.

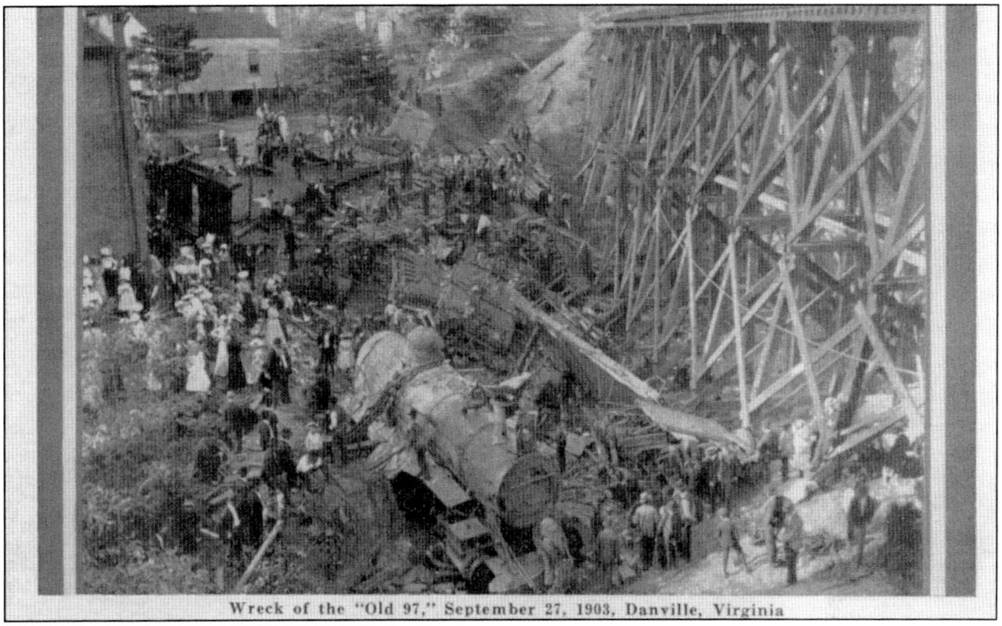

On the afternoon of September 27, 1903, an express mail train of the Southern Railway Company jumped the track and fell from the trestle that was built over Stillhouse Creek on the north side of the Dan River. From this tragedy a folksong evolved that became the first country recording to sell 1 million copies.

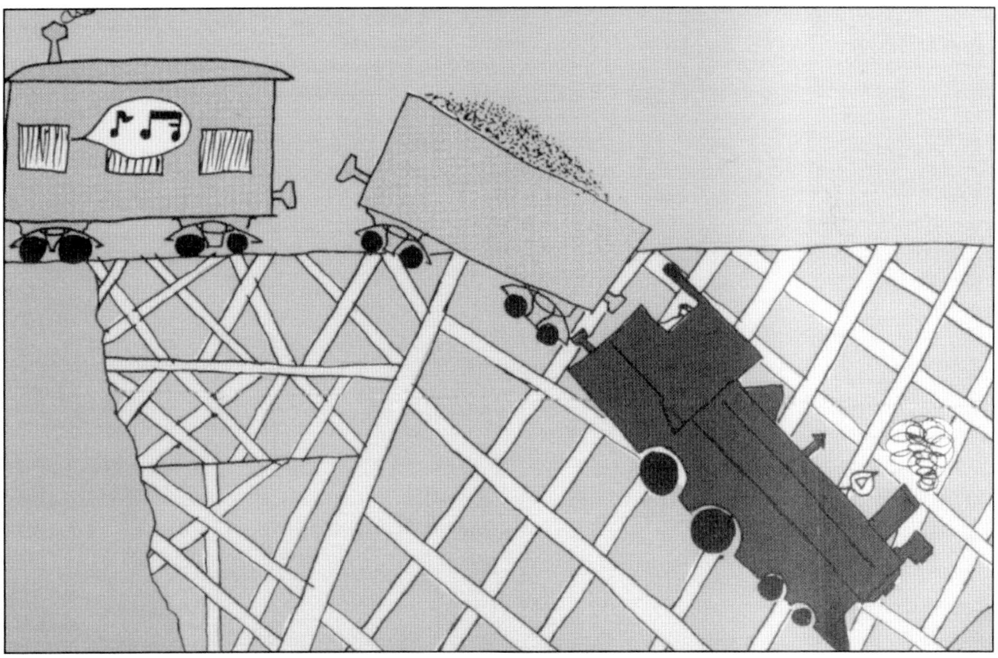

In 1976 a children's version of *The Wreck of the Old 97* was published by this author with the assistance of the third and fourth grade children at Grove Park Elementary School. At age 11, Marc Fountain, the author's son, drew the cover illustration that was also published as a postcard.

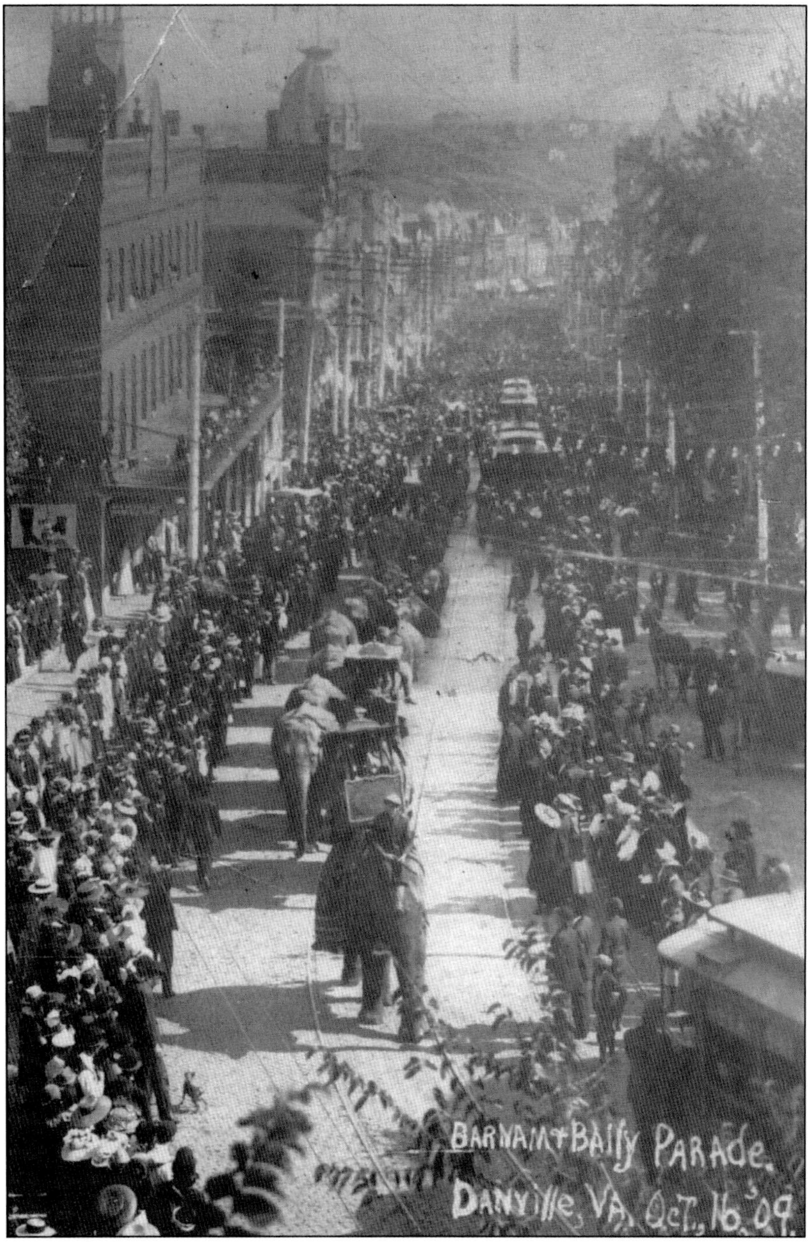

On Saturday, October 16, 1909, the great Barnum & Bailey Circus came to town. Since the circus required 14 acres for setting up their show that year and since the fair grounds weren't large enough, the City provided room at the old race track. A grand street parade was held at 10 a.m. that morning, a feature that had not been offered to Danville in four years. This spectacle was like nothing in the past, with a parade consisting of 1,500 people and 700 horses. The parade, which included other animals (some in open cages) and ornate floats typical of many exotic countries, traveled up Main Street and created such excitement that more than 30,000 people attended the two performances that day, one at 2 p.m. and one at 8 p.m. that evening. On Sunday morning the circus packed up and loaded onto five long trains of double-length cars and headed to Lynchburg, Virginia.

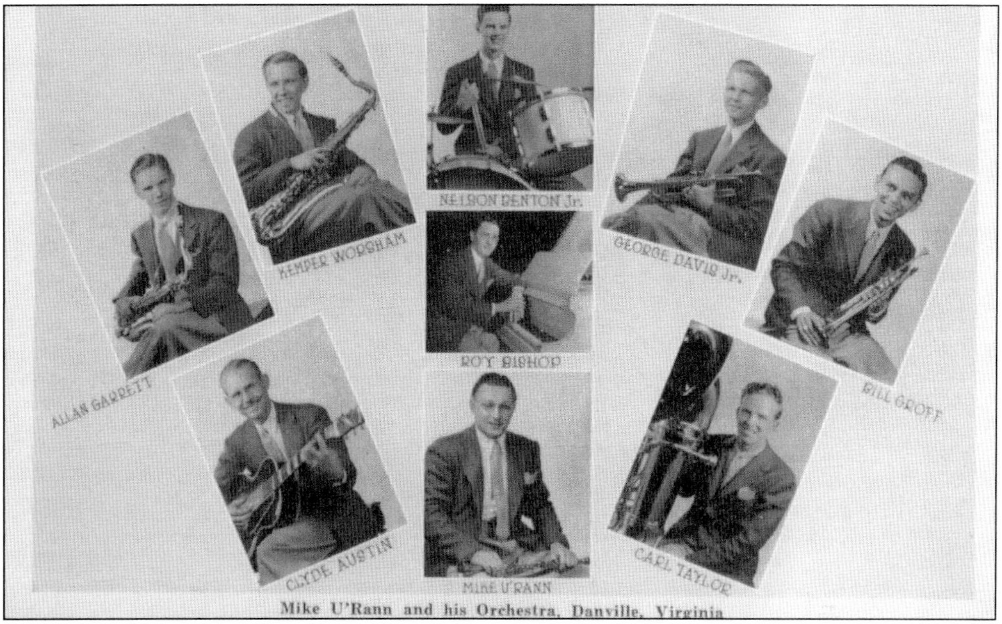

In the 1930s and 1940s music and dancing were some of the favorite entertainments of young people of Danville. The Mike U'Rann Orchestra was made up of eager local musicians; they are, from left to right, as follows: (front row) Clyde Austin, Mike U'Rann, and Carl Taylor; (center) Roy Bishop; (back row) Allan Garrett, Kemper Worsham, Nelson Benton Jr., George Davis Jr., and Bill Groff.

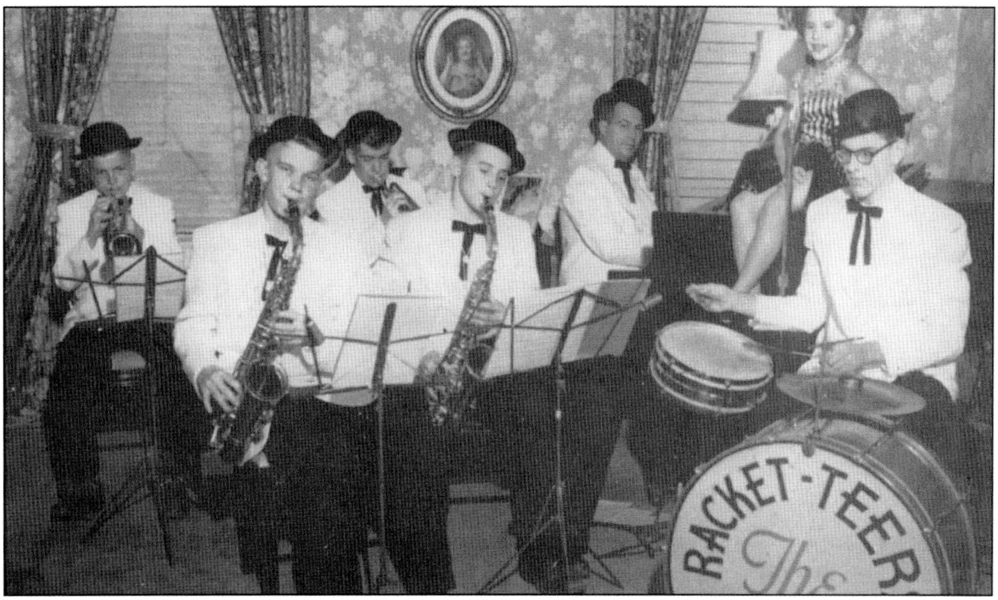

In the mid-1950s Johnny Westbrook, seated at the piano, encouraged these young people to form a dance band, the Racket-teers. Playing often for dances held at the County Club Inn and other places, this teenaged band was composed of (from left to right) Sutt Farley, Ebb Williams, Ken Overcash, George Penn, Lambsie Penn (on the piano), and Fred Winiker.

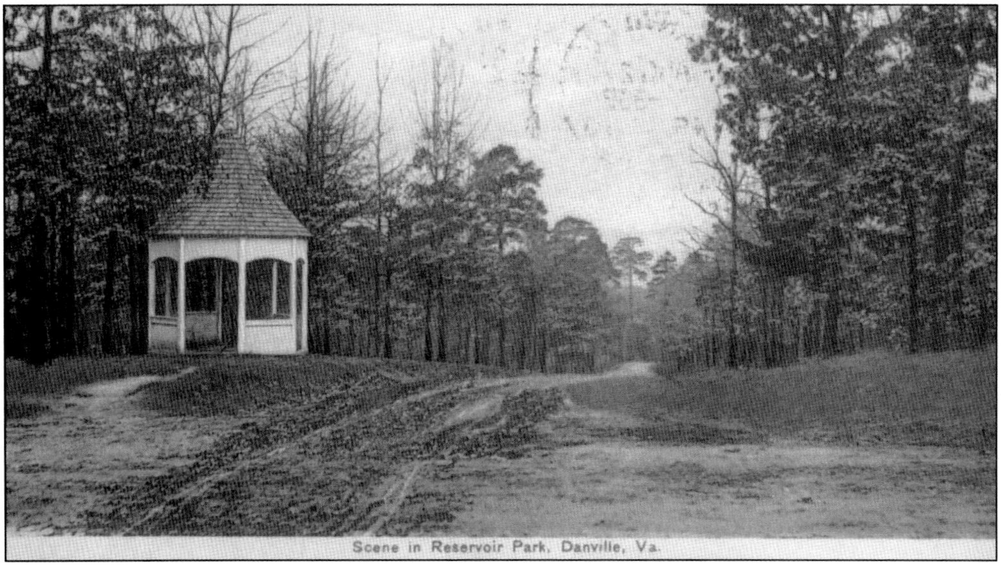

In the 1880s City Engineer C.A. Ballou recommended to City Council the construction of a water reservoir on land first called Reservoir Park, but later renamed Ballou Park in his honor. Since 1975 Danville has held a Festival in the Park there every May. Artists and craftsmen are invited (for a small charge) to exhibit their wares. Free entertainment is provided for large crowds that are drawn to Danville for this event.

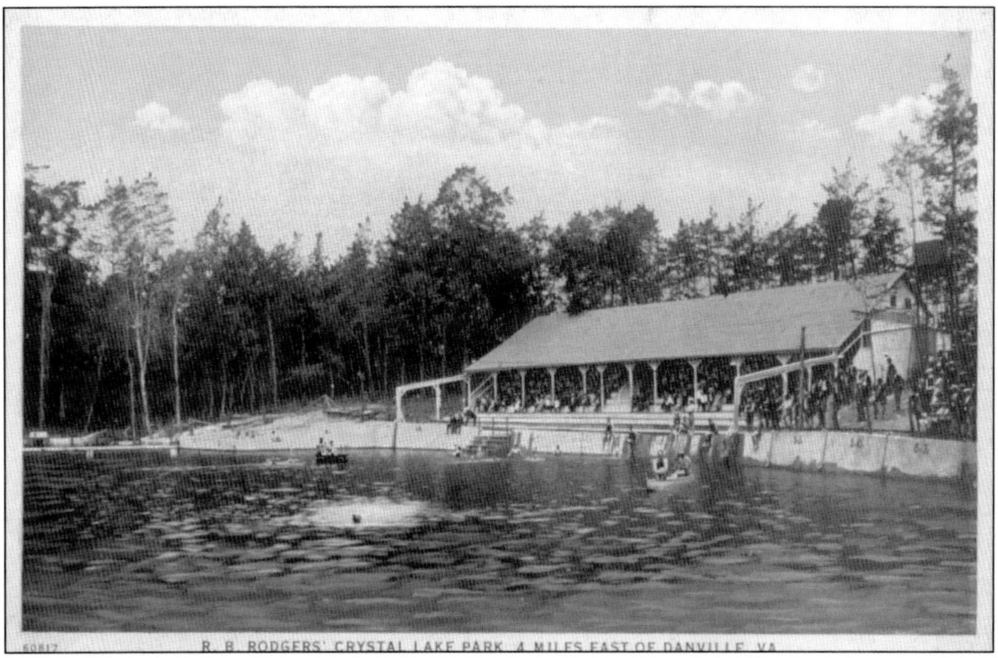

Public swimming places in Danville have been few and short-lived. Luna Lake, Pine Lake, and Crystal Lake exist no more. Crystal Lake was located on Highway 58 East at the lower end of the site of the current Baptist Tabernacle. In 1953 (the year pizza pie stormed the nation) the cost for a swim at Luna Lake was 74¢ for adults, 50¢ for children under 12, and free for children under 6 years old.

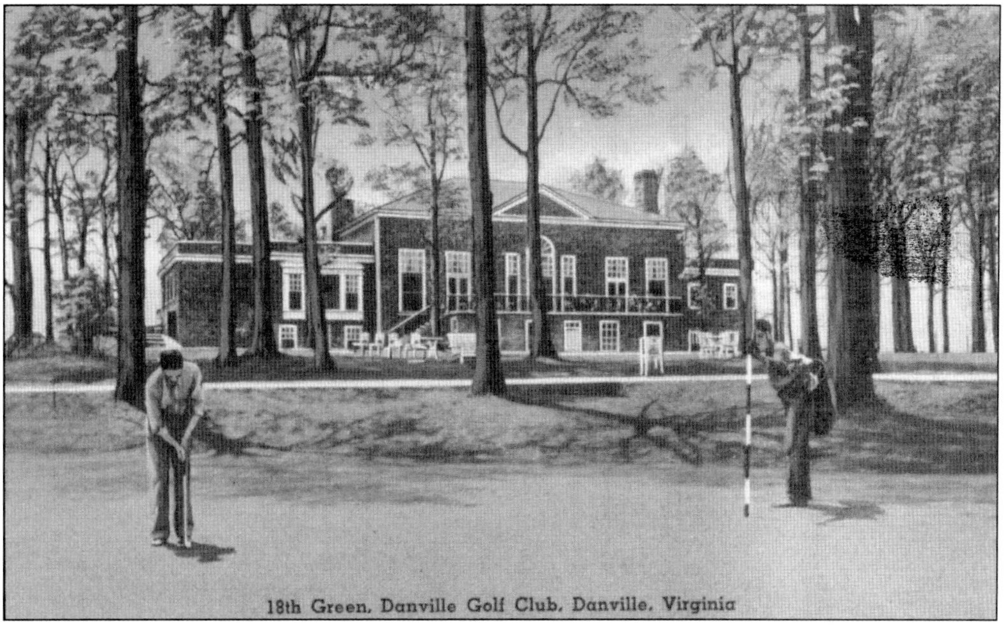

The Danville Golf Club, located at 2725 West Main Street near the outskirts of town and just off Highway 29 South, was founded in 1916. E.H. Miller Sr. was the first president of this private club established for the recreation of its membership. Many parties, dances, and wedding receptions have been held in this clubhouse.

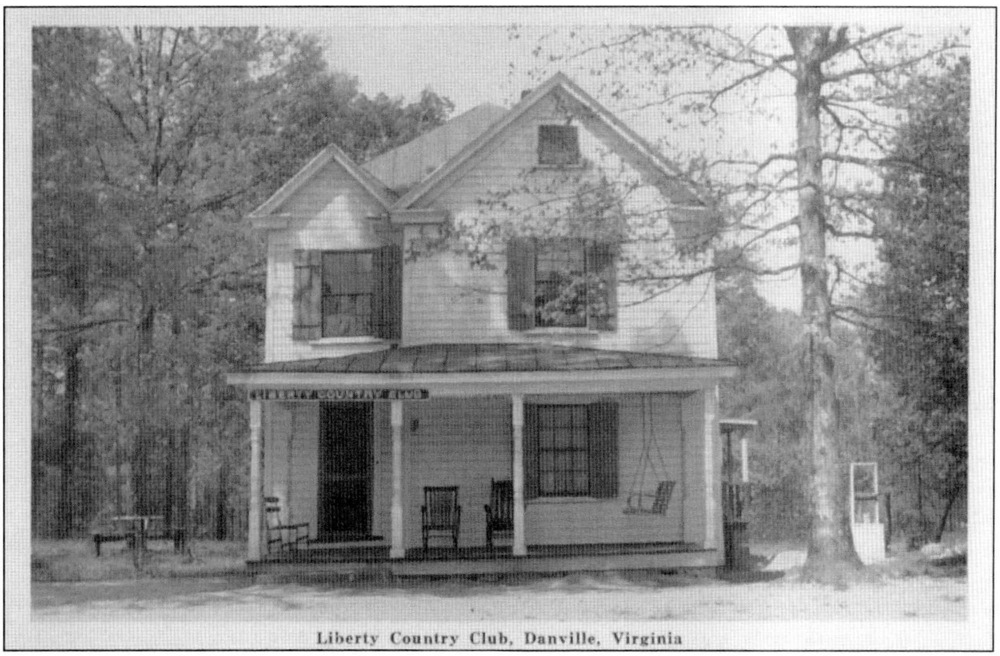

The Liberty Country Club on Seeland Road was granted a charter in 1944 as a non-profit corporation to be used exclusively for the recreation and enjoyment of its members. Liberty Country Club was founded by M.C. Martin, who served as its first president. Martin was later to serve as president and chairman of the board of First State Bank.

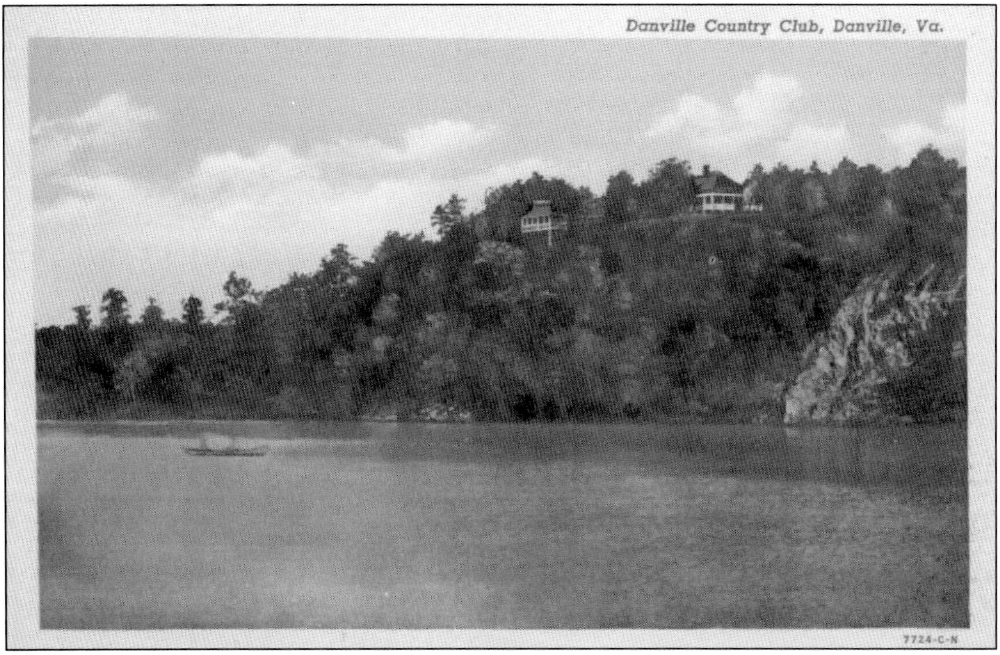

Before the days of tennis courts, golf courses, or even movies, Danville citizens managed to have fun riding bicycles or bowling. Both sports were made available at the House Rock Wheel Club, which stood on a cliff overlooking the Dan River above the Schoolfield dam. The large rock at the cliff gave the club its name.

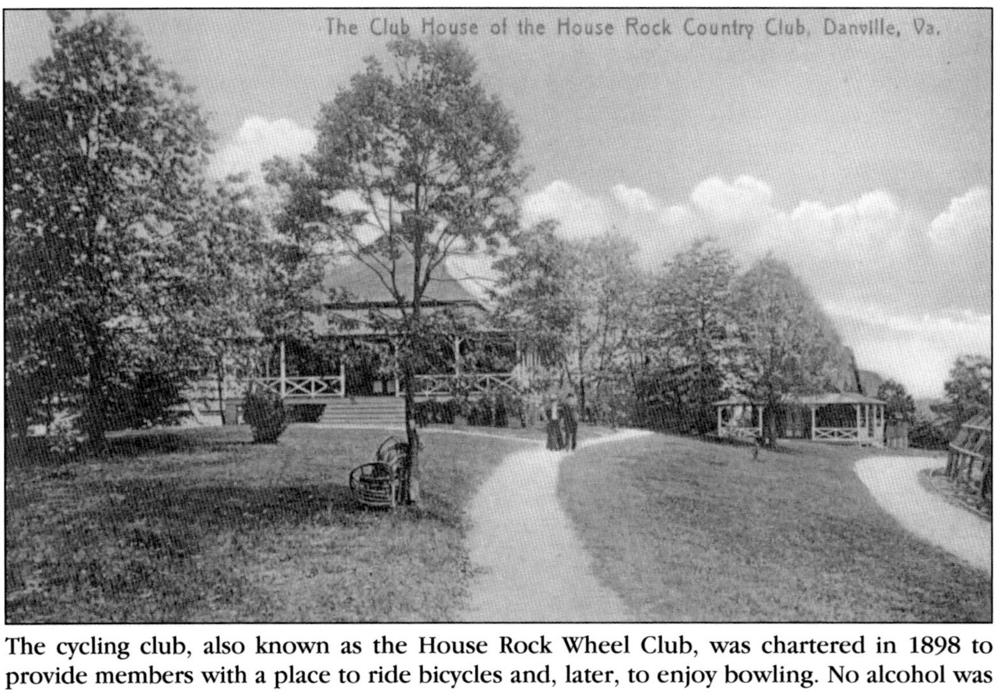

The cycling club, also known as the House Rock Wheel Club, was chartered in 1898 to provide members with a place to ride bicycles and, later, to enjoy bowling. No alcohol was permitted on the premises, nor was card playing or dancing.

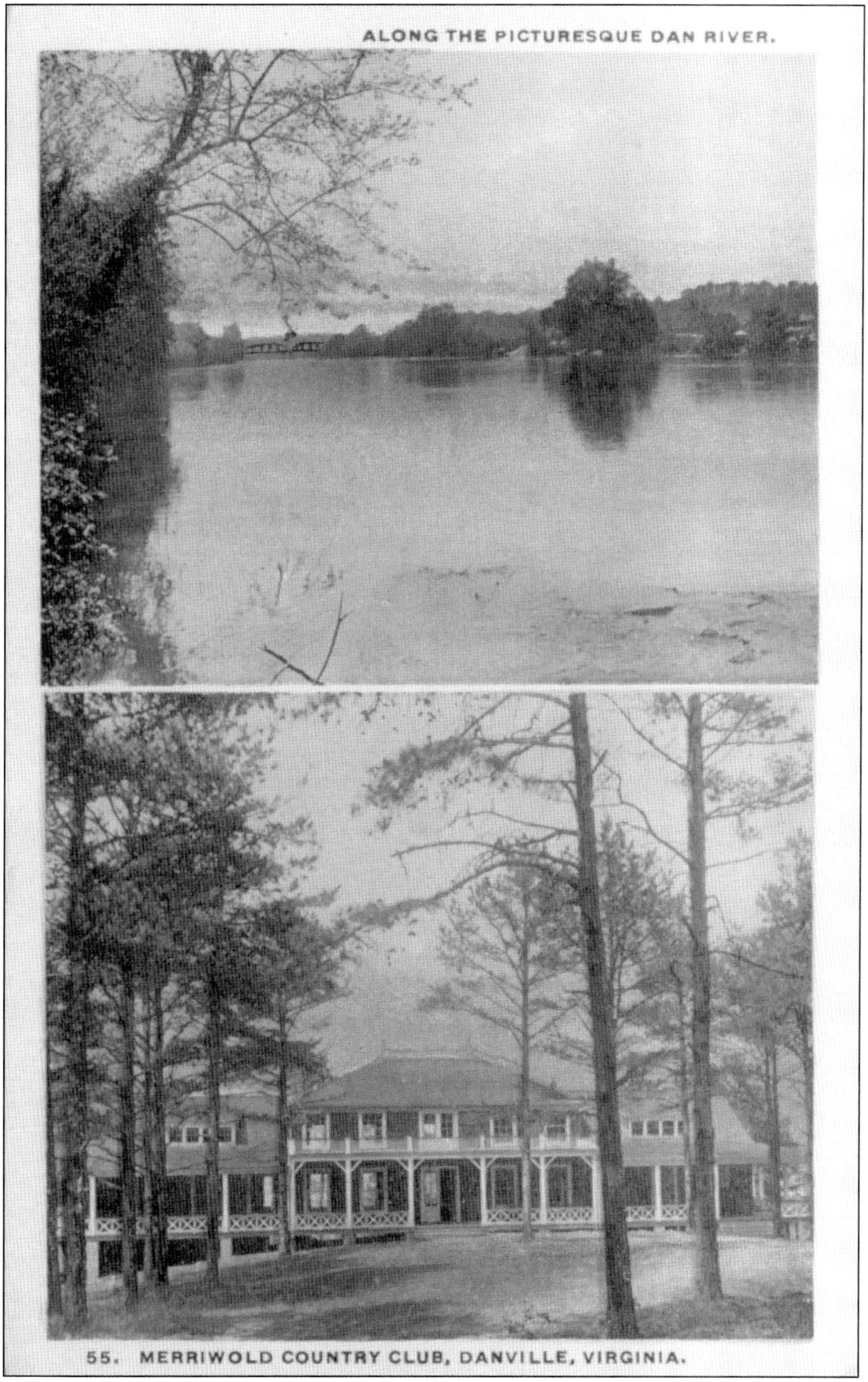

The Merriwold Country Club, formerly the House Rock Country Club, was established by Dan River Cotton Mills as a place for holding meetings, dinners, or even dances for large groups. Later known as the Country Club Inn, this clubhouse provided an elegant setting for social events.

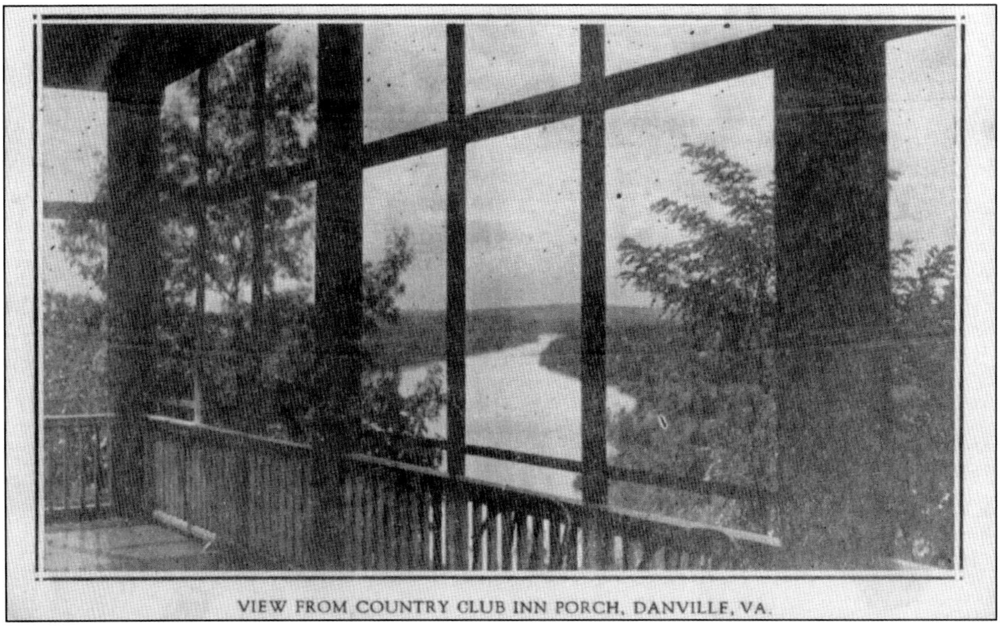

After every social gathering, whether an afternoon reception or an evening dance, people would slip out of the dining hall and go outside onto the wrap-around porch of the Country Club Inn. The view of the Dan River to the west has always been a captivating sight.

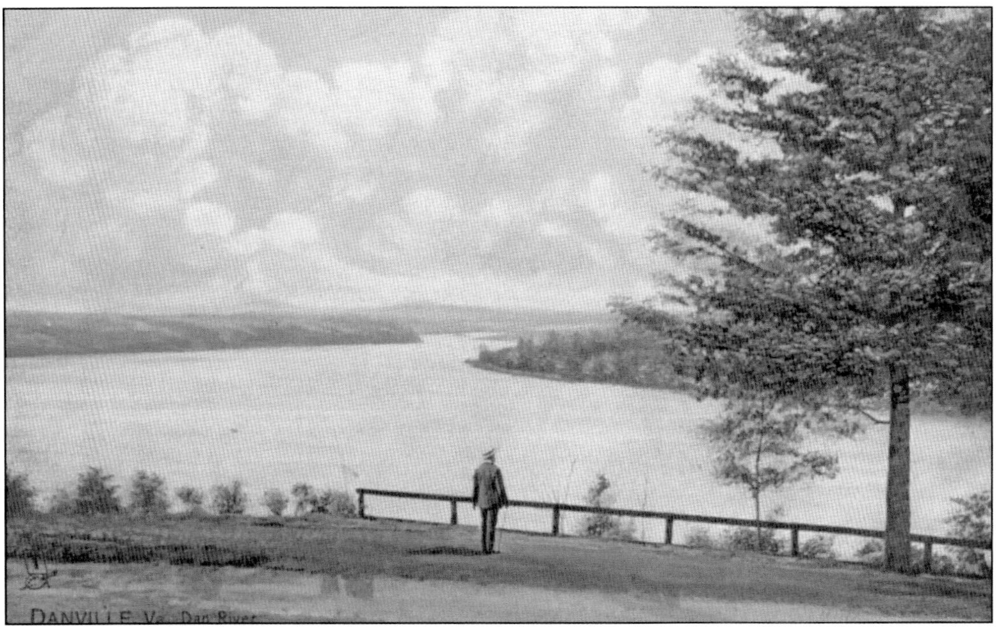

The Dan River was the cause of the founding of the city of Danville in 1793. The future of the city may also lie in these slowly moving waters that still manage to entrance the viewer. The future may also prove the common picture postcard to be the most accurate mirror of Danville's past as it grew from a town into a thriving city.

INDEX